Welcome to Empire City, metropolis of fantastic adventure and startling danger. It is the heart of a world where armoured madmen bunkered in impregnable island fortresses threaten peace and progress, giant monsters creep from time-lost lairs to topple buildings and trample hope, and aliens from beyond the stars invade mankind's dreams. Empire City is a place beset by criminals armed with superscientific weaponry, its citizens the chosen prey of uncanny creatures that do not fear death.

And Empire City is the home of heroes:

Sentinel: America's eternal supersoldier. Born in atomic fire but tempered in post-war peace, he is the world's greatest protector.

Caliburn: The modern-day knight touched by tragedy, he prowls the darkness to defend the helpless and to punish sinners.

Mother Raven: Ojibwa teacher, poet, mother, and messenger for the Raven, spirit of illusion, trickery, and sunfire.

Slipstream: An alien refugee who loves Earth and uses his enhanced metabolism to guard his new home.

Red Phoenix: The latest incarnation of the female warrior, a champion of justice armed with the devastating Phoenix Blade.

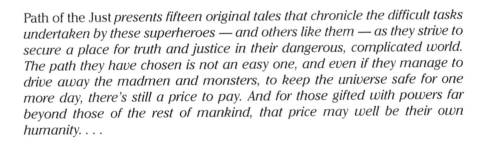

Path of the Just *presents fifteen original tales that chronicle the difficult tasks undertaken by these superheroes — and others like them — as they strive to secure a place for truth and justice in their dangerous, complicated world. The path they have chosen is not an easy one, and even if they manage to drive away the madmen and monsters, to keep the universe safe for one more day, there's still a price to pay. And for those gifted with powers far beyond those of the rest of mankind, that price may well be their own humanity. . . .*

SILVER AGE SENTINELS

THE SUPERHERO ROLE-PLAYING GAME

Silver Age Sentinels core rulebook

SAS Game Master's Screen

SAS Character Folio

Shields of Justice: The Hero's Almanac

Emergency Response 1

Roll Call 1

Roll Call 2: The Sidekick's Club

From the Files of Matthews GenTech

<u>FORTHCOMING</u>

Criminal Intent: The Villain's Almanac
(OCTOBER 2003)

Emergency Response 2: Sphinx Engine
(DECEMBER 2003)

Roll Call 3: Country Matters
(JANUARY 2004)

Artificer's Almanac
(SPRING 2004)

Empire City
(SUMMER 2004)

Whispering Winds
(FALL 2004)

<u>FICTION</u>

Path of the Just

Path of the Bold
(MARCH 2004)

PATH
OF THE
JUST

EDITED BY
JAMES LOWDER

SILVER AGE SENTINELS
LINE DEVELOPER
JESSE SCOBLE

Path of the Just is published by GUARDIANS OF ORDER, INC.

This collection © 2003 by GUARDIANS OF ORDER, INC. and James Lowder.

Cover art by Ed Northcott. © 2003 by GUARDIANS OF ORDER.

Introduction © 2003 by Dennis O'Neil.
"Ghosts of London" © 2003 by Matthew McFarland.
"War and Hell" © 2003 by Brett Barkley.
"Citizens" © 2003 by Steven Grant.
"Decisions" © 2003 by J. Allen Thomas.
"Covalent Bonds" © 2003 by Erica Schippers.
"The Final Equation" © 2003 by Robin D. Laws.
"Apocalypse" © 2003 by Daniel Ksenych.
"The Man in the Wall" © 2003 by Ed Greenwood.
"Ion Shells" © 2003 by Steven Harper.
"Stormcloud Rising" © 2003 by Jim C. Hines.
"The Whispering Wars" © 2003 by Lucien Soulban.
"Hardball" © 2003 by John Ostrander.
"Evening With the Minotaur" © 2003 by Jon Hansen.
"Arcanum's Last Card" © 2003 by Bradley J. Kayl.
"Mirror, Rust, and Dark" © 2003 by Alexander Marsh Freed.

Please address questions and comments concerning this book, as well as requests for notices of new publications, by mail to: GUARDIANS OF ORDER, INC., PO Box 25016, 370 Stone Road, Guelph, Ontario, CANADA, N1G 4T4.

Visit us at http://www.guardiansorder.com.com.

FIRST PAPERBACK EDITION
10 9 8 7 6 5 4 3 2 1

GUARDIANS OF ORDER publication 13-901, August 2003.

ISBN 1-894525-82-5.

Printed in Canada.

TABLE
OF
CONTENTS

INTRODUCTION

BY DENNIS O'NEIL

You're lonely and you're afraid. Don't worry — you're not alone. People have been like this for a long time. That's why there are superheroes.

Superman wasn't the first, not at all, though I once thought he was. When I began to look, really look, at comic books I agreed with the conventional wisdom, which maintained that a teenager named Jerry Siegel got a bright idea one summer night in 1934 for, in his words, "a character like Samson, Hercules, and all the strong men I ever heard of rolled into one — only more so." You probably know the rest of the story, but just in case you don't I'll give it to you as briefly as I can: Jerry shared his vision with an aspiring artist named Joe Shuster, who translated Jerry's idea into graphics. They called their joint creation "Superman" and for the next several years tried to peddle it to newspapers as a comic strip. Finally, in 1938, they sold it to something new: a comic book. Now, comic books — little magazines containing comic strips — had been around for a while, but only as reprints of stuff that had already appeared in newspapers. Superman's new home, *Action Comics*, was different; it was filled, cover to cover, with original material, including the first Superman adventure.

Instant success.

If you'll allow me to digress and get just a tad academic here, I'll tell you that what Jerry and Joe had done was create a meme and if you'll allow me to extend this shabby exercise in erudition another few words, I'll proffer the *Oxford English Dictionary*'s definition of *meme*. "An element of a culture that may be considered to be passed on by non-genetic means, especially imitation." So a song's a meme. Fashion's a meme. Anything you pass on by imitation is meme. So costumed superheroes are memes and Jerry Siegel and Joe Shuster perpetrated one when they created Superman — call it "the costumed superhero meme." It was almost immediately imitated in dozens, then hundreds, of supranormal vigilantes wearing tights and capes and masks who went around fighting crime.

Many, if not most, of these heroes had double identities — that is, they pretended to be ordinary citizens with ordinary lives and jobs until some criminous menace came to their attention, whereupon they dealt with the problem, usually violently.

They've been with us ever since, a pervasive part of popular culture. At first, their domain was exclusively comics, though the peculiar kind of fantasy-melodrama they embodied was exported to radio and the movies within five years of Superman's debut. Arguably, they were a major part of the creation of the comic book industry; almost certainly, the comic book biz would not have grown so quickly and so healthily without them. Eventually, and maybe inevitably, they were attacked: accused of promoting everything from unwholesome sexual attitudes to laziness. But they have more than survived; they have prospered.

Although comic books have only a small fraction of the circulation they once did, before competition from television, video games, and the thousands of other distractions of our electronic age marginalized them, superheroes are prospering. Spider-Man, the X-Men, Batman, Daredevil, the Hulk — all these comic book refugees have been featured in mega-successful movies within the last five years, and more are on the way. There have also been successful television series featuring them and/or their counterparts, and at least two best-selling novels (plus dozens of others that did not qualify as best-sellers), CDs, videotapes, and, most surprising to me, attention from academia. Comic books are actually being studied, sometimes at institutions with ivy on their walls.

The reasons for superheroes' persistent popularity may not be immediately obvious, but squint a little and you can see it. Jerry Siegel and Joe Shuster created the costumed superhero meme, but they did not conjure it from nothing. What they added or borrowed, depending on which authority you consult, was the costume; superheroes have been around a long time, possibly from the very beginning of narrative storytelling. The Epic of Gilgamesh, for example, is full of mighty deeds, and that was composed about 2000 BCE. Homer's epics are populated by warriors who are, by any reasonable definition, superheroes. Then there are the Arthurian legends and the tall tales of the American West and all the world's mythologies. . . . The list is not exactly endless, but it wouldn't fit on the back of a trading card, either. Jerry himself acknowledged his debt to his forebears in the quotation cited above: "a character like Samson, Hercules, and all the strong men I ever heard of."

Nothing in culture, popular or otherwise, lasts for millennia without answering some deep human need, and I submit that superheroes are no exception. Remember what I wrote at the beginning of this essay, an astonishing 802 words ago? "You're lonely and you're afraid." Well, I'm sorry: You are, at least some of the time. We all are. We cope with our loneliness and fear in various ways. One of them is to imagine someone like ourselves, but someone bigger, stronger, smarter, tougher, perhaps a bit better looking and, mostly, braver. Someone who embodies our values. Someone who, unlike ourselves, will always prevail against the chaos and evil that have always plagued humankind. Next, we label this phantasm who lives in our skulls. We use the word *god*, or *hero*, or *superhero* — whatever's appropriate to where and when we live.

Finally, using the alchemy of our ever-resourceful imaginations, we merge with our god/hero/superhero. It is the world's first and best magic trick, this ability to become someone who never existed. We assemble this splendid creature in our minds and then, clever devils that we are, we identify with him or her. We call the process *ritual, myth, fiction, drama*: in a word, *storytelling*. And we do it wherever and whenever conditions are propitious. Throughout most of our history, that meant people gathered around fires listening to the narratives of elders or shamen or bards; now, our tales are told on screens or through electronic devices or — cast your eyes down and become aware of what you're holding! — on printed pages.

Which brings us to a thing many of you may have begun to think we'd never arrive at: this book. It is proof that memes, like their biological counterparts, genes, and like everything else, undergo change. Read on and behold what the superhero meme has evolved into, some of the variations that have proceeded from Jerry and Joe's inspiration and its multiple predecessors.

Maybe the stories herein will give you some help with that loneliness and fear problem we all seem to have. Maybe they'll inspire you. Maybe they'll provide you with insights. Stories can do all that.

Or maybe they'll just entertain you. That's okay, too.

— Dennis O'Neil
June, 2003

GHOSTS OF LONDON

BY MATTHEW MCFARLAND

October, 1995.
London. Friday.
Ben kicked a pebble into the gutter. "Where is he, then?"

"How should I know?" North spat his gum onto the street. "S'posed to be here. Gets out of school same time's us." North pulled his collar up around his neck. His mother had told him to wear a muffler today, but he'd run out without one. He'd never admit it, but mum was right.

Ben looked down the street and wiped his nose on the back of his gloves. Both gloves were developing a crackly yellow film from this habit, but Ben didn't much care. "Don't supposed he tried it?"

"Tried what?" North was attempting to peer into the tinted windows of the adult bookstore. He thought he could almost make out a pair of —

Ben shoved him. "Stop it. The owner'll come out and chase us, and I don't fancy running." He stole a glance in the window himself, then looked back at North. "Anyway, you *know* what I mean. Maybe he tried it. What we was talking about yesterday."

North furrowed his brow and laughed. "Are you cracked? That's just a story, Ben. Watch." He walked back to the window and stared into it. "Bloody Mary."

Ben tugged his sleeve. "Don't. North, please don't."

"Bloody Mary." North smiled, trying to make out anything beyond the darkness of the tinted glass. *Ben's a baby*, he thought. *Bloody Mary. Bloody stupid, more like.* "Bloody Mary."

"North, please!"

North's voice dropped to whisper, but Ben could swear it was the only sound in the world.

"Bloody Mary."

North put his hand out to touch the glass, even as Ben backed away. His fingers touched the glass, which rippled like a lake on a moonless night. North's hand disappeared. "Bloody Mary."

Ben screamed. He screamed with all his breath, and then he ran, still shrieking. Even so, all he could hear was his friend repeating her name.

Empire City. Sunday.

"He still hasn't said anything?" Around a table sat three of the Guard, along with a sallow British detective in a dark blue suit. The man speaking was Slipstream, and he looked quizzically between his teammates and the Englishman.

"Nothing useful, I'm afraid," the detective replied. "He keeps insisting that he saw his friend disappear into a window, and that 'Bloody Mary' took him. The London police might have dismissed it as a prank, or as some sort of reaction to a different traumatic shock, but it turns out that one of the officers who heard the story was something of a . . . hobbyist with regards to superhumans such as yourselves. Not that London doesn't have its own protectors, you understand —"

"And a fine job they do, too," interrupted a muffled voice. The other four turned to glance at Caliburn. They couldn't see his face, of course — he insisted on keeping that hidden from visitors — but even the stranger in the room felt the tension in his voice.

"Well, quite," the detective continued. "The problem, however, is that we need some assistance. Our city's defenders are not —" he paused, as though trying to phrase something difficult "— *available* for this sort of assignment just at the moment."

The woman at the head of the table stiffened slightly. She leaned forward and the sweat on the Englishman's forehead began to bead. "Not available? You have four missing children cases in twenty-four hours. Evidence points to a costume being involved . . . and your people aren't *available*? Where are they, then?"

The man cleared his throat. "Afraid I can't tell you that. It's not really relevant, anyway. Believe me, Ms. . . . ah, Phoenix, if we didn't appreciate the gravity of the situation, I would not be here. But the fact remains that the Guard and the Regiment have worked well together before, and I was hoping to enlist the aid at least of Caliburn in this matter."

Caliburn didn't move or speak. He waited for the man to continue.

"We will, of course, grant you full access to any of the intelligence we have on this Bloody Mary, but frankly, there's not much to be had. Your country's FBI has had more dealings with her than we have. There's never even been a recorded instance of her appearing in Europe before."

Slipstream smiled. "Bad batch of the Guard to meet with, then. None of us have tussled with her, to my knowledge. Sentinel's gone for the moment, too. Not sure about Mother Raven; maybe she could be of some help."

"I'll do it."

The three of them turned to Caliburn. He was standing. "I'll do it," he repeated.

The detective smiled. "Splendid." He opened a briefcase and pulled out a thick manila envelope. "This is all the information on the missing boys, along with your plane tickets and a diskette containing what we know about Bloody Mary and what the FBI has shared with us on the subject. See you in London, sir." He stood and left the room, not sparing a glance back.

"Friendly guy," muttered Slipstream.

Red Phoenix shook her head. "Adam."

"Don't say it, Sarah," Caliburn rumbled.

She stood abruptly. "You don't have to do this."

The masked hero sighed. "It's like you said. Kids are going missing. I've not read much on Bloody Mary, but what I have read scares me white. I can't let that go on. What happened to me in London doesn't matter."

Red Phoenix looked helplessly at Slipstream. He shrugged. Johnny Smith had little real idea of homes and nations; his home was on another world, and he could run across continents in moments.

"Adam," Phoenix pressed, "let me find Katherine. She's probably better suited to this, anyway. You're a detective, not a mystic. She —"

"No." The tone was more forceful than most people would even dream of using with Red Phoenix. "Katherine may know the occult, but she doesn't know London. The city's got a pulse. It's got a soul." He paused, and although his teammates couldn't see it under his mask, he chewed his lip thoughtfully. "If Bloody Mary's there, something's wrong with the city itself. Katherine wouldn't be able to tell the difference, not without knowing the place already." He grabbed the envelope from the table and left the room.

Red Phoenix sank back into her chair. "He may know the city, but that doesn't mean he's ready to face it."

"Why?" Slipstream asked, eyebrows arched. "What happened there?"

En route to London. Sunday.

Adam Sinclair didn't much like flying. Anything could happen on a plane. Because he chose to keep his true identity secret from everyone except his teammates, he couldn't fly with his usual complement of weapons. The alternative was to fly suited up as Caliburn, and even on good days he found that uncomfortable. There was no way he could have handled that today.

He'd spent the first few hours of the flight memorizing the plane's layout, idly deciding what objects could be used offensively or defensively in a crisis. He'd read through every word of the magazines in the seat pocket in front of him. He'd even chatted with the sweet old lady from Yorkshire, who'd probably been too nearsighted to be upset by his scarred face. She was presently fast asleep.

So far, he'd left the file unopened. Only as the plane soared quietly over the sea and the sky began to darken did he allow his mind to drift to London.

"Blood on your hands, hero. . . ."

Sinclair turned to the window and focused his thoughts. *Right. What do I know about Bloody Mary? Steals children. Costume, but not necessarily human. Speculation is that she's some sort of spirit or even an alien being. Probably has powers far beyond mine. . . .*

As Caliburn, Adam Sinclair had faced opponents who ran the gamut from ordinary street thugs to well-equipped mercenaries like Iron Bow to the freakish creations of Mister Matthews. It was ironic that the worst of them had simply been a man.

"Blood on your hands forever. . . ."

He shook the thought out of his mind. Janus — Zachary King — had been apprehended in the United States. The police didn't know who they had in custody. The world at large still believed King was dead, and Sinclair was afraid that if he came forward to identify the man, King would unmask him. Sinclair wasn't sure why he was still clinging to his secret identity. Perhaps out of respect for the memory of —

He shook off the thought. He had nothing to fear from King in London — this time. Besides, Bloody Mary looked to be a more dangerous foe than King ever was, simply by dint of the lack of information about her. He'd printed the files about her before leaving Empire City, but it was a lamentably thin dossier. Most of the people who had given statements in the 1990 case were children. As such their testimonies were filled with helpful little conclusions drawn by the FBI, which probably skewed the truth badly.

Sinclair thumbed the call button and asked the attendant for a cup of coffee, then opened the files.

★   ★   ★

Detroit. Sunday.

"Quit singing that crap."

The man speaking hadn't used his real first name in years. Most folks just called him "Pit," and that suited him fine. It was short for "Pit Bull," as the tattoo on his arm indicated. He'd gotten that tattoo the day he was arrested, and he'd barred the door of the ink parlour securely enough for the artist to finish the work before the cops broke in. Pit stood close to seven feet tall and wider than most doorways, and his mouth was populated by his last ten teeth. He looked like what he was, and he was proud of that. His new cellmate didn't seem to appreciate that, though, and it was getting on Pit's nerves.

"Hmmm? Oh, sorry, Pit. I've got a song in my head. You know how that can be." The man on the lower bunk went back to singing quietly.

Pit slid down off the top bunk and peered at the man. He was a skinny white guy, probably not thirty years old. He wore the same orange county issues as everyone else, but on him they seemed as classy as a tuxedo. That annoyed Pit, too. "Quit it," he growled, "or I'm gonna knock your teeth down your throat."

"'Sixteen, clumsy, and shy —' Sorry. Did you just threaten me?" The man smiled. "Knock my teeth down my throat, was it?" He pulled himself forward and stood up in front of Pit. "That's not terribly original, is it?"

Pit balled a fist. Even the guy's accent was annoying! He sounded like he was from Canada or something. Yeah, this jerk *needed* to get hit.

"No need for that," Pit's cellmate said, gesturing calmly at the meaty fist. "What I meant by my comment was that you look like you've won some fights." He waited for the seeming compliment to sink in, for the big man's brows to knit in confusion. Then he continued. "Yes, I recognize that you're a tough customer. So if you thought about it, you could come up with a threat that would really scare me. That's all I meant. Give it a try. I'll just wait on my bunk until you come up with another." He sat back down, a slight smile twisting his thin lips.

Pit took at step back. This guy didn't seem the least afraid of him. That was just . . . wrong. He was thinking about that when the man started to sing again.

Pit reached down and grabbed his cellmate's arm. He planned on jerking the man from the bed and planting him on the filthy prison floor. Instead, he found himself lying face down on the lower bunk with a piece of wire pressed against his eye. "Here, I've thought of a better threat," the older man said with his strangely accented voice, the playful tone replaced by one of ice and blood. He whispered something into Pit's ear.

The bedding swallowed Pit's scream, which didn't last that long anyway.

Zachary King — known to some as the hero-murderer Janus — walked down the moonlit hill from the prison fence exactly twenty minutes later. He glanced at his blood-spattered prison issues in disgust. *First thing*, he thought. *Change of clothes. Also need to get the hell out of Detroit. The cops here don't know who they're looking for, but my picture'll still be on the news any minute, and I don't need half the bloody Guard looking for me.*

He jogged down to the road and hid on the verge until the coast was clear. Finally, he threw himself into the dirt, partway onto the asphalt. A moment later a car approached and passed the night-obscured form, then slowed to a full stop.

Janus smirked even as he let out a loud, dramatic groan of distress and rolled farther into the tall grass. Had the motorist been paying attention about a kilometre back, he'd have noticed a sign saying *PRISON AREA: DO NOT STOP. DO NOT PICK UP HITCHHIKERS.*

Thank God for illiterate Americans, Janus thought as the helpful young man exited the car and started toward him.

London. Tuesday.

Sinclair had expected to be jet lagged, but his body had adapted — or, more properly, returned — to London time quickly. He sat on the bed in his hotel room with pictures, printed pages, newspaper articles, and FBI datasheets strewn around him. As big as the mess was, however, it contained precious little information.

He'd spoken via secured transmission to eight masks in five different countries. Of the eight, six hadn't any new information for him. Only two — a strange character in New Orleans called the Baron and a federal agent called Countdown provided anything at all helpful. He'd recorded both conversations, and as the city began to darken and change from busy metropolis to concrete jungle, he played back the tape of the Baron.

A burst of static jolted Sinclair from his thoughts. He turned down the volume. He didn't know how, but the Baron's tape had been damaged. His testimony hadn't been particularly helpful, anyway — his accent was hard to understand, and he'd made a lot of cryptic references to "unquiet spirits" and "fallen angels." Sighing, he tossed it aside and slapped in Countdown's.

A deep voice with a Texas accent boomed from the recorder: "We had us a rash of missing children — oh, six, seven years ago. Ten missing kids all told. Never saw eight of 'em after that. State of Texas called me in along with a couple of freelancers. One was a fella named Whisper — he was like a mystic or some such, and he said he could smell where the kids were. Other was a lady named Succour; she was there to keep the kids calm, if we found 'em. I was there for muscle. We did find two of the kids, but they was all shaken up. I think they're still in the hospital."

Caliburn's own voice: "Yes. I'm sorry, but did you ever see Bloody Mary?"

Countdown paused. "Yes, I surely did. Succour leaned over to help those kids, and this white crow flies in an open window. Both kids started screaming to beat the band, and then there she was. She didn't look like much — kinda weird and scary, I guess. Black streaks on her face. Anyway, she just raises up her hands and Whisper falls over clawing at his own face. Succour grabbed the kids and lit out, and here's me squaring off with this gal. I didn't have much choice; I threw Whisper through a window and used my power."

Sinclair glanced down on a fact sheet from Texas. *Agent: Countdown. Powers: Enhanced strength and endurance. Able to emit explosive force equal to ten pounds of TNT. Requires thirty seconds to build the charge.*

"Anyway," the voice on the tape continued, "when the rubble cleared, she was gone. No body, no nothing. I know that means she ain't dead."

"Thank you," muttered Sinclair's voice. He switched off the tape.

Some sort of emotional attack, he thought. *Enhancing fear. Might work on grief or rage, too. I'll have to keep myself under control if I fight her. And she seems able to change shape. . . .* He sighed and rubbed his temples. He knew a little about her potential, but almost nothing about her motives. He grabbed the dossier on the missing children and flipped through it again.

They were all boys. The youngest was only six, the eldest eleven. Two witnesses — one had seen his friend Nicholas "North" Ulner disappear into a window. The other had seen her older brother vanish into a bathroom mirror. Clearly Bloody Mary could open some sort of gateway through glass or reflective surfaces. But there was something else, something obvious, that Sinclair was missing. He knew from experience that he couldn't will himself to find it; he'd just have to wait. He fell back on the bed and his eyes drifted shut.

What was frustrating was how little the police knew about her. Not all masks were flamboyant; Caliburn himself could very easily have remained completely out of the public eye for years. But Bloody Mary was stealing children, and that sort of thing always garnered attention from the authorities. Why, then, did the FBI, the British government, and the Guard all have virtually no information about her?

He'd heard stories about creatures similar to Bloody Mary, of course. Growing up, his mates had told yarns about horrible monsters from the bottoms of lakes, ghosts in shrouds lurking in old houses. He'd been more interested in tales of Arthur and his knights, but everybody had already heard those stories. . . .

Sinclair sat bolt upright in bed. "Idiot," he growled. He opened the dossier again. Both witnesses had referred to "Bloody Mary," but they hadn't met and the police hadn't used the term.

The police, the adults hadn't heard of Bloody Mary. But the children knew her.

Moments later, Sinclair had rolled a deceptively heavy case from beneath the bed and was suiting up.

London. Tuesday.

The city was much as Caliburn remembered it. Grey, rain-slicked buildings, the smell of concrete and exhaust. It wasn't so different, in those respects, from Empire City. But it was London, and every step he took was a step back to a life he couldn't find again.

He'd run eight blocks, operating on instinct alone, before a thought entered his head. As it happened, the thought was the one he wanted least.

"Blood on your hands, hero. . . ."

King in Whitechapel. King, the new Ripper, standing over his latest kill. King had beaten him that night. It didn't matter that King had no powers, no special gifts beyond his intellect and his heartless nature. He'd found out who Caliburn was and murdered the woman he loved. Sentinel had later told Sinclair that it was much easier to best a hero than a villain. "Villains," he said, "return wearing different masks. Heroes have only one face, one heart. Kill that, and it's over. Injustice doesn't die."

"Blood on your hands forever. . . ."

Caliburn ran on through the London night. He'd planned on going to the home of Lizzie Metcalf, the little girl who'd seen her brother John disappear into a bathroom mirror. But he had overshot her street by two blocks before he noticed.

He ducked into an alleyway and leaned against a wall. *Got to pull this together. I can't do this if I'm not focused.* A high-pitched giggle caught his ear. A small gang of kids was spray-painting the walls across the street.

Caliburn didn't care much for vandals, but they hardly merited special attention. There were much worse crimes than spraying some vulgarities on walls. Tonight, though, he had his reasons for interfering. He crept across the street and leapt into the alleyway.

Three of the six kids present bolted immediately. The others, none of them older than ten, backed away from the menacing blue figure.

They probably think I'm a cop, thought Caliburn. "Listen," he said. "I'm not here for you tonight. But I need to ask you something."

The children quaked. One looked about to cry. This kind of thing wasn't Caliburn's style; he was better suited to striking fear into criminals, not relating to kids. "You're not in trouble," he said, trying to sound reassuring. "I just need to know about something."

One of the kids plucked up some courage. "You're Caliburn, right?" The hero nodded. "I've seen you on telly. From America. You're in the Guard."

"That's right."

One of the others piped up. "How come you left England? They pay you more over there?"

Caliburn took a step back. He'd been asked the question before, of course, but by reporters and interviewers, and he had always refused to answer it. "I was —" Then he stopped. He didn't know how to answer, how to tell these children that he'd left because he could no longer face London. Because he couldn't wash the blood from Whitechapel, couldn't erase the memories from the loft he'd shared with Jennifer. To Caliburn, London died along with her.

"It's not important," he said. "But it's not about money."

The children didn't look convinced. "What'd you want, then?" asked the older boy.

"Bloody Mary," he said.

The effect was immediate. The three kids turned white. One moved as if to run, but stopped when he saw the dark alley behind him. The youngest child — a boy of about eight — actually began shaking. Caliburn faltered; he wasn't sure how to be tender here. Not from behind a mask. So he simply pressed his question. "What do you know about her?"

They looked at each other. Finally the older boy spoke up. "Well, she's a murderer, isn't she? Like, she was hanged way back when there was hanging. And now, if you say her name, she comes for you."

"No, that's not right." The second boy shoved his friend. "That's not right at all. She comes from mirrors. I heard she was like a demon or something, and if you stare into a mirror, you see her face and she grabs you."

The youngest boy didn't speak, but looked about to cry. Caliburn knelt down. "It's all right, son. What did you hear?"

The boy stared at Caliburn's masked face helplessly. "I heard she takes boys away for being naughty. I heard she comes to you like a spider and spins you up in a web. Then she drags you back to her house and eats you."

The older kid pushed him. "No, she not a spider. She's a ghost. She don't eat you; she just takes you away." The three boys started arguing. Caliburn took the opportunity to disappear. He was half a block away when he heard one of them say, "Where'd he go?"

He hadn't really learned much. They all had heard different stories about Bloody Mary, but they all believed they were telling the truth. Bloody Mary was a legend, and legends, as Caliburn well knew, had the power of people's belief in them. He turned and began to circle back toward the girl's house. He wasn't sure what else she would be able to tell him, but he had little else to go on and it seemed unlikely he'd get much sleep tonight.

From somewhere nearby, a woman's muffled cry for help sounded. Behind the hero's mask, eyes narrowed. This was the wrong night to cross Caliburn.

London. Wednesday.

Adam Sinclair woke to find a copy of the *Times* outside his hotel room door. His run-in with a pair of muggers hadn't made the morning edition, but that was just as well. He skimmed through the articles — no coverage of his presence in the city, no mention of the kidnappings or of Bloody Mary. Sinclair was relieved; he knew from experience that releasing the name of the supposed perpetrator would result in nothing but copycats and crime confessors, especially if Mary, as he feared, were somewhat removed from human spheres of influence.

He showered and dressed, and walked out into the sunlight. In the years following Jennifer's death, he'd avoided working by daylight, either as Adam Sinclair or as Caliburn. Now, seeing London by day was surreal, as though someone had chosen the hues of the city without any thought of what the sun might do to them. The streets seemed to shimmer as Sinclair walked to the bus stop. The passing cars gleamed, and their colours played across his mind as if tempting him to think of something other than his mission.

He boarded a bus and sat down. The bus wasn't quite full when he got on, but within two stops it was stuffed to capacity. Sinclair didn't mind the crowd; he found the murmur of conversation somewhat soothing.

A woman next to him got up and left the bus, and a young man replaced her. Sinclair glanced at him, then returned to his thoughts: *Bloody Mary. There has to be a way to find her turf, her realm. I've seen things pop in from other dimensions; this can't be much different. But maybe she only opens the gateway to kids.* For a split second he considered finding a child to open a portal for him, but dismissed that thought. *I'm not putting anyone else in harm's way. I'm not that desperate.*

The man next to Sinclair was singing quietly. Sinclair knew the song, but couldn't quite remember the band. He glanced over at the man, and his eyes widened.

The young man was gone. Zachary King sat beside him.

Sinclair's hands began to sweat. He couldn't act against King, not here. Perhaps he could trail King when the murderer left the bus — but that assumed his nemesis hadn't recognized him. Sinclair hadn't bothered to make his face up before leaving the hotel, so the scars King had given him were easily visible.

Sinclair turned his face away and tried to act nonchalant.

"You know the song, Adam?"

Sinclair sighed and turned to face King. He knew King wouldn't hesitate to murder innocents if things turned violent. As if reading his thoughts, King continued: "I've got two guns right now, both aimed at little old ladies. People's grans, I'd guess. Behave yourself, and I won't pull any triggers."

Sinclair glanced at King. His hands were both visible, but that didn't mean anything. Sinclair guessed he had one gun worked into his boot and another in the sleeve of his jacket, but he wasn't going to push the issue. "What are you doing here?"

"Why, I was homesick." King smiled. "I was languishing in an American prison, surrounded by idiots with no idea who I was. You can imagine what that's like for me."

"Yeah. You're a self-aggrandizing bastard. I imagine it was hell." Sinclair gritted his teeth. He wondered if he could get the shock-bomb out of his pocket without King noticing.

"Well, it wasn't fun." King sighed, then looked down sharply. "You'll want to keep your hands on your lap like a good lad — if for no other reason than a city bus wouldn't make for a very interesting coming-out party." Sinclair's hand, which had been creeping toward his pocket, came to rest on his leg. "Now then. I'm in London because *you're* in London. I missed you in Empire City by a day, but the wonderful thing about you is that you're so delightfully easy to track. 'Welsh gent, about my height, strongly built, ugly scar on his face.' The porter knew just where you'd gone." King leaned in conspiratorially. "Of course I killed him anyway."

"You're a monster." Sinclair clenched his fists. King yawned.

"Yes, I've heard that. Anyway, what are *you* doing here? I didn't think anything would get you back to London."

Sinclair didn't answer. This was more than he could bear. He was not going to lose control and attack, not with lives at stake. But King couldn't stay on the bus forever. He decided to keep him talking. "Looking for missing kids."

"Really? How delightful. But don't the mundane police have that sort of thing in hand?"

Sinclair paused. King looked away, and Sinclair followed his gaze to an old lady across the bus reading a romance novel. He wondered if the madman was mentally targeting her, imagining her skull shattered by a bullet. "Apparently not," Sinclair said, trying to draw King's attention back to him. "There's a costume involved."

King smirked. He was obsessed with costumes, no matter what side of the law they were on. "Mmm. What's this one called?"

Sinclair licked his lips. "Bloody Mary."

He was completely unprepared for King's reaction. The older man lurched forward and grabbed Sinclair by his collar. Sinclair could feel a sharp blade tickling his throat, and realized that King must have been palming a razor. "Right, Caliburn," King hissed. "Where'd you hear her? *No one* knows about her."

"I don't know what you talking about." People were starting to stare. "Bloody Mar —"

"Don't say that name!" King's eyes darted frantically.

"Okay, okay. Anyway, she's taken four boys so far."

"There'll be more. She never stops." King relaxed and sat back in his seat. He stared down a few of the people looking at them. "She's never satisfied."

"What do you know about her?"

"Enough," he hissed. "I know enough. I know what she is."

"Go on."

King regained his composure and cocked his head. "Give me one good reason to tell you anything else, Sinclair. And don't try to appeal to my good nature; I don't give a donkey's balls if she kidnaps a few snipes. No skin off my nose."

"No, I shouldn't think so." Sinclair looked out the window. He knew what to offer King, but every fibre in his being screamed against it. Again, King guessed his thoughts.

"Come on, man. You know what I want. Give it to me, and I'll tell you all about her."

"What if I just promise to leave you alone while I'm in London?"

King laughed. "Fat chance. Besides, we both know that you're too gutless to kill me and I'm too clever to stay in jail, so what's the difference if you leave me alone for a while? No, you know what I want. And that's the final price, mate. No haggling, no bargaining, no quibbling. Yea or nay?"

Sinclair buried his face in his hands. What King wanted was harmless enough, all things considered. And while King was probably the one person on Earth that could lie to Caliburn successfully, something in the way he'd reacted to Bloody Mary's name made Sinclair think he'd be honest this once.

Sinclair looked up. "All right."

London. Wednesday night.

Caliburn knew where he was going this time. He'd been close the night before. Idly he wondered if the same instinct that let him sense truth had also been leading him to Bloody Mary, and he'd been too distracted to follow it.

He passed by the same gang of kids he'd seen the night before. All six were there, and they were arguing over whether Caliburn could beat a local mask called Prism. Caliburn had never heard of her, but the kids seemed fairly convinced she could trounce him.

He ran on, replaying King's words in his head. He had been very helpful indeed, and though Sinclair made no promise to allow the murderer to leave the city unmolested, he couldn't help feeling that King had derived a sense of satisfaction from the whole arrangement. Perhaps he had once been stolen by Bloody Mary himself. He'd seemed terrified of her. More likely he was simply delighted by what Caliburn had traded him in return for the information.

The buildings grew more decrepit and the streets choked with trash. This was a neighbourhood Caliburn knew well; the crime rate was so high that he'd spent entire nights on patrol here when he'd first donned the mask. That seemed like lifetimes ago now.

He soon found the house and slipped into the shadows under one of the windows.

From inside, he heard voices. They sounded like children's voices, but they echoed as though from the bottom of a well. He hoisted himself up to the window and peered in.

The glass in the window was gone, but he couldn't see into the room. All he saw was blackness, the deep dark of the ocean at night or the countryside beneath a new moon. The voices grew louder, and he realized they were all repeating her name: "Bloody Mary. Bloody Mary. Bloody Mary."

Caliburn took a step back and jumped through the window. The instant his body crossed into the house, he felt as though he'd been doused in icy water. His feet hit the floor, but soundlessly. The room was completely dark — he might as well have jumped into a vat of black paint. All around him, the boys' voices continued. "Bloody Mary, Bloody Mary. . . ."

He crouched low and tried to focus. Grabbing a flare from his boot, he lit it. He heard the crackle as it blazed to life, but couldn't see a thing. The light simply could not break the darkness. The voices grew louder, and he heard something scrape against the floor.

Caliburn crouched low and reached out, trying to find any of the boys in the gloom. He tried to single out one voice, but the sound seemed to come from every direction at once. "Nicholas!" he called out. "North! Are you there?"

One of the voices faltered briefly. In that instant, Caliburn saw his flare dimly, as though from a mile away. He could barely make out the face of a boy sitting on the floor, swaying and chanting. "North," Caliburn said. "Can you hear me?"

The boy stopped chanting, stopped swaying. In the growing light from the flare, he looked about the room as though just waking up. His eyes widened. "Help me!" he cried.

Caliburn reached forward, then stopped. He heard the hiss of a cat from somewhere in the darkness. If what King said was true, Bloody Mary could take the form of a white cat.

He stood and waved his flare around, but the light seemed only to function when he stood near the boy. Desperately he tried to remember the other boys' names. "Willie!" he called. "Willie Desmond, are you here?"

Another voice dropped out of the chorus, and the room brightened considerably. Caliburn could see all four missing boys now, sitting crosslegged on the floor. Two were still chanting, but the others were trying to stand up. They looked, however, as though they were mired in something — they could only get to their knees before falling back again.

Caliburn took two steps toward North, thinking to help him up. And then white fire surrounded him. Pain forced him to his knees. Whatever had hit him, it had bypassed his armour entirely. He felt weak and nauseated, but wasn't bleeding or bruised. He looked up and saw the woman advancing on him.

Bloody Mary towered over him. Red hair cascaded down past her shoulders, and black tears stained her face. Her eyes glowed with a pale, white witchlight, and her clothing seemed woven from spider's silk and fresh blood. She glanced down at North and Willie, and they resumed their chant, obviously terrified for their lives.

The room grew dark again, but Caliburn could still see Mary's silhouette. "What are you?" he gasped. He was rewarded with another blast. The attack drove him to the ground. He struggled with his wrist pouch and dug out a flash-bang. He flung it at Bloody Mary's feet, and rolled away from the blast.

Caliburn pulled himself to his feet. The children had stopped chanting, and the room was lit as brightly as his flare could make it. Mary was nowhere to be seen. Caliburn staggered toward the children, all of whom were trembling and shocked, half blind from the flash. "It's all right, boys," he said, though he knew they couldn't hear him. The blast would leave their ears ringing for days. He reached down to help North up and noticed a white spider clinging to his shirt.

He tried to knock the spider away, but Mary was too quick. She jumped from the boy's collar and, in an instant, grew to her human form. She reached out and placed a hand on Caliburn's chest, and suddenly the world turned to ice. He felt his body shutting down, the cold beginning at his chest where she touched him and spreading from there. He remembered what King had said: *"She's a vampire or a demon or something like that. She can't live normally — she steals life from others. I saw her touch a man for ten seconds once. In that time, he was dead. His hair turned white and his skin ash grey."*

And as he reached for a special compartment in his armour, he heard King's voice again, gloating as he stood over Jennifer Randall's body. *"Blood on your hands, hero. Blood on your hands forever. You'll never stop the blood, because it began long before you."*

Caliburn was going to black out. The cold had reached his face, and he shook so badly he could barely see. His hands trembled in his gauntlets, but he managed to open the compartment and pull out a tiny silver cross on a chain.

"She's a vampire or a demon . . . she's afraid of His Judgment. Just like all us proper monsters."

Caliburn held out the cross, and Bloody Mary backed away. The cold stopped, but Caliburn could still barely move.

"I cast you out," he croaked.

Bloody Mary raised her hands as if to strike him with another blast. Nothing happened.

"I cast you out, and banish you from my sight. Begone." He staggered forward, legs barely able to hold him. The cross dangled from the end of the chain, and Mary fixed her gaze on it in horror. "Begone, whatever you are. Go back to Hell."

Mary glowered at the children, as if trying to force them to take up the chant again. Caliburn ground his teeth and barrelled forward, knocking her off balance. "I said, begone! Go back to whatever hell you're from, but leave these children alone and never trouble them again."

She regained her footing and looked over the faces of the boys with an expression that was almost tender. Then she turned to Caliburn. The look on her face now was simple, unabashed hatred. "Who are you to banish me? You are no believer. You are no angel."

Caliburn didn't think he had the strength to withstand an actual strike, and he wasn't sure what his weapons would do to her. "I am justice," he said. "Justice doesn't change. Justice began long before me." He felt tears roll down his cheeks. His mask felt uncomfortably warm. "Get out of my city," he said, his voice breaking. "This city doesn't need monsters." He held out the cross, and Mary's face twisted into a horrible grimace. She let out a hideous shriek that left the boys on the ground clutching their blast-deafened ears, and changed into a white crow. With one flap of her wings, she was gone.

London. Thursday morning.

"I had no idea it was the same creature." Slipstream's voice seemed tinny and rushed over the web camera. "But after hearing your description, yes, I'm sure you faced the same being that Mother Raven fought in Empire. She was called something else — the Chinese children gave her a name, but I don't remember it. It's in the report." He paused, then leaned in toward the camera. "According to Mother Raven, she was more powerful then."

"*More* powerful?" Caliburn still felt like he'd been run over by a lorry.

"Yes," continued his teammate. "She apparently draws power from children, but we're still not sure why. All the different theories about her seem to agree that she grows in power as she steals and enslaves kids. You probably set her back considerably."

Caliburn slumped in his chair. "I'd better have."

Cardiff. Friday.

Sinclair stood in front of the grave. Jennifer's parents hadn't wanted her buried here, but Sinclair had won them over eventually. He'd told them that the site was important, that he'd proposed to Jennifer here. That was a lie; he'd proposed in London. But he wanted to keep her gravesite a secret.

King knew everything about him: his real name, his occupation, his powers, his weaknesses. All of his secrets — save one. King didn't know where Sinclair had buried his love. And that information was what he had demanded in return for his aid.

Sinclair knelt at Jennifer's grave, as he had many times before he left England. He'd always felt that he could come here and be alone, be safe from his life as Caliburn. No longer.

He wanted to cry, but he couldn't. He didn't know who was watching, besides the ghosts.

WAR AND HELL

BY BRETT BARKLEY

Jack Pitt, private in the 2/1st London Regiment of the Fourteenth Division, carefully selected a target from the many rushing German soldiers. He waited as the man charged toward him . . . waited . . . waited. Then he fired. His shot found its mark. The German soldier jerked awkwardly midstride and crumpled to the cold muck, no more than thirty yards from the British trench. Pitt's hands shook as he ejected the spent round, quickly loaded another, slammed the bolt back in place, and selected his next target. The soldiers standing on either side of him did the same, the report of their rifles echoing down the line. There were many targets to choose from. The Germans were attempting to overrun the regiment's position — again. It wouldn't be their last try, either. All the men in the trenches had been given the same order: Conserve ammunition at all costs.

It was late March, 1918, and over the course of the last week, the Germans had made a strong surge back against the line, catching Pitt's battalion terribly off guard. The British had suffered tremendous losses. Word was, the Germans had regrouped and were trying to push through all along the Western Front. Pitt and the rest of his regiment hadn't learned much about the goings-on to the south, but they had heard the Germans were using gas and massive amounts of artillery, driving many divisions back. The 2/1st hadn't yet seen either, but had hastily dug in, preparing for the worst.

They hadn't anticipated the worst would include being cut off from supplies or reinforcements when the various divisions to the south retreated. And with the Germans' near-constant attempts to overrun the British line, their supplies were now despairingly low. Morale was far worse. Runners had been sent to summon help. Word returned that the lines had been strained or smashed all along the front, and that holding their position was imperative. Help would be sent when it could be spared. So, with dwindling supplies and support, failing morale and hope, the men of the 2/1st dug in. They would wait. They would fight. And if that weren't enough, they would die.

The Somme River valley, where they had been ordered to make their stand, was a dead and desolate place. Winter snows and thawing rains had soaked the earth, and the booted feet of thousands of men had churned the resulting mud until the terrain was beyond treacherous. For miles around, the trees were splintered and broken; only jagged stumps and trunks remained standing in most places, stripped of bark and charred. Manmade trenches sliced across the landscape, deep furrows angling against those of the enemy. Between these gashes, hastily laid barbed wire stretched and coiled, waiting to ensnare those daring to cross No Man's Land.

Private Pitt stared out across that wasteland and chose another target. He fired. The recoil of his weapon and the strong smell of gunpowder no longer registered in his mind. There were so many Germans. He watched some of them stagger and fall, watched his own target drop unceremoniously, claw at the ground, then stop moving. Still the Germans came. Some ran, crouching low, darting erratically, trying to dodge the hail of British bullets. Others charged directly at the line. All fired on the trenches as they came.

Pitt found a cold, distant comfort in the mechanical movements of his hands: disengage bolt, empty chamber, reload, engage bolt, raise rifle, aim . . . carefully . . . carefully.

A bullet struck the ground near Pitt's head, spraying his face with foetid mud, forcing him from his daze. The numbness lifted, and it all became real for him — the suffocating expanse of the grey sky, the sound of the rifles discharging all around him, the bullets whistling past, the cries of his fellows as they fell to the duck-boards lining the trench floor. Two positions down, on Pitt's left, Corporal James Gatby from Whitehall suddenly dropped limp to the boards. A large section of his head was missing. His remaining eye stared blankly ahead.

Pitt had seen too many corpses in the two years since his conscription to be unsettled by the gruesome sight. It only reminded him that today, with the Germans closing in, his own time to die might be upon him.

Private Owen Crouch, directly to Pitt's right, screamed something at him. Pitt stared at his friend for a moment, uncomprehending, until his attention was drawn away by another man to his left falling back from the trench wall. Crouch grabbed Pitt's arm and shook him. "Are you hit? Are you hit?" he screamed.

Pitt replied, but the words were swallowed up by the battle's cacophony. The Germans were close, as many as twenty or so approaching Pitt's small section of trench; between the rifle reports he could actually make out some of their shouts as they crossed the last dozen meters of No Man's Land. But there was something else. Barely audible at first over the fight, an odd roar echoed from somewhere behind the British line, a distant sound, now getting louder.

Then, out of the corner of his eye, Pitt saw the source of that feral roar. Others saw it, too. All along the trench, men looked up to watch the large motorcycle rocket overhead toward the onrushing gang of German soldiers.

"Tommy Gun," they whispered. "He's come."

Somehow Tommy Gun had ramped his motorcycle, jumping it high into the air on a course straight for the advancing German line. The Triumph was a strong machine. Over the past several months, it had served him well up and down the Western Front. Today it would serve one last, great purpose. In midair, he kicked himself free of the Triumph. As he did, he drew his signature weapons — twin Thompson submachine guns — from two large sling holsters across his back.

The machine guns, it was said, had been crafted specifically for Tommy Gun's hands by an American gunsmith. No others like them existed. Rumours abounded as to why the craftsman had refused to make any others, though most assumed the weapons were too deadly, too devastating to be mass produced. Others believed the twin guns had been a gift from the Devil himself. The sound they made was surely hellish, unlike anything the soldiers of either army had heard before — shockingly loud, with a growl that was anger incarnate.

Hot brass shell casings fell to earth as the guns called out. But Tommy Gun did not aim at the German soldiers now staring wide-eyed at the spectacle before them. He targeted the Triumph's fuel tank as it dropped from the sky into the midst of the advancing enemy. The motorcycle ignited with a concussive blast of startling size, spitting blazing metal and shrapnel. The Germans scattered, but they could not flee fast enough. The sizzling steel fragments caught some, the ball of fire still others. The wounded slipped in the muck, writhing, before they eventually fell still. The less fortunate, their bodies savaged beyond all reckoning by the blast, mewled sad, terrible things as they blindly tried to drag themselves away from the carnage.

Secondary explosions caused the motorcycle's burning husk to jump and pop as Tommy Gun stood on the battlefield, still firing at the fleeing Germans. Pitt stared at the hero, awestruck.

He was tall, a large man with broad shoulders. His long grey trench coat billowed wildly. Underneath his coat was what appeared to be a standard-issue British infantry uniform, with an unusual number of pouches and belts of various sizes, most likely holding his shells and supplies. The boots he wore were similar to those issued to Pitt and his fellows, though his gloves were thick and long, strapped at the wrist, extending halfway up his arm. On his head rested the familiar round, wide-brimmed steel helmet. His face, though, was concealed by a Union Jack moulded tightly to his features. The flag's bright red and blue contrasted starkly with the dull greys, greens, and browns of his uniform.

Tommy Gun began to move, slowly, methodically, firing his weapons now in quick bursts, selecting targets as he walked. His long trench coat, spattered with mud, flared at his sides like the wings of an avenging angel. Some of the enemy turned to flee. Others attempted to exchange shots with the towering warrior, but their bullets seemed unable to strike him. Every shot aimed his way arced wide and buried itself impotently in the earth.

The men in the British trenches finally followed Tommy Gun's lead and opened fire. And within moments, the tide had turned, the disruption in the German advance widening into a broad retreat. The 2/1st had been spared.

On that muddy black battlefield strewn with broken and burning bodies, their saviour stood alone, unscathed. Around him, the wounded cried out. Small fires crackled softly. Overhead, the sky faded from the cold grey the men had come to expect of the winter days. To the east, the leaden hues of night had already laid claim to the horizon.

Tommy Gun turned then, still-smoking guns hanging loosely at his sides, head lowered so that the round rim of his steel helmet obscured his face. Slowly he made his way back toward the British line and the cheering soldiers. They had survived the day. He saved them, that powerful figure silhouetted against the darkening sky. The soldiers quieted as he approached the trench.

"Good show, old chums," Tommy Gun said brightly. "But there'll be more of that before we're through." Unceremoniously, he leapt down into the trench to stand amongst the men. "Who's in charge of this outfit?"

It was Lieutenant-Colonel McCrae, a weary man in his late thirties, who responded. "I am," he said as he stepped through the crowd of men.

Tommy Gun turned to him, "Right. Well, then, we'll be needing to talk." His voice was strong, controlled. The men surrounding him watched his every movement, hung on his every word.

McCrae cleared his throat and summoned Major Baylie and Captain Pollack. Then he struggled for something to say to the hero.

"I want to thank you," he murmured. "For what you've done today. And my men — they thank you, too."

Tommy Gun shook his head slightly. "Not at all."

The two officers arrived abruptly to flank the lieutenant-colonel. "Follow us, if you would, Mister . . . er —"

Tommy Gun cut him off with an easy gesture of his hand, "No formalities here. I'll follow you."

The four departed for the dugout, leaving the gathered men shocked and amazed behind them.

"A whole battalion," Corporal Gowdy remarked with wonder. "He pushed back a whole battalion."

Coming in closer, Gowdy put his arm over Pitt's shoulder. He smiled as he announced to the group, "We're going to make it, boys. The lot of us."

"More than that," someone added. "We're going to take it to them."

"Ol' Fritz is in trouble now!"

"Too right!"

Tommy Gun heard those exclamations, and others like them, as he trailed the officers winding their way through the trench. But there were many more soldiers who remained wearily silent. They parted solemnly as the procession passed. Lean as starved dogs, caked with mud, clinging to their battered rifles, they fixed sunken eyes on the hero. Even in this cold, the men wore their hair closely shorn, a means of combating the lice that plagued the trenches. They were cloaked in an overwhelming stench of sickness and rotting flesh, a smell that cut through even the pungent odour from the chloride of lime used to kill the bacteria that thrived in the mud.

Throughout this long war, Tommy Gun had spent a great deal of time fighting beside men much like these. He did not expect them to rise to attention as he passed, to make themselves presentable. He understood it was a small victory if his presence inspired them to smile despite their soul-sick fatigue.

Still, there were some who shook off their weariness to call out a greeting or rush forward to shake his hand in gratitude. He tried to acknowledge all those who did. These men, he hoped, might show similar spirit in a time of crisis, when their pluck would mean the difference between victory and disaster.

As he entered the dugout, Tommy Gun turned and waved.

Of the soldiers nearby, Altaridge, a young man of seventeen, did the least to mask his excitement and awe. "Did you see what he did out there? Did you see?"

Altaridge was talking to no one in particular, but that made his enthusiasm all the more infectious. "And he's with us now," he added. "Here in the trenches to fight beside us!"

Before long, many of the men were smiling right along with him. They had to admit, there was something in the air, something big.

Tommy Gun wasted no time once he entered the dugout. He retrieved an official British army document from his trench coat and handed it to the lieutenant-colonel.

Before McCrae could break the seal, Tommy Gun began: "It's from General Sir Byng of the Third Army. We're in a terrible way out there. I just came from the front, and I can tell you myself it's a massacre. We're taking heavy losses all along the line." The lieutenant-colonel had begun reading the document; Tommy Gun addressed the major and the captain, his blue eyes impassioned with the urgency of the situation. "If this stretch of front collapses, they'll be completely cut off. We'll likely lose them all."

Lieutenant-Colonel McCrae sank into his seat, his brow furrowed as he read. The makeshift command dugout was little more than a hole with a roof. There was no radio, no electric, and the men were forced to stoop. In the centre of the uneven boarded floor stood three chairs and a small table. Several maps were hastily strewn over the table. A flickering oil lamp lit the space, casting an orange glow. The air hung heavy with the cold and the smell of burning lamp oil.

McCrae looked up from the document in shock. "But this can't be. We don't have the necessary forces to take that German position. We're at half strength — at best! Our machine guns have been lost. We've no artillery support. We can't even evacuate our wounded." McCrae set the document on the table. "We've been requesting reinforcements for a week. We've gotten nothing so far. Can we at least expect them before we're to mount this attack?"

Tommy Gun squared himself to the men, looking the lieutenant-colonel directly in the eyes. "I'm your reinforcement," he answered.

The officers stared blankly at the masked man, their faces registering their utter disbelief. McCrae and Baylie paused. Pollock stepped forward and reached out with one hand, appealing for the hero to tell him he hadn't heard correctly.

"No," Tommy Gun said in response to Pollock's desperate gesture. "No mistake about it." When he again addressed the three, his voice was reserved, yet strong. "Simply put, there aren't reinforcements to spare."

Tommy Gun crossed his arms over his chest. "If we can't take that German position, they'll have an easy road straight to Ham. If they beat the French there, our boys are completely cut off. And we haven't time to debate and delay. You may have heard that artillery to the south. It's been pounding away there for the last several days. Well, its work is almost done, which means it will be coming through here by no later than tomorrow evening."

The lamplight flickered orange across his masked face. He waited, allowing the gravity of his words to sink in. When the proper apprehension showed on the officers' faces, he went on. His voice now was stern, hard.

"What happened today, what's been happening for the last week, is just a taste of what's coming for you. You're in Fritz's way. Either you move out of his path now, let him through, and hope you're not caught in the crossfire when he cuts the rest of the retreating British forces to ribbons —" he leaned forward, his gloved hands gripping either side of the small table "— or you can be soldiers. Take that position, buy our boys the time they need. And maybe, just maybe, hold the Germans off long enough to get the reinforcements you need."

Lieutenant-Colonel McCrae rested his face in his hands. He sighed heavily and addressed his men, "Major Baylie, Captain Pollack, we'll need to be moving tonight. Arrange to meet with all company sergeants. Whether or not a proper chance presents itself, we'll have to strike before dawn."

Baylie and Pollack paused for a moment, watching the lieutenant-colonel in disbelief.

"Go on," he snapped. "You've got your orders."

After they had departed, he turned to Tommy Gun, "I trust you won't fail us now, because I have no intention of letting my men fail you."

"I appreciate that, sir." Tommy Gun noted. "But there's nasty business ahead, and how he chooses to face it down is a decision every man must make for himself. . . ."

Tommy Gun returned to the front line trenches some hours later. The new orders had since been handed out, and the men were preparing for an unprecedented early morning attack. Despite the hero's continued presence, the mood in the trenches had dramatically shifted. And as Tommy Gun himself trudged back through the sombre crowd, even he appeared weary, discouraged. He paid little attention to the soldiers busily preparing for battle as he moved past, lost as he was in his own thoughts and concerns.

Tommy Gun passed through Pitt's area as many of the men were eating their evening rations. Altaridge was the first to greet him, jumping up from his position, hurrying to the hero's side.

"I guess you heard about our orders, eh?" The boy spoke with excitement and admiration. Tommy Gun nodded. "Don't that beat all?"

The masked man looked at the boy for a moment before responding simply, "Yes."

"What you did out there today was bloomin' mad!" the boy effused. "I mean, I've never seen anything —"

"For God's sake, lad," Corporal Longley interrupted, "give a man some rest!" He was seated against the trench wall. There was a tin of canned beef and several army biscuits laid out in front of him. "You'll have to excuse Altaridge," he said to Tommy Gun. "He gets a bit daft occasionally."

"To be expected hereabouts," Tommy Gun replied with a laugh. He sat down on a makeshift timber chair someone stood to offer him.

"Excuse me, sir," Longley said, "but would you care for a bit of bully beef and biscuits?" He raised one of his biscuits, looked at it quizzically. "Well, they're not all that much like biscuits without soaking them in water for a day, or so. Still, anyone who can fight like you would stand a fair chance against one of 'em."

The men gathered around the hero laughed, nodding in agreement. Tommy Gun chuckled softly, but declined with a simple gesture.

"No, but if one of you blokes has a fag to spare, I'd appreciate it."

Private Blankenship quickly offered Tommy Gun a cigarette.

Tommy Gun removed his gloves and rolled his mask up over his nose, revealing a square, unshaven jaw. He gratefully accepted the cigarette, offering a strained, awkward smile in return. But the men hadn't noticed. They were watching his hand. It was shaking — a noticeable and sustained tremor. Cigarette clamped in his thin lips, he produced a match from a small pouch on his belt and struck it against the timbers. It wouldn't light. Again he swiped it over the wood, only to break the matchstick. He managed a slight chuckle. "Wet matches. . . ."

Blankenship hurriedly found his own lighter and struck a light.

"That's a chum," Tommy Gun said. He took a long drag, held it in, then exhaled the smoke into the cold March air. His body rose and slumped with the effort. He did not speak. He did not make eye contact with the men crowded around him. He simply stared ahead into the distance.

Private Pitt watched a large brown rat scavenge for food just down the trench from him. Vermin grew large in the trenches; the abundance of corpses provided them with frequent and ready feasts. At night they would scamper over the soldiers, trying to sort out the dead from the sleeping. Gowdy had actually gotten quite good at spearing the foul things with his bayonet. He claimed it was the only thing bayonets were good for. Normally, there were scores of rats. In the last few days, however, he had seen fewer and fewer. Even the vermin were smart enough to clear out before the big push — though they'd surely return to claim their spoils, once the fighting was done with.

Shivering, through clenched teeth, Pitt muttered to the group, "Sometimes I think we've already died and this is hell."

The men around him grunted their agreement. Tommy Gun did not react.

From somewhere in the dark, Gowdy spoke up: "Here we are deceased, and poor Altaridge's never even been kissed." They laughed at bit at that, more at the way the boy blushed and bristled than at the jibe itself.

"This isn't hell. . . ."

Tommy Gun's words hung in the air, silencing the men.

"The death, the suffering. . . ." He paused for a moment. "It's not hell."

His words were distant and paced, coming with effort. In silence, the soldiers watched him closely. He appeared alone, forlorn. He wrapped his arms tightly around himself, and they waited for him to finish. The sounds of shelling to the south — closer, it seemed, all the time — filled the silence. The wind blew a sombre chill through the trench.

"No, this isn't hell," Tommy Gun repeated distantly. "We can leave this place. We can escape. Some day, maybe we will." He raised his head then, as if only just realizing there were others around him. He searched for something in their faces — recognition, understanding — before concluding. "Hell is a place that stays with you no matter where you go, no matter what you do. . . ."

The men watched him carefully. Tommy Gun sat, motionless, against the trench wall.

It was Corporal Longley who spoke first. "Why do you do it, Tommy? You don't have to stay here. You've got no C. O. after you."

The masked man turned to him, cocking his head to the side dramatically. "Well, I can't let the fun all to you blokes." He managed an unconvincing chuckle.

"No, really, Tommy," Longley pursued. "You like doing away with old Fritz that much?"

"No," he whispered. The soldiers leaned in close, each in his own way studying the enigmatic man.

Tommy Gun lowered his head again, appearing for a moment to withdraw. He began slowly, deeply searching for the words. "An obligation. A promise I made to myself."

Again, he chuckled self-consciously. "It seems so long ago now." He reclined a bit, relaxing his arms. His fingers toyed with the frayed cuff of his sleeve.

"It was early in the war. I was here in the Somme. I was alone. It was nearing on to dusk, and I happened on one of our boys. He was lying on the ground — dead, of course, but all alone. Now, I'd seen corpses before. I'd seen plenty. I'd been responsible for a good many, I'd say. But he was all by himself. There was literally no one else around."

He paused and took off his helmet, running his hand through his short brown hair.

"And I knew that was where he would stay, at least until something got to him. But it had me wondering: What would his people think? Someone back home had to be missing him. But they wouldn't ever know for certain he was gone. They'd just wonder. They'd never know where he died, how he died.

"I felt in his pocket for his pay book. I wanted to know him. I don't know why. I could've just left him there." He leaned back against the trench wall, watching the sky as he reflected.

"Walter Rimmley. That was his name. And when I pulled that pay book out, a couple of photographs fell on the ground, see? I had a look at them. His wife and son, apparently. I thought to myself, I thought, 'What's she thinking about him now? Will she ever know? And what about that boy?'

"I'd seen a lot of men killed, but I never thought about the people at home. I guess I never considered there's a life they have to get back to, people who are waiting on them. So I took those photographs. I had the pay book. And I promised myself, with poor old Private Rimmley as my only witness, that when this war was all over, I'd find them. I'd find his people. I'd hand them those photographs, and I'd tell them he died thinking of them and that he hadn't really been all alone."

Tommy Gun reached a trembling hand into his trench coat. He searched for a moment, then slowly, carefully retrieved a thick stack of ragged, dog-eared pay books, photographs, and stationary. It was loosely wrapped with a dirtied white ribbon. He stared at the bundle in his hand for a moment.

"I've got a lot of these, you know. They're each one a life." He caressed the papers as he spoke. "I guess some people would think it morbid to gather up these mementos of dead men."

He held the bundle up, raising it, presenting it for men to see.

"This — the men bundled up here. They're the reason I'm out here." Carefully, he replaced the packet in his coat and again wrapped his arms around himself.

"If I had my way, that would be the lot. I don't want to add to the collection. But I will if I have to. I made a promise, after all. . . ."

None of the men spoke. They bundled themselves as best they could, huddled together against the cold, each alone in his thoughts. A three-quarter moon was reaching its zenith. On the horizon, the German artillery bombardment lit the skyline in brilliant golds and oranges.

Pitt awoke from an uncomfortable sleep at approximately a quarter to four, to whistles shrilling in the darkness, sounding the British charge. His sweating hands fixed on the cold rifle and he stood, breath shallow, eyes wide, heart racing. Each man waited his turn to take the ladder out of the trench. "Going over the top," they called it. As they queued up, the soldiers didn't speak. They exchanged glances, but the world around them was mostly a fear-hazed blur. All that mattered was the ladder and the dark unknown to which it led.

Tommy Gun was the first over the top, the first to hurdle the parapet, the first to embark on what seemed the impossibly long march across No Man's Land. From the trenches, the men watched the hero as he moved confidently across the wasteland, hunkered low to avoid sniper fire. He was several steps out before he realized that he was alone. He glanced over his shoulder; the men had stayed behind.

In the feeble pre-dawn light, Private Pitt caught Tommy Gun's questioning gaze. The private and a few of his fellows returned that look with one of stark fear. Others turned, eyes quickly averted in shame. They couldn't move.

Down the lines sergeants barked orders, screaming at the men to do their duty. Scattered soldiers had climbed the ladders and now found themselves caught in the confusion of the moment. Seeing themselves alone and exposed, these few quickly retreated to the relative safety of the trenches.

Pitt felt the warm blood spray across his face before he heard the bullet's impact. Instinctively his hands moved to cover his face and he fell to the duck-boards, tumbling through the soldiers directly behind him. His first thought was that he had been hit, though he couldn't feel any pain. He screamed for help, but none came. As he regained his senses, he found the rest of the 2/1st standing on the firing steps and hanging on the ladders, looking out at something on the battlefield. He could sense their panic, read the horror in their stiff backs and clenched fists. He heard their frightened, nearly insensible mumblings: "Oh, God, what should we do?"

Tommy Gun was hit.

Pitt rose unsteadily to his feet, dreading to peer over the parapet but incapable of doing otherwise. His eyes took in the barren landscape, searching desperately for Tommy Gun, hoping for proof that he was reading the signs incorrectly. Then Pitt saw him. Though he could barely make out the form, he saw a dark mass lying in the mud a short distance in front of them. Tommy Gun wasn't moving.

Someone had grabbed Pitt by the arm. It was Altaridge. He was screaming at him, screaming that they had to do something. The young soldier's eyes were wide with terror, and tears streamed down his cheeks. Pitt jerked away from him, then numbly watched the boy move on to another soldier, still shouting. The private turned again to the others around him. They stood in silence. Absentmindedly he wiped the blood — Tommy Gun's blood, he realized with a shudder — from his face. The commanding officers were calling for the men to move, but Pitt didn't hear. He didn't see the handfuls of soldiers who had been forced out on to the battlefield, didn't see them nervously making their way toward the German lines. He saw only the dark form crumpled in the mud.

Slowly the echoes of distant rifle reports registered in his mind. The German's were waking now. Soon the Somme River valley would ring with their gunfire. Enough of the enemy had taken up their rifles that the confused soldiers out in No Man's Land were already falling, one by one, to the growing hail of bullets.

To Pitt's right, Altaridge crawled up over the trench wall and dragged himself toward where Tommy Gun lay. He made it only a short distance beyond the parapet before a sniper's round found him.

Altaridge was still alive. The men of the 2/1st could hear his screams from where they stood. But he was too far to reach, too many steps beyond the safety of the trench to risk a rescue. Some of the men turned away, moving down the line. But Pitt couldn't turn away. He watch as Altaridge dragged himself through the mud — not toward the trench, but away from it, in the direction of Tommy Gun. The young soldier was calling for a medic, but not for himself.

Pitt swallowed hard. Another round passed just over his head. Absently, he ducked, but only after the bullet had passed. Altaridge was sobbing now, long sustained wails of pain. Some of the men behind Pitt were screaming at one another in panic. They were arguing about how they were going to drag the boy back, who would take that terrible risk.

Pitt was shaking, his body tense, numb. He glanced down at his rifle and checked the safety, checked the bayonet, checked the safety again. Briefly, he thought of his home, his mother, his younger sister; their images were quick flashes in his mind.

Altaridge was calling to the men by name now.

"Charlie! Albert! Jack! For God's sake . . ."

No one moved to him.

The familiar sounds of war enwrapped the 2/1st. Shots rang out and sergeants howled orders in to the night. But there was another sound, too. Pitt heard it first. It was almost like the growling of a wounded animal. It wasn't Altaridge. It didn't even sound human. Slowly it grew, built up by rage and pain. The others heard it. Some cowered from it. Some cautiously craned their necks over the parapet to find the source.

It was Tommy Gun.

The wounded hero was rising from the mud. Stunned, the men of the 2/1st watched as he pulled himself to his feet. He was roaring at the top of his lungs, screaming denial in the face of death, defying the German snipers, defying the bullets themselves. He would not be taken. He raised his left arm and unleashed a fiery burst from his submachine gun. The muzzle flash painted his hunched form in bloody hues, but not even the clatter of his weapon could drown out his howl. It was a sight, a sound those nearby would never forget.

Right arm hanging limp at his side, numb fingers still gripping his famous weapon, Tommy Gun lurched back toward the trench. Through the darkness, Pitt could make out the glint of moonlight off the steel of his helmet and the vaguest hints of the Union Jack covering his face. More clear still was the wound on his right shoulder. Even from this distance, Pitt could see the ugly, wet stain spreading to his chest.

Altaridge had collapsed into the mud. Though consciousness seemed ready to desert him at any moment, he still managed to blindly lift up a hand as Tommy Gun approached. "The other way," he croaked. "Got to save Tommy Gun. . . ."

Tommy Gun dropped his weapon to the half-frozen earth and took the trembling hand raised before him. There was no indecision, no hesitation. With great effort, he pulled Altaridge toward the trench.

The boy was still murmuring about saving Tommy Gun and their duty to overtake the Germans when he was hefted over the parapet into the hands of a waiting medic. Pitt and another soldier reached out to help Tommy Gun into the trench, but he waved them off. Bullets tore up the ground all around him, but the hero did not flinch. Silently, he stared at the soldiers. His breathing was heavy, laboured, his form trembling with the effort of staying on his feet.

He leaned in close to Pitt, speaking with difficulty. His words were raspy, yet strong.

"That's not hell." He pointed through the darkness to the German lines. "That's our only way out of it."

The words hung in the icy air for only a moment before Tommy Gun rose, turning again toward No Man's Land. He retrieved his gun from where he had dropped it. Then, managing somehow to raise the weapon with his wounded right arm, Tommy Gun disappeared in the night. The angry bark of his submachine guns and the distinctive, but dwindling flash of their muzzles marked his progress toward the German line.

As Tommy Gun's words made their way down the line, the soldiers of the 2/1st London Regiment of the Fourteenth Division clamoured over the trench walls and charged into the night. As they surged forward, they roared as one the cry of the battle worn, defiant to the end. Private Jack Pitt took the trench ladder in two steps, clearing the parapet with his third. He did not look behind him to see if the rest of the regiment were following. He didn't need to.

CITIZENS

BY STEVEN GRANT

The legend goes that thunder roared where the Citizen walked. If it did, I never heard it. We live in an age of legends, but I can only give you truth, and the truth is this: Six times the Citizen and I fought, and six times he won.

So I was baffled when they came to me to put an end to him.

It made no sense then. I had no reputation as a killer, unlike the Jackanape or Doctor Malice, and had, frankly, no taste for it. They could have gone to myriad other criminals the Citizen had no direct experience with, powerful men like Janus or the Iron Duke. I'd been driven by narcissism — a conviction in my physical and intellectual superiority, a conviction that crumbled a little more each time the Citizen beat me — and, I realised later, by a latent desire to commit patricide. My father came from a line of thieves and profiteers who had never paid a day for their crimes; time had sanctified the family fortune, so delusions of superiority ran from generation to generation, as did scorn and abuse. "Great men make their own law," he'd drummed into my head until I was sick of it, and he delighted in proclaiming that I'd never be a great man, that I'd always be nothing more than his shadow.

I didn't hate my father. I despised him. Though I pretended a life of crime would show I was worthy to be his son, in truth it brought me great glee — still does — that my initial capture destroyed his political career. When I fell my family fell with me, as the papers dredged up long-buried allegations that ended any hope he'd ever had for public office. I was cut off, of course, but that was irrelevant. The last I heard, he was cut off, too, scorned by former friends and allies, just another failure drinking himself silly all alone in our mansion. Where the money went after he died I couldn't say, except that none came to me. Which was fine. I'd gotten what I wanted.

They appeared without warning, after lockdown, two of them in guard uniforms. But not guards. They took me down with a taser, cuffed my wrists behind my back, slipped an opaque bag over my head, and dragged me down endless corridors. I thought they were going to kill me. I was roughly strapped into a painful wooden chair, able to move only my fingers, eyes, and jaw. When the hood came off, I was in a small, dark room with sweating brick walls, centred under a bright light. Across a table, a stone-faced blond man in a nondescript grey suit studied me passionlessly through wraparound charcoal sunglasses, like a coroner examines a corpse. There was something unreal about him, as though he were a projection, a cartoon. Nebulous. He neither smiled nor frowned, merely told me what "they" wanted me to do.

He didn't twitch when I abruptly laughed.

"Don't you want revenge?" he asked with implied disinterest, as if we were two strangers passing time in forced conversation on an airplane.

I know we "villains" are supposed to leap at such offers. But I'd had my revenge — against my father. The Citizen, I realised, I couldn't have cared less about. Our first fight ended in my humiliation, true. The papers called me Lord Adonis then, and I was as close to a Greek god as anyone was likely to see. How could such a seemingly normal person — that was his gimmick: the ordinary citizen — have defeated someone as obviously superior as me? My first loss I chalked up to my inexperience and his trickery, my second to bad luck, the third to the unexpected, coincidental appearance of Tom Foolery and the Amber Prince as their battles spilled from Detroit onto our turf. By our fourth fight my father was dead, and without him for a mortified audience my interest was already on the wane. The last two battles were more like games, two old sparring partners testing their skills against each other, but my passion had already fled.

"Do I want revenge? Not really," I admitted.

Again Nebulous showed no visible reaction. A thin hand went to his breast pocket. He slid a folded sheaf of papers across the table, topped by a pen. I knew he wanted me to pick them up. I didn't. We gazed at each other for what seemed like forever. At last he nodded, so slowly the threat couldn't be missed. I smoothed the papers open and read them.

Bearer bonds, in the sum of a quarter million dollars, and pardons. Blank lines where my name could be written in. Signatures from the mayor and the governor. And the president. And, reading between the lines, I recognized the real message: Unstoppable forces were arrayed against the Citizen, and soon he'd be destroyed, regardless of my decision. Whoever ended him would be a free man with a sizable bank account, his record totally expunged.

So it might as well be me.

I took the pen and wrote my name onto the pardons. Nebulous took the pardons and left the bearer bonds with me. As he turned away I thought I saw him smile.

Then darkness slammed all thought out of me with the cold finesse of the executioner's plunging blade.

As a television crackled on, I woke, in the sort of room I grew up accustomed to: large and decked out in fine linens and rich woods. A huge, panoramic flat-screen hung from the ceiling like a mobile, directly above the foot of the king bed upon which I was sprawled. Only the light from the screen and a trace of bright sunshine from around dense curtains disturbed the room's twilight.

"I trust you're comfortable," Nebulous said, somehow more real on the screen than in person. "You'll find a wet bar near the door. Room service is always available. Everything's paid for, so feel free." By then, my eyes were adjusting to the light, and I saw the desk to the left of the bed and the notebook computer sitting on it. "That's your weapon. The fastest, most capable portable made, with broadband Internet access, password cleared for every database in the world," he continued. I realised it was no pre-recording or simple broadcast. Somewhere he was watching me. Without clothes, I suddenly felt conspicuous.

Nebulous went on in that same inflectionless voice: "Off the bathroom there's a walk-in closet decked out with a selection of today's fashions. Wear whatever you like. We didn't want to make that choice for you. Hit 88 on the phone if you'd like some companionship, and we'll send it up. I presume you prefer woman?"

"The more legal the better. Am I allowed to leave here?"

"Go wherever you like. You're a free man — as long as you do what you were hired for." He paused a moment, theatrically letting the silence foment enough gravity to give his next words special weight. "Don't think about running out on us. You wouldn't make it."

"And I'm to do *what* exactly?"

"Find him — who he is, where he lives, what he does. Find him. You'll find a cell phone in the desk drawer. If you need to contact me, switch it on and it will automatically connect to my number."

"I'm not a killer," I said.

"Perhaps," he replied. "Perhaps in finding him you'll find yourself as well."

"Who do we work for?" I asked. The screen abruptly went blank. A small triumph: I knew now how to get rid of him.

It was beginning to sink in that this was no longer prison, or, if it was, it was a prison that could be easily cracked. The computer was evidence they'd chosen me for my intelligence and cunning — my old delusions of superiority kicked in reflexively, and I had to force them out of my mind — which meant they knew I was already working out a double-cross; why else would he have warned me against it? It also meant doubt. Whatever their power, they were nowhere near as confident of it as they pretended to be. Which meant?

Like me, they'd fought the Citizen before, and had been beaten. Maybe many times. Were they the ones who wanted revenge? Unlikely. Revenge is a petty ambition, difficult to sustain in the absence of the frothing madness you see only in movies. Oh, I had no doubt that these "men of power" were mad. In my experience, men of power almost always are, because only the mad are drawn to that much power. But theirs was a crueller, colder madness, excising the sorts of plebeian desires that had gripped my father and grandfather, and had even wrapped their fingers around me now and then. No, they didn't want revenge. They wanted an obstacle removed, a threat eliminated.

So why recruit me? Simple. Despite viewing themselves as beyond mere humanity, "they" were — extrapolating from my family — uniquely susceptible to the most ancient and prehuman emotion of all: fear.

But what would make them fear the Citizen so much they'd bring me into it, leaving a trail back to them, if anyone cared enough to follow it?

There was only one possibility: He knew who they were. He knew where to find them. The Citizen could reach the unreachable and drag them down.

Knowing that gave *me* power over them, though they certainly wouldn't realise it. I wasn't about to let them. It was a hand I had no clue yet how to play. I'd know the proper time and place for that when I saw it, but there was no reason to force things. Besides, knowing such great men feared the Citizen so much made me truly curious about him. I wanted to know what made him great.

I guess I did still have my own demons to cast out.

I fished out a mineral water and a Toblerone from the wet bar, and switched on the computer, instantly calling up a search engine portal. In a box prefaced with *Find results with the exact phrase* I idly typed in *"the Citizen"* and tapped *Enter*. 3,443,278 results.

Not how I wanted to spend my first day out of prison. I closed the computer. From room service I ordered a barbeque platter and a dessert buffet tray, then immediately picked up the phone again and tapped *88* on the keypad.

I'm not stupid.

Charlene — so she called herself — dropped her card on the nightstand before she left, so I could call her again. I knew Nebulous had been watching. A dirty little secret of the costume types, both hero and villain, is that to be one you need a taste for exhibitionism. You have to see the world as your stage, and being on stage is the ultimate kick, even if you lose. That's why so many villains keep coming back.

Charlene and I had put on quite a show. Next time I'd ask them to send up three. But not Charlene.

I took a hot bath, then slept for four hours. It was dark out when I woke. I called room service again for breakfast, watched some Japanese cartoon on a cable channel, and, after the food and coffee arrived, settled in front of the notebook and began to work.

William Pendleton, better known as Lord Adonis, passed away in solitary confinement at Lourdes Penitentiary yesterday afternoon of a respiratory ailment. . . .

A short piece on a news site, effectively summarising my accomplishments, if you can call them that, and my family history. They could've encapsulated it in a single phrase: *He did nothing*. For the first time, I felt I'd wasted my life.

The piece concluded with the news that my "ailment" had been the result of a highly contagious disease that necessitated fumigating the solitary confinement wing. Authorities were at a loss to explain how I had come in contact with the disease, and the warden speculated that, given my genius, I'd been able to surreptitiously use the prison's scant resources to gen-engineer the germ myself, perhaps as part of an escape scheme gone wrong. It was a flight of imagination that appropriately capped the myth of Lord Adonis.

I wasn't Lord Adonis anymore. I wasn't William Pendleton. Both were gone for good. Well, almost.

Though he didn't know it yet, the Citizen would set me free.

Three days after I started, I discovered how to access bank records. I was into it by then, forgetting women and food, living off mineral water and Toblerone, only leaving the room to visit the hotel's well-equipped gym for my daily workout. The room was always cleaned in my absence. I never saw a maid.

I started by cutting out all information about the Citizen that predated the beginning of the year, bringing the number of available articles to a workable 447,000-plus. Within forty-eight hours, I'd mapped out the Citizen's appearances for the year to date, noting with special interest the eyewitness reports of apparent injury. That was the key. Whatever else he was, the Citizen was a man, as prone to damage as anyone in his line would be. I'd damaged him myself, once or twice, though that had never stopped him.

I guessed at the type and extent of injury from the reports, and calculated his subsequent absences. There was an inescapable pattern: His absences were growing longer. Maybe he was getting older, maybe there were other factors, but statistics suggested recuperation was harder to come by. Maybe "they" had noticed that fact, as well, and had chosen this moment to strike because of it.

Or maybe the Citizen was taking his crusade to "them," moving to their realm beneath the horizon of public and media notice.

I cross-referenced his adventures against city and state maps. I had his movements charted. There was no locus, no central point of activity, no area he seemed to favour over any other. A dead end.

For two weeks I cross-referenced credit card receipts against areas of Citizen activity, starting at three mile radii and narrowing the field as necessary. For another week I analysed the results. Five names showed up with greater-than-statistically-reasonable frequency. I searched their records. One was black, another Asian, which let them out; there wasn't much I knew for sure about the Citizen, but I knew he was Caucasian. The other three were white, of similar build and age. Benjamin Pearson, an attorney over in Hasselgate. Bryan Wickline, a session musician; bassist. Michael Lloyd, sportswriter and ex-ballplayer. There was nothing to suggest any one of them over the others.

Some supervillains would've killed them all. The Iron Duke would've just obliterated the city. But Lord Adonis was an artist of crime, not a butcher.

Returning to the injuries, I cross-referenced the names against hospital reports. Another dead end. It made sense; had the Citizen gotten treatment at a hospital, or through a random physician, there'd be a trail back to him.

But the absence of data is also data.

Conclusion: He had his own doctor, someone who didn't report gunshot wounds to the police and had the knowledge and experience to cope with a variety of traumas. Someone within fairly easy access. If the Citizen paid him at all, it was cash under the table, or barter. Nothing that left a paper trail. But the doctor would leave a trail, whether he wanted to or not. He'd need special equipment, extra supplies. That was my next search: unusual purchases by doctors matched against the time and nature of damage most likely sustained by the Citizen.

No immediate matches, but the odds were very good their relationship had been set up for some time, suggesting that the doc would order supplies needed to cover most crises well in advance. Probably even blend them in with normal orders. This was a problem, but nothing insurmountable. It was still easy to extrapolate what supplies and equipment would be needed to treat the Citizen. Tediously, over days, I snagged doctors' purchase orders from a period of years, and sorted the data.

This time a dozen names popped up. Still, there was nothing to distinguish them from one another, no smoking gun. There were ways to explain the anomalies in their purchases, and nothing apparently connected any of them to the Citizen. I was a month into my search, and my interest was waning. The assignment seemed more of a prison than anything I'd known in the past eight years, with no end in sight. I spent my time playing online games, all ridiculously easy to beat. The Citizen became more a ghost the closer I tried to get to him.

It was while playing go against a gaming site that a pop-up ad appeared on the screen, peddling a service to find old classmates. Sometimes you read the arcane signs and piece together minute clues. Sometimes the solution to a problem walks in and beats you over the head.

I should have called Nebulous. He would have taken over. I would have finally been free. What happened to the Citizen, or even the doctor, was no concern of mine. But the month had changed me. In studying the Citizen, I'd read of his exploits — a far different and more encompassing perspective than our first-person encounters — and slowly came to what I believed was a larger understanding of him. It's possible he had hidden, darker motivations, but I didn't think so. Everything I read drew a picture of nobility and altruism: civic duty in the finest sense of the term. He was a man who gave completely, endlessly, to protect other citizens, without any desire for reward, glory, or personal gain. This was not a type of man with which I was familiar.

I was, I hate to admit, impressed. He was too good a man to be surrendered to Nebulous and his hidden bosses. There was no question the Citizen would die. I couldn't stop it. No one could.

But the Citizen deserved a proper, glorious death.

Both of us did.

I had no doubt Nebulous had my computer tapped, and was following my progress. Men like his bosses weren't known for patience, or trust, but I hadn't heard from him since I arrived at the hotel. I was watched constantly; it was the only possible explanation.

I finished a game and started a program, downloaded from the Internet, that would obliterate my research. I'd long since found and disabled the programs intended to prevent that.

I'd also started complementing my weight regimen with an aerobic run three times per week, partly because it made exercise sense and partly in anticipation of my eventual escape, when I would go out for a run and never come back. I knew "they" would never trust me, but "they" — perhaps even Nebulous — would be lulled by my rigid fixation on routine and never realise it was a ploy. Hopefully.

I started on my run, taking the cell phone. Had I not taken it, they'd have been on me in a flash. The phone contained a tracking device, but I'd found it and could remove or disable it whenever I chose.

It occurred to me, as I jogged through a spacious park, that there had been no reports of the Citizen since my release from prison. Under the circumstances, I thought that odd, as if it meant this whole thing was some Byzantine trap. Not for him. For me. As paranoia gripped me I considered dropping my escape plan, but that would just put me back in my captors' hands, and I knew their patience must be running out. I could never be returned to prison. I expected far worse if they decided I had failed.

At a point I had mapped out weeks earlier, I broke from the path into a full sprint through thick woods. It was, I considered proudly, a stunt only a superior athlete could manage without serious injury. Short of superpowers, no one could've kept up with me. No doubt Nebulous wouldn't bother. There was no need to stay near me when he could track my moves.

As I ran I opened the back case of the cell phone and flipped out the tracer, a cybernetic wafer not even as big as my thumbnail. I cut right through the woods and back, emerging at a dog walk near the park entrance. Crashing out of the woods, I almost ran into a pretty brunette and the Samoyed she had on a leash. Both were startled. The dog barked rabidly to warn me off, but I apologised, claiming to have gotten lost. Crouching before the Sammy, I spoke calmly and sweetly and held my hand out for it to sniff, charming dog and owner with the same gesture. As the animal calmed, I petted its ruff, slipping the tracer under its collar. Under other circumstances, I'd have listened in mock fascination while the girl gushed small talk, but I had other things on my mind. I took off running until I was out of her sight. Out of everyone's.

No one saw me shimmy over the wall and onto the street outside the park. Hordes milled by. I blended in. Just another citizen.

Stopping periodically to check behind me, I abruptly changed directions several times. When I was satisfied no one was following me, I went to the library.

I loaded the classmate seek site on the library's Internet hook-up and ran combinations, doctors' names against my suspects'. Only twenty minutes in, I caught a match: a high school yearbook, eight years before the Citizen's first appearance. Two seniors on the school's baseball team.

Doctor Mitch Rundle.

Michael Lloyd.

I logged off and went to the phone books.

* * *

I wasted half an hour hunting for a security system before I realised there was none. It made no sense. Why would the Citizen leave his home unguarded, open to enemies? The latch jimmied so easily I could think of only two explanations:

I was wrong, and Michael Lloyd wasn't the Citizen.

Or it was a trap.

I'd committed crimes my whole life, some clever and some horrible. Prison never fazed me, nor any threat of the law, including the constant possibility of disability or death. Only weak men had such concerns — that had been my philosophy. Yet, on the cusp of a simple B&E, I was filled with a dread that my next action would change, maybe destroy, what little was left of my life. This was no game, like my fights with the Citizen. I was betraying men who would never forgive; by escaping them to face Lloyd on my own I had effectively killed myself. An impulse said run, forget them and the Citizen and blend in with the crowd I'd tried so long and hard to stand out from, put as much distance and time as possible between myself and the hammer that would inevitably fall.

I should have run.

But I had gone there not only to prove I could find the Citizen, but to warn him. He'd fought long and hard, too, against overwhelming odds. He deserved to know they were coming for him, that if I had found him anyone could. Eventually.

Slipping the latch was ego, another show of my cleverness, but it wasn't clever. Or smart. It was the vestige of a lifetime of crime: Pavlovian response. There was another, simpler way in.

I rang the doorbell.

The door popped open with a buzz and a metallic cough. I entered what seemed to be an old-style railroad apartment, spartanly furnished. A faint, sour smell, like old fever sweat, soaked the air, growing stronger as I moved through the living room and kitchen to a bedroom in the back, as austere as the rest of the place: a small dresser, a thirteen-inch TV on a stand, and, on the floor, a mattress with a lamp and alarm clock nearby.

A tall, withered man lay on the bed, propped up by several pillows. His eyes and cheeks were sallow and sunken. He was sick, that much was clear, maybe terminally ill. But he smiled as if we were long lost friends.

"Lord Adonis," he rasped, though I hadn't identified myself. "I was hoping they'd send you. You're looking good."

"Citizen?" I asked, though I couldn't believe it.

"I read about your death," he said. "Sorry I couldn't make it to the funeral."

"There wasn't one."

"Oh, that's right. No body. All burned up." We both laughed at that. "Cancer," he said then, answering the obvious question. "Came on very quickly. The Radium Brothers."

"Yes, I heard about that. They're dead, aren't they? They blew themselves up."

"I hope so, 'cause they sure killed *me*. Of course, you still have time to finish the job, if you want."

"I'm not a killer," I said. He seemed disappointed. As he twitched in pain, I could understand why. His body was slowly devouring itself, taking him away bit by bit. An assassin's bullet would be a mercy compared to that.

"No, you never were. Take a look in there." He gestured to the closet.

It was tiny, with boxes stacked on the floor and clothes hung in no particular order. There, amidst jackets and shirt, hung the suit he wore as the Citizen, and the mask. "This?" I asked, showing him the outfit.

"It's yours," he said.

"I don't understand. . . ."

"I won't be using it again. I have maybe a couple more weeks."

"What am I supposed to do with it?"

He shrugged. "Burn it. Give it to Goodwill. It doesn't matter to me. You *could* try it on; you might like how it fits. You're smart. You'll think of something."

"But we're enemies!"

"Us?" he said, as though the thought had never entered his head before. He propped himself on an elbow and sadly shook his head. "William, didn't the last few weeks teach you anything? You and me, we were the sideshow. Entertainment. A moral lesson. Men like Lord Adonis, they don't exist to *win*. They exist to lose, to show that no matter what kind of power or brains or skill or even luck you have, you don't challenge the system — the Law — and expect to do anything but suffer for it. That was your role. Mine was to be the instrument of your defeat. Everyone goes to bed happy at night, certain that Truth and Justice are triumphant."

The condescending lilt in his tone reminded me of my father.

He convulsed in dry hacking; all the talking was ripping at his stricken throat. When I moved to help him, he signalled me back, and, as the coughing subsided, he continued. "The *real* show takes place behind the curtain."

I understood then what it was all about. Why they feared him. He had stopped playing the game. Or maybe he had always used the game as a cover for his true purposes. Irrelevant. He was onto them, which was the one thing they feared and the one thing that could — probably already had — hurt them.

It hurt me, too. I was angry at the way he spoke to me, like a wise teacher patiently tutoring a torturously slow student, and at having to hear these things from *him* when I could easily have worked them out myself.

All I could think to say was "I know."

Then Nebulous came through the wall.

★ ★ ★

I heard thunder then, an explosion that spit a torrent of plaster dust into the room, blinding and choking me. By the time I cleared my eyes and throat — mere seconds — Nebulous had a hand around Lloyd's bony neck. "Get out," he snarled at me, finally showing some emotion.

"You're slipping, Wallace," Lloyd rasped. "You used to leave no witnesses."

"You know each other?" I asked.

"Oh, yes," Lloyd said. Nebulous glared uncertainly at me, then let him go and drew an odd pistol from a latex holster strapped across his chest. He levelled the gun at Lloyd, who said flatly, "This is Wilmer Wallace. You can understand why he changed his name. He used to be Doctor Malice."

Nebulous pistol-whipped him silent, and, barely wasting a glance on me, said, "Get out now."

I gaped. I couldn't help myself. All the schemes and subterfuge, all the Citizen's fanciful paranoia, and what was it really? Just another insane criminal's revenge. He had used me as a stalking horse, I had found the Citizen for him, and now . . .

And now Lloyd was right. It didn't add up. I'd done nothing Wallace couldn't have done himself. While Nebulous — Doctor Malice — might have busted me out of prison, he couldn't have arranged a pardon. Why *was* he letting me leave? Why wouldn't he kill me, now that I'd served my purpose?

Unless my real purpose was just beginning. . . .

"No," I said, surprising myself as much as them. Wallace's face tensed with fury, and I thought he might shoot me on the spot. But the old thrill was back; I was a player on the stage again. "If anyone kills the Citizen," I continued, almost unaware of the words, "it will be Lord Adonis."

I *was* Lord Adonis again, one last time. Wallace could see that. Anything else and he would have killed me. Instead, he laughed.

He actually laughed, making it clear Lord Adonis was a joke to him. But he replied, "As long as I see him die."

With a gesture of mock courtesy, he handed me the pistol. It felt warm in my hand, heated by energies pulsing within it. I shot Nebulous twice in the face. He toppled backward, nothing but scattering ash above the neck. He was no longer laughing. Lloyd let out a shocked gasp, eyeing me with newfound respect and a touch of fear as I turned toward him. Those shots had shattered his cosy preconceptions of Lord Adonis, and he now faced a man far more unpredictable than he — than even I — had supposed.

"You killed him," he said sadly, without accusation. A statement of fact.

"He was going to kill you."

"I had hoped . . ." he began, but his voice trailed off.

"That I'd take your place? Become the new Citizen?"

His eyes widened. I knew now why I had always lost when I faced him; it was not luck or circumstance. He'd had sources of intelligence I couldn't have fathomed, but here, with just the two of us, his resources were failing him. Whatever he knew, he didn't know me, and that pleased me.

"I wouldn't know where to begin."

He studied me for a long time, as if deciding how to salvage the situation. At last he said, "I could give you a key, and an envelope. In the envelope is money, enough to keep you going for a while. You'll have to find out what the key is for yourself. But it's the key to everything." He fixed on my eyes and became utterly serious. "Great men don't make societies great, William, or make them just. Heroes don't, and laws don't. Greatness and justice originate with a society's citizens, and even a single citizen can choose to make a difference. Anyone can make a difference, if they're motivated. You could."

"And I might," I said. "If it's any consolation, Lord Adonis ends for good tonight. There's just one thing I was wondering."

"Yes?"

"Why was he going to let me go?"

"So —" he began, and abruptly stopped.

"So I'd carry the word that the Citizen was dead, and it had nothing at all to do with secret societies and everything to do with an arch-enemy with a grudge. Which strikes me as a reasonably good idea." The gun felt warm in my hand. "And it's only fair that Lord Adonis should win *once*, don't you think?"

"You don't have to do this," he said, but offered no resistance.

"I think I do," I said. "They'll know something went wrong otherwise. They'll keep after me. It was going to be their cover. Now it can be mine."

"No one will know," Lloyd said, his voice trembling.

"The right people will," I said.

I put a pillow over his face and shot him.

I lied.

I used to have a fantasy where Lord Adonis battled the Citizen and won. Now it's realized and I feel nothing. Which, when you think about it, is the right response; there should be no joy in killing. Anyway, we both lost, and both won. I'd had nothing to do with my life, and he gave me that. It was what he always gave: hope, courage, purpose. His legacy. So now I have a suit, and a mask, and a key for what I don't know. His secrets, I think. I found him, I can find out what the key goes to. And I'll know what he knew about "them," and they'll pay for their crimes.

But I realized Lord Adonis can't die yet. They'll need him, now that Wallace is gone. I did what they wanted. I did well. This morning's paper ran a headline story about Sentinel battling the White Rooks in Empire City, while Lloyd's death was a square inch on page sixteen. I think Empire City's the place to go, if I really want to catch "their" attention. I won't have to find them. They'll come to me.

Then Lord Adonis will be truly dead, and William Pendleton, too. I'll become nobody, nobody special. Just another face in the crowd.

Just a citizen.

DECISIONS

BY J. ALLEN THOMAS

Liberty. Justice. Security. Peace. These are the four pillars of a better world; a land of hope, freedom, and truth, where life is not a burden to endure but a joy to experience. There are threats you cannot conquer, tragedies you cannot avoid, and sins you cannot punish. We are here to help. We will support you when you stumble, keep watch when you sleep, and help you achieve the unreachable. We will show you how to touch Paradise.

— Sentinel

Liz catches my eye. She's standing across the room with some people I don't know. Wine glass in hand, she gestures for me to come over. A big, expansive, expressive gesture . . . to make sure all the people at the party see her and understand that I'm her boyfriend.

I shake my head — a terse refusal. I jab a finger at the couch.

She tilts her head, a dramatic frown on her lips. Shoulder-length blond hair falls across half her face. Her shoulders slump. Her hand covers her heart and clutches her blouse, pulling the silk tight over her small breasts.

Behind her the people continue to talk, but I see one, then another glance at her, glance at me, note the exchange.

I frown and turn away. Before I do, I see her turn back to the group. She laughs at something someone said. She takes hold of a guy's upper arm. Her hand stays on his arm while she sips her wine.

I squeeze through the crowd, say "Excuse me" and "Hey, how you doing?" when appropriate, and bum a cigarette somewhere along the way. I fall back onto the couch, patting my pockets for a lighter with one hand, holding my beer steady and away from me with the other.

Two people, a guy and a girl, are already on the couch sitting next to each other. They're talking. The guy's excited; the girl's bored and interested at the same time. Bored with what he's saying; interested in him.

"Your first time?" she asks.

"Yeah, I've seen it on TV, on the news, but —"

"Not the same."

"Right, right. On TV, it's just like a show or something."

She smiles, nods. "Different in real life."

"Exactly! The sounds . . . you can hear the punches. Like . . . like explosions. And they shake you, like you're on a roller coaster or something. And the wind as they swoop by — having to lean into it or be blown over." He shakes his head. I can't see his face, but know the expression: He's at a loss to describe. He finishes, "Bigger than life, yet there it is right in front of you."

He must be new to Empire City. I glance at the girl. She pats him on the knee. At least he's made a new friend.

I lean forward, put my beer down on the coffee table. I dig out my lighter and light my cigarette. The crowd in front of me parts. Between the people, over my hand cupped around the lighter's flame, I catch a glimpse of Liz.

She's let go of the guy's arm. She leans toward a different guy, this one on the other side, bumps her shoulder against his. Playfully.

Talk about supervillains.

"You know what I wanted to be when I grew up? I wanted to be a superhero."

Still in bed on a Sunday morning, I pull the pillow up behind my head, prop myself against the headboard. I look over at Liz. She's turned away, curled up under the covers, hands tucked beneath her pillow. She lifts her head, squints at the clock, lets her head fall.

"Not just when I was a kid, either. In high school, too. Heck. Even in college."

I'm breaking the rule. An unspoken one, but a rule nonetheless. We talk about today. Not about yesterday, when we hurt each other with slights and little hurts — itsy-bitsy jabs. And not about tomorrow, when we'll do it again. No future or past for us. We only have today. That's how we've stayed together this long.

"I kept hoping my parents would tell me I was an orphan — that they'd found me among the wreckage of a spacecraft. I kept my fingers crossed for a meteor to crash right at my feet. The government to approach me about a secret project. A chemistry experiment to go awry. Anything. . . ."

She sits up. The sheets fall to her lap. She knots both hands in her hair, pulls it away from her face. Then she arches her back and stretches. She reaches across me and takes her cigarettes from my night stand. I grab her wrist, pull out a cigarette for myself before letting go.

"Superheroes don't smoke," she says.

No, I suppose they don't. I keep talking about the past. "Even in college, I still hoped. What the heck? It seemed as likely as winning the lottery — lots of people buy tickets every day. Why should I give up hope of becoming a superhero? I had names picked out so I'd be ready. Maxi-Man, when I was a kid. The Cynic in high school. Cipher Null and Getaway Kid in college."

"A superhero would light my cigarette," she notes.

I light my own first, then hers. Itsy-bitsy jabs.

"When I was a kid, I wanted to fly and be superstrong. Maybe shoot lightning from my hands. Later, it was something else. I wanted clear-cut choices. I wanted the opportunity to make the *right* decision — not the best one given the circumstances and not the best one for me. I wanted to confront evil and fight villains and know I was doing good.

"Yeah, I really wanted that."

She draws on her cigarette. She holds it between her first two fingers; the other two are curled toward her palm, making a loop with her thumb. She cups her elbow with the other hand. She lifts her chin, tilts her head back — blows the smoke out, first a cloud drifting from her lips and nostrils, then a thin, tight stream.

She doesn't look at me. "Going to tell me you're a superhero now?"

"No." I throw back the sheets. "I gave on that. I realized it's got nothing to do with opportunity. I wouldn't — don't make the right decisions. If anything, I would've been a supervillain."

She draws on her cigarette.

I roll out of bed and leave the room.

The next day, while walking through the plaza to meet her for lunch, I think about decisions: right decisions and best decisions and wrong decisions.

Lunch is the best time to break up with a girl. Lunch has a time limit — a short limit, maybe an hour, tops — then it's back to normal life. Only so much time to argue and fight; only have to see the girl, sit across from her and watch her expression, for an hour or less.

Nothing I see will be good. Either she'll be happy one of us finally said something. Or angry she didn't beat me to the punch. If she's happy, I wasn't good enough. If she's angry, I'll hear about it.

Neither outcome is good . . . neither is the best for me, at least. One hour and I can get on with my life. Have a future where something good might happen. Have a past I'm fond of remembering.

Right decisions and best decisions — whichever one this is, I've been making the wrong decision for too long.

A shadow hurtles over me. A rush of wind from behind and I stagger forward. A rush of wind from ahead blows my suit jacket back, flips my tie into my face, sends it rippling over my shoulder.

As one, all of us in the plaza look up to the sky.

Eyes locked and faces grim, chests out and hands balled into fists, they collide fifty feet above us — Sentinel and a villain I don't recognize. Likely a two-bit loser from out of town if he's fighting Sentinel.

The boom when they collide makes me hunch my shoulders. A whoosh of air blows grit up from the ground. I duck my head and hide my eyes in the crook of my arm. My pants cuffs flap around my ankles; the grit stings my cheeks and chin.

The sizzling roar of atomic fire — my face burns from the flash of heat, and sweat soaks my undershirt — then a second boom, followed by a rumble.

I look up again.

The rumble sounds like a glacier, an ice floe. Ice breaking apart and grinding together — quick, sharp cracks on the surface and longer, muted cracks deep below. Just like the sound of a skyscraper — four hundred feet of concrete and metal — struck by a hurtling superhero.

Vectors of force spread out from the impact, from the epicentre. Concrete rips and metal groans as the shockwave passes. Cracks spread along the skyscraper's towering height, both on the surface and below. There's a rumble like rolling thunder — a growling sound that grows louder, until one massive chunk of concrete breaks off and falls.

I look across the plaza. I scream, "Liz! Lizzie!"

She's wearing a white blouse and grey business suit, nylons a darker shade of grey, almost black, and sunglasses with white plastic rims — she calls them her Jackie O. glasses. She's looking up. Her head's back, neck straining. She's trying to run, but she keeps looking up. Her eyes are locked on the chunk of concrete torn free from the building and tumbling down.

I'm running toward her. The others running from the plaza make way for me. One guy's hand brushes against my shoulder. He shouts, "Wrong way!" Then I'm past him, still heading toward Liz.

The heel of her shoe twists; the other heel twists opposite. Her knees are knocked and now she's staggering.

I'm ten feet away — five feet away — less than five. Another boom, the third one, and the ground shakes. She falls to a knee. Both my feet leave the ground, breaking my stride. I stumble forward . . . fall.

Toddling forward on my knees, I close the distance between us. Eyes screwed shut, I wrap my arms around her. I cradle her to my chest, shield her with my body, lay my cheek against the top of her head.

A shadow covers us.

"Hold her tight," a voice says. It's deep and filled with authority and comfort. Like a father's voice. I look up. Sentinel stands over us — floats above us, his toes pointed downward, inches above the ground..

"Hold her tight. Keep her safe." He looks me in the eye. He nods in approval. "I will keep you both safe."

His cape snaps hard as he rushes into the air. The villain has fled the plaza, and Sentinel gives chase, disappearing after him.

Liz looks up at me. Her mouth is open. Her front teeth are stained red — whether from blood or lipstick, I don't know. A shudder runs through her bottom lip. Her sunglasses are pushed up from her eyes and crooked across her forehead, one plastic arm pressing against her ear, the other bent at the hinge and tangled in her hair.

Gently, I pull them off.

She presses her head against my chest.

I haven't held her like this in a long time.

I look across the plaza. A chunk of concrete — three hundred? four hundred pounds? — is sunk in the ground. It looks like a megalith, a standing stone with rough edges. Twenty feet away . . . probably farther than that.

However far, not very close.

That evening, after work, I pause outside her door. I pull my key ring from my pocket. I finger through my keys and find the one to her apartment. I stare at the brass-coloured key — the raised letters on the round end worn smooth by my fingers, and the key's narrow length of peaks and valleys, jagged highs and lows.

Supervillains. . . . Nothing to do with opportunity. . . . Right decisions and best decisions. . . . "Hold her tight. . . ." However far, not very close. . . .

All that — words, fragments of things said and thought — goes through my head while I stand at her door.

I take her key off my key chain. I slip the rest of my keys into a front pocket. I toss her key into my palm, knock on the door — three hard raps — then I slip her key into the lock and open the door.

I find her in the living room. She's on the couch, curled up under a blanket. She stretches toward the coffee table, puts out her cigarette in an ashtray. She presses a button on the remote and mutes the TV.

I make a fist around her key. I don't take off my jacket. I sit down in a chair, crouching forward and resting my elbows on my knees.

"You all right?" I ask.

She doesn't answer.

One moment wasn't enough. One time that reminded me — maybe her, too — of a past walled off. A past we don't talk about anymore, because we can't see over the piled up slights and little hurts. The itsy-bitsy jabs. The pile is too high. I knew it before I came over; she knows it now.

She doesn't answer my question. It's in the past — nothing worth talking about. Nothing we can talk about.

I look at the TV. The six o'clock news is on, and they're showing the fight between Sentinel and the supervillain. I recognize him now. He calls himself Jawbreaker. He wears a black bodysuit with purple and green striping. A black cape. His hair is black, too, and his jaw seems too wide.

The footage shows Sentinel and Jawbreaker colliding in midair. Eye-beams scorch the villain square in the chest, burning away his costume. Hands clenched together, Jawbreaker hits Sentinel. Knuckles crash into his midsection. Sentinel hurtles back through the air, striking the skyscraper.

The scene cuts away. The camera shows a chunk of concrete tearing free of the building. The camera returns to Sentinel. He pulls himself out of the shallow crater in the skyscraper's side. He rushes downward. On the TV screen, he's little more than a blur of red, white, and blue. He reaches the chunk of concrete. With his left hand, he bats it one way. With his right, he bats it the other. When no one's below — everyone's safe — he hammers it into the ground.

The third boom in the plaza — the one that made Liz fall to a knee and me stagger — the chunk of concrete hitting the ground.

I see myself enter the picture on the very edge of the TV screen. There's Liz. There I am, lurching forward on my knees. The program returns to the news anchor as I wrap my arms around Liz.

I laugh — a single, short, sharp laugh. I turn my head away. My voice is bitter. I say, "Too late. I got there too late. Didn't matter anyway. Stupid."

"It mattered . . . at least to me it did."

I look at her.

Her voice is quiet, almost shy. "You weren't the only one who wanted to be a superhero. When I was kid, I mean . . . I was too mature for that in high school." She laughs, embarrassed. "What was I thinking? I can't even run in heels."

I raise an eyebrow. But don't smile. "A superhero?"

"Super*heroine*, thank you."

Her voice is teasing, but not harsh. A voice from the past.

"Did you have a name picked out?"

She doesn't say anything. I wait and wait for her answer, but in the end, all I can do is nod my head. A nod of recognition and resignation. Too hard to share; the past is just too hard for us to share.

She asks — no more shyness and no more teasing, now she's matter-of-fact: "Going to break up with me?"

I look down at my hand. I'm holding her key between two fingers, holding it like a cigarette. I look up. She's picked her head up from the couch. She's staring at me, her face expressionless.

I swallow.

She gestures for me to come over. A small, hesitant, expressive gesture. A gesture just for me.

I stand up, still holding her key between my fingers. I tap its jagged, narrow length against my lips.

Keep each other safe. . . . Never having the opportunity. . . . I wouldn't — don't make the right decisions.

Sentinel is on TV again. Letters on the bottom of the screen read *Live*. He's holding the supervillain, gently but firmly. Reporters are clustered around, asking him questions. Sentinel pauses, looks at a reporter, then straight into the camera. He shakes his head slowly. His face is stern, but not hateful. His expression is patient, without anger. He speaks.

The TV is still muted, but I can imagine what was asked and how he answers. Everyone in Empire City — maybe everyone in the world — has heard at least once the question asked and answered before. The question is about the fate of the supervillain, whether he can be reformed.

Sentinel's answer is always the same: "If he will meet us halfway, he deserves our mercy. But we must meet him halfway, and we must not make him crawl. If he will meet us halfway, we must give him a second chance. If we are truly heroes — all of us, both you and me — this is what we must do. . . ."

I remember what he said to us: *"I will keep you both safe."*

"Mizz Glam," Liz says.

I look away from the TV. "Miss Glam?"

"Mizz Glam — two Zs. I liked Zs when I was a kid."

"I didn't know zzat, Lizzz."

We both laugh.

Again she gesture for me to come over.

I sit down next to her on the couch, slide her key into my pocket next to the others.

She lays her head in my lap.

COVALENT BONDS

BY ERICA SCHIPPERS

Emma Boltzmann, 2003.

"Looks like it's going to be another one of those nights," sighed Emma, eyeing a pair of science-villains. Their conversation had obviously moved from the negotiation stage to the "it's my plan — you are merely a lackey" stage. They were still shouting, but something more physical seemed likely, and soon.

"I got it, Alice," Emma said, tucking a bar rag into her apron and picking up a tray. The bartender, Alice, shot her a grateful look.

"Thanks, girl. Nothin' I hate worse than the smell of fried science-villain."

Emma grinned at Alice and strolled toward the feuding pair. Twenty-five was a good age for the grin-and-jiggle approach. If she were fifty she would have tried looking over her glasses and pursing her lips in disapproval. It was amazing how many hardened criminals would behave themselves if reminded of their mothers. Still, you worked with what you had, and it would be a long time before Emma bounced back to fifty. In a few years she would be too young to work in a bar and have to quit until she started getting older again. Emma rather looked forward to her childhoods. She usually needed the break.

"Hi, fellas. Can I get you something? Another round? Some hot wings?"

The two villains were standing as much as the booth seats allowed, leaning over the table and almost nose-to-nose. They continued to glare at each other, ignoring Emma's cheerful interruption. Numerous empty glasses cluttered the table

"The acid lizards were *my* idea! All you could come up with were dinosaurs! *And* you got the species wrong! The seismosaurus doesn't have anything to do with earthquakes! It ate plants!"

This close, Emma could see the smaller science-villain's helmet quivering in outrage. It was painted red, and had probably started out as part of a car. The face behind it was young, earnest, and still had a few pimples.

"Silence, dolt!" boomed the other science-villain, who was a little bit older and a lot larger than the first. He sported a series of metal implants placed carefully around his shaved head. The implants were sets of concentric silver circles, all connected to each other by curly wires, giving the science-villain's head a see-through afro look. He was red-faced and sweating, and Emma could see that the adhesive holding one of the implants had started to give.

"Don't call me a dolt, you dundering buffoon!" screamed the first villain, and started groping underneath his cape. He was probably reaching for a weapon.

"Hey!" shouted Emma, putting some diaphragm into it and slamming her tray onto the table's edge. The two villains turned to stare at her as though she had suddenly teleported into the middle of their argument.

Emma pointed to one of the many signs that decorated the walls of McLarney's, one that said simply, *TAKE IT OUTSIDE*.

"Or what?" sneered the larger villain. "You some sort of superbouncer?"

"I don't need to be," said Emma, maintaining her smile. "Our security system was designed by Doctor Deimos. It tends to be lethal."

"That old has-been? He's in jail. Why should we be scared of anything he came up with? It's got to be fifty years old by now." The smaller villain, the one with the red helmet, had decided to get in on the sneer action.

"Your funeral." Emma shrugged and turned as though to walk away.

"Will you kids shut up? I'm trying to have a drink, and the only meat I want to smell burning is in the kitchen." The beastman in the booth across from the two villains punctuated the end of his sentence with a rolling snarl.

The two villains looked at each other and then at the beastman, who was wearing an expensive suit. His manicured claws looked extremely sharp, and his professionally whitened fangs gleamed from behind his twisted lips. They sat down slowly, still muttering.

"Thanks, Ralphie," said Emma to the beastman, who was a regular.

"Sure thing, toots. Can you get me another Laphroaig?"

"On the house," she said, and headed back to the bar. Alice was already pouring when she got there.

"Huh," she said, sliding the Laphroaig across to Emma. "This new crop of villains — it's enough to make me change my business. I bet I could sell this place and set myself up someplace warm. On a beach."

Emma nodded, having heard this refrain many times before. Alice would sell a kidney before she would sell McLarney's. The waterfront bar had been in her family for four generations, and had been a supervillain bar for three of them. It was a life span pretty much unprecedented in the watering holes of evil, but luckily for McLarney's, Doctor Deimos had adopted it in the 1930s. Between his security system and his actual presence, the place had gained a reputation for being neutral ground. Anyone who tried to bust up McLarney's ended up dead or sucked into an alternate dimension, and word had gotten around. The only thing that Deimos had asked in return for his protection was that nothing change. Bill McLarney's half-West Indian great-granddaughter presided over a bar that had remained as untouched as possible for close to seventy years. Deimos had been in prison for the last fifty, but when he got out, McLarney's would be waiting.

There was a loud *zappity-POW*, and the smell of ozone and burning hair drifted up to the bar. The smaller of the two young science-villains lay slumped across the table, some sort of weapon clutched in one hand. The other was sitting very still, his face gone white. One of his "implants" had come off completely and dangled from the end of its wire like strange jewellery. He held his empty hands in the air as though he were facing the police, instead of Deimos's fifty-year-old security system.

"Damn," said Alice with feeling. "The last one who got himself fried was booby-trapped."

Emma Boltzmann, 1933.

I well remember my first meeting with Doctor Deimos, that brilliant scoundrel who would render himself so influential to the second great world conflict. It was a cold, rainy evening in March, and McLarney's usual clientele had been largely discouraged from venturing out by the gusts of chill wind that are March's defining characteristic. As it was Monday night, I was attempting to tune the radio dial to WABC in order to discover what mischief the nefarious oriental, Doctor Fu Manchu, was going to wreak in that night's episode. I had been at this task for about ten minutes, but had produced only static. The proprietor, Bill McLarney, stood behind the bar polishing shot glasses, a favourite activity of his and one that he said prevented "idle hands," those potential tools of the devil. We were soon to discover that busy hands were far more useful to him.

"Might as well give it up, Emma," Bill said. "Why don't you put some Duke on the phonograph or something? That static is drivin' me nuts."

"One more minute, Bill," I said.

We would have continued our familiar argument, but at that moment the door opened, letting in both a burst of chill, damp air and one of the largest men I had ever seen. This behemoth, who truly had hands the size of hams, stood to one side, holding the door open with an attitude of deference. A tall, slender figure entered, followed closely by another huge man. The thin man removed his hat and hung it on the coat rack, then stood with arms held slightly away from his body as though waiting for something. One of the thugs hurried to remove his overcoat, nice as a valet, and hung it beneath the hat, which was a black fedora with a brim too wide to be in keeping with the current fashion. Only then did the thugs divest themselves of their own outer garments. Their boss straightened the shoulders of his black suit jacket with a shrug and a tug at the lapels, and headed for the bar.

"A whiskey and soda, please, barkeep. And beer for the fools in my employ." An accent coloured his words, upper class British with an underlying strata of something from farther east.

Bill shrugged and started to pour. The thin man seated himself at the bar and

57

began to remove his gloves — fine black kid, of course — tugging at each finger with slow deliberation. His bodyguards seated themselves to either side of him. He had a lean, intense face and dark hair that was slicked back from a precise part. I almost expected to see a narrow moustache, but his face was clean-shaven, and I could smell the sharp scent of his aftershave lotion from several feet away. There was something neat and fastidious about him, but it seemed more to be an addiction to order than a dandy's vanity.

"Quite a night out there," said Bill as he set the drinks out in front of the men, serving the neat one first.

"Indeed," said the thin man with a thin smile. He removed a five-dollar bill from his pocket and slid it across the bar toward Bill, using only his fingertips. "Tell me when we have exhausted this."

Bill's eyebrows went up. Prices were still high from Prohibition, but the three men would be hard pressed to walk away from the bar if they consumed five dollars' worth of drink at Bill's prices. McLarney's was a working man's bar, and charged accordingly.

"Mister, you all three could drink here for a week on that."

"Then you may keep the excess when we are finished. Let none say that Doctor Deimos is ungenerous to those who serve him well!"

The thin man's voice had risen and his eyes had taken on a manic gleam with those last words. This animation enlivened his saturnine features and rendered his narrow lips and long nose more attractive than not. Bill's eyebrows arched again but his expression remained otherwise unchanged. We had heard of this new breed of madmen, dubbed "science-villains" by the newspapers. These publications reported every move and utterance of the same. If Doctor Deimos was not a science-villain, then he had taken great pains to fashion himself after the type.

"So," said Bill, "what brings you to Empire City?" He had gone back to polishing glasses, and didn't seem terribly interested in the answer.

"Conquest!" shouted Deimos. "I plan to hold the city for ransom with my army of beastmen and giant mutant octopi. When they rampage through the harbour, wreaking havoc and destruction the likes of which this city has never seen, none shall refuse my demands! None shall gainsay me! They shall fall down upon their knees and beg to call me 'Master'!"

Bill seemed largely unfazed by this abrupt change of character, but I was rather alarmed. I took advantage of the fact that I had not yet come to Doctor Deimos's notice and backed slowly toward the door to the kitchen.

"That so," said Bill, looking up. "They hard to make, them giant octopi?"

"Only a genius of my calibre could design something so ingenious, so utterly beyond the bounds that Nature has set forth. . . ."

"That sounds like thirsty work." Bill slid another drink across to Deimos, who had spilled most of the first with his wild gesturing. He seemed to have forgotten that he had a glass in his hand, although none of the liquid had landed on him. His muscle had dodged the flying liquor with the ease of long practice and now sat looking resigned and vaguely embarrassed.

"Thirsty work? Oh, it is," said Deimos. "Thirsty and lonely, with none but fools and bumblers for company. But I persevere. Tell me, do you serve food in this establishment?"

"I expect we could come up with something. Won't be fancy, though."

"Oh, I don't require fancy, merely filling. Perhaps some corned beef?"

"Sure thing," said Bill. He turned to me just as I was ducking through the door. "Emma, go fire up the grill. And see if we have any of the missus's chocolate cake left." He looked back at his customers. "My wife makes the best chocolate cake in Empire City. Make your whole trip worthwhile all by itself."

"Excellent," said Deimos, and sipped his drink.

I headed into the kitchen, more interested now than troubled by our visitor. It had been a long time since I had encountered something truly novel, and Deimos promised to be very singular indeed.

Over the next few months, Deimos became a regular at McLarney's. Bill and I had expected trouble between the mad scientist and our usual clientele, but they quickly accepted him as a familiar and harmless eccentric. This was facilitated by the fact that he soon employed many of them, and any job in that time was a powerful cement for loyalty. The night he did loose giant mutant octopi on the shipping lanes, there was a strange undercurrent of pride in McLarney's. It was as if the regulars were happy that their pet lunatic was a man of action, however strange and destructive that action might be, and not merely a blowhard with a good wardrobe and maniacal laugh. I began paying more attention to what he said.

Let me say now that I was a forerunner to that breed of metahuman that has become so common the modern person takes them for granted. I never grow older than sixty-five years, or younger than twelve. At first, I believed that this strange aging was the extent of my condition. Later I noticed that cards and dice tended to favour me, and that my possessions remained much more durable than those of the people around me. Shoes refused to wear out, clothes to stain or tear.

It was not until the beginning of the twentieth century that I was able to effect changes in the world consciously and purposefully, and those initial changes were very minor: I could reheat a cup of coffee, or create ice from the water in a drink. These strange powers mystified and excited me, but I told no one about them for fear of attracting the attention of one of the less benevolent science-villains. In all other ways I remained utterly human and only able to defend myself in human ways.

As Doctor Deimos proceeded to make a name for himself as a science-villain, his enemies, both among the heroes and the other villains, took note of his habits and haunts. It was, therefore, not surprising when McLarney's came to the attention of a villain who figured, quite unfortunately, that taking Bill and me hostage would give her a lever to influence Doctor Deimos. Her name was the Lacquer Dragon, and she was a Chinese sorceress.

★　★　★

"So, do you still think your friend will save you?" The Lacquer Dragon ran one long and intricately painted fingernail down the side of Bill's face and smiled at him. Malevolence rendered her lovely features quite unpleasant.

"Lady, I keep telling you, Doctor Deimos is not my 'friend'! He drinks at my bar. He comes in every Friday for the corned beef platter. So do lots of other guys."

Our captor frowned at Bill for a moment, as though unable to believe that he could have said quite what she had heard. Then she stalked away, giving us a narrow glance over one shapely shoulder.

"Defy me all you like. In the end, it shall come to nothing."

Bill looked at me, his blunt Irish face an incongruous map of helpless terror above his exotic silken robes. We had both been clothed in them before being bound to thrones of elaborately carved jade. I could feel my eyes well with tears at the thought of the horrible fate that awaited us at the hands of this foreign madwoman. A scant few hours before, her dragon-masked servitors had invaded the bar and rendered us unconscious with a narcotic gas. When we woke we were in an elaborately panelled and screened room that the Lacquer Dragon referred to as the "Chamber of the Black Sun."

On a table before us sat a bowl of water, the bowl itself carved out of an enormous piece of obsidian. Intricate patterns traced its sides, and on the surface of the water floated a closed black lotus blossom. When the sun rose, its light would enter the room through a concealed slit in the ceiling, fall upon the lotus blossom, and cause it to open. The pollen of this rare breed of lotus was extremely deadly. Once it filled the air, Bill and I could anticipate nothing but hours of agonizing insanity leading to our deaths.

"Why won't you listen?" I shouted. "We haven't seen Doctor Deimos in weeks! He's probably not even in the country!"

"Oh, he'll be here. I sent him a . . . *special* . . . invitation." The Lacquer Dragon chuckled evilly, and would probably have moved onto a full-fledged laugh if the door had not burst inward at that moment.

"Which I received," said Doctor Deimos, striding into the room in a swirl of black greatcoat. He threw the smoking corpse of a dragon-masked minion at her feet.

"Foolish woman, to seek to strike at Deimos through others! Your pitiful sorcery is nothing in the face of my unchallenged mastery of science. The trap you had planned crumbled at the touch of my genius. To think you were a match for Doctor Deimos? Now reap the rewards of your arrogance!"

With that, a horde of Deimos's thugs rushed into the room, two of them grasping the Lacquer Dragon's arms tightly and holding her despite her struggles.

"You shall never defeat me!" she shrieked. "I shall return and make you rue the day that —"

"Silence her," said Deimos, and one of the men grasped the Lacquer Dragon's face tightly enough that I could see the hold must be painful.

"Take her to the blossom."

The sorceress was dragged, kicking and twisting, toward the bowl where the black lotus floated. Her muffled screams took on an edge of real terror. From the corner of my eye, I saw a glimmer of sunlight high up in the room.

"Now," said Deimos, grasping the back of the Lacquer Dragon's exquisitely arranged hair, "you shall learn."

In the very instant when light found the lotus blossom, exactly as it began to open, Deimos thrust the Lacquer Dragon's face deep into the water and held it there. He maintained his stance until her struggles had died away completely. Then he motioned to his servants to release her arms. As her body slumped lifelessly to the floor, I could see that open flower plastered over her face. The petals mercifully concealed her features from view.

I don't believe I shall ever entirely forget the look on Deimos's face as he drowned that woman, or the sight of his black-gloved hand buried in her black hair. There was no joy in his expression, but rather a grim determination underlaid with that terrible aphrodisiac that is power.

As Deimos's men untied us, he said, "Now we shall return you to your rightful place. I have much work to do before this evening, and the machinations of this insufferable creature have delayed me quite long enough."

We were stripped of our robes, given our old clothes back, and taken to an autogyro. I could tell the machine impressed Bill terribly, although we both remained shaken by our ordeal. As the craft rose into the air, Bill produced a flask of whiskey. We fortified ourselves thoroughly before either of us felt settled enough to speak.

"So, this is quite a machine," shouted Bill, not trying to keep the admiration from his voice.

"It is but a trifle, built solely to aid me in my other endeavours. Did I not have immediate need of it, I would not have wasted my genius on such a simple mechanical device."

Despite his words, I could see that Deimos was pleased. It struck me, not for the first time, that his chosen path was not one that led to many convivial interactions.

"Soon my greatest plan shall come to fruition! The gold I shall liberate this evening will allow me to build a large store of incendiary rockets — rockets such as none have dreamed, filled with an explosive compound of my own devising, far more powerful than mere dynamite. Already my minions have placed radio transponders throughout the nation's capitol, and each of the rockets shall thus be attracted to a specific location. When Washington falls, none shall stand against me, and I shall attain my rightful place as supreme ruler of, first, this great nation, and then the world!"

"Won't that kill a lot of people?" I asked, horrified.

"What matters the price if it brings my genius to the forefront of human affairs? I am Deimos, and all shall bow before me!"

I opened my mouth to protest, but Bill shot me a warning look. We were, after all, several hundred feet in the air and entirely at the mercy of a man we had seen commit murder that very evening.

"I'm sure you know your own business best," shouted Bill, and we spent the rest of the flight listening to the details of Deimos's plans to steal a federal gold shipment that was being moved through Empire City that evening.

Throughout this recitation, I wondered desperately what I might do to stop Deimos. The police had been entirely unable to deal with him so far, and I had not the faintest clue as to how to get in touch with any of Empire City's science-heroes. It seemed the autogyro figured largely into his plans for the gold heist. If something went wrong with it, it would at least delay him. In that time perhaps Bill and I could figure out what to do, to whom we might go. I couldn't imagine which part to sabotage, or how to do it while we were flying and not draw attention to myself. Still, the thought haunted me until we landed near McLarney's. Stress, horror, and the motion of flying had given me a vicious headache. Bill and I clung to each other, disoriented and trembling, as Deimos, with a cheery little wave, flew off into the night.

Bill offered to give me the next night off, but I felt safer in the bar's familiar surroundings than huddled alone in my apartment, so I was there when Deimos burst through our door, soaking wet and bleeding. One glove was gone, and his hair hung limp, streaming water and blood into his eyes. There was a rent down one side of his black greatcoat, and he smelled charred underneath the wet. The radio blared jazz in the background.

"My autogyro!" he gasped. "I don't know what could have happened. I built it with my own hands. I barely let the lummoxes I employ refuel it! Imbeciles! They will pay!"

"We interrupt this broadcast to bring you a report of an attempted robbery gone wrong. Infamous science-villain Doctor Deimos . . ."

The radio blared the story of Deimos's misfortune. His autogyro had malfunctioned and crashed into the river. The authorities were uncertain whether he had survived, and from the state of him it seemed to have been a close thing.

"There now, son," said Bill. "Why don't you let Emma take you into the kitchen and get you dried off and patched up. Maybe find a cup of something hot to warm you."

"That would be — that would be most appreciated."

Deimos seemed a little unsettled by Bill's easy generosity. He sat in uncharacteristic silence while I wrapped him in towels and dabbed his cuts and abrasions with iodine, a process that he endured without flinching. As for myself, I couldn't image what to say to him. I was not in the least unhappy that his plan had failed. His height and enthusiasm were such that I had not realized before how thin he was, and I found myself feeling a little sorry for him as he slumped dejectedly in Bill's kitchen, flowered towels around his shoulders. I reminded myself of his treatment of the Lacquer Dragon, and my pity evaporated.

His cuts were almost completely bandaged, and he was drinking whiskey and hot water with honey when Bill stuck his head into the kitchen.

"The police are coming. Better take our guest downstairs."

"There is no need to hide me. Doctor Deimos can outsmart a few flatfoots, or he is not worthy of escape!"

"Son," said Bill, "you're in no shape to run, and you're smart enough to know that. Go with Emma."

Deimos paused for a moment, then said, "Your words have some merit. I shall follow your advice."

That was how I found myself crouched in the root cellar with Doctor Deimos. The "root cellar" was really a secret room off the basement where Bill had concocted illicit liquor in the recent past. We heard the police arrive, and heard them enter the basement. We also heard them question Bill, and heard Bill tell them that while Deimos was known to show up on occasion, he hadn't seen him these many weeks past; they'd best look somewhere else. Later, Bill even gave Deimos five dollars, a clap on the shoulder, and a bit of advice when he left.

"Maybe you want to be thinking about what you're doing with your life before you lose it," he noted sagely.

"I am Deimos," he said, then shrugged. "But I shall not forget what you have done for me."

Emma Boltzmann, 1985.

"What do you want, Yuri?" Emma fiddled with her club soda and glared at the man seated across from her. His steel grin glittered in the strobing light. Tattoos gave his face an inhuman topography that Emma knew was reflected in his character.

"Ah, what it is, I think we need a little talk, yes?"

"What do we have to talk about, Yuri?" Emma tossed a note at him. It was composed of mismatched letters clipped from magazines, and demanded that she show up at Flix, a neo-Japanese wirehead bar. "If this is your idea of asking me out, you really need to work on your technique."

"Ah-ha, no date, pretty lady. I think you have a secret, and that you want to share your secret with Yuri."

"What possible secret could I have that would interest you?" Emma scanned the mesmeric chaos of writhing black latex and shiny fake body mods that filled the bar. The club flickered in and out of reality with each multi-collared strobe. It was a bad place to look for an ambush, and even with a bullet-proof vest on she felt much less than safe. She knew, too, that she possessed two secrets that might interest Yuri. A low, cold terror began deep in her guts.

"This is you," said Yuri. He held up a copy of an old sepia-toned photo that showed Deimos, Bill, and Emma standing by an autogyro in front of McLarney's. Bill had his hand on the nose of the machine, and had obviously just said something to Deimos, who was laughing and gesturing. Emma stood to one side, arms crossed but smiling at the two men.

"That's my grandmother," said Emma. Relief washed over her. The more dangerous secret was safe.

"No, pretty lady, I think is you. But you are too young, so how is this possible? I think Doctor Deimos goes to McLarney's so long not just for the corned beef, eh? And Deimos — he is in prison now. But he does not age. You do not age. So, what am I to think?"

63

"I think you're crazy," said Emma, and started to get up. Yuri grabbed her arm, the servos in his prosthesis whirring audibly through a pause in the music. His grip was warningly painful, not quite hard enough to do damage. Emma sat back down. Unlike most of the Flix crowd, Yuri possessed real cybernetic enhancements, the product of illegal and highly classified Soviet technology.

The flashing light limned Yuri's face to a mask as he leaned across the table, steel teeth still showing in a feral grin.

"I think Doctor Deimos, he wants to have something waiting for him when he gets out of prison. I think he keeps you young, and I think you need to tell me how. Or you just be a young, pretty corpse."

Emma closed her eyes and tried to think past the pain in her arm and her rising panic. Yuri would kill her. She thought she had come prepared to do whatever proved necessary, but now that the moment was here, she wasn't certain she could kill, even to defend herself. The music drove to a crescendo again, then died.

"So, pretty lady, what will it be?" Yuri's whisper rang harsh in the sudden silence.

"It was my grandmother," said Emma. She heard her own voice crack with the beginning of tears.

"I think what we have here is misunderstanding," said Yuri. "I think you believe you have a choice." With the word *choice* Yuri grabbed the back of Emma's hair and dragged her halfway across the table. She cried out in pain and terror and opened her eyes. Yuri's patchwork features and foetid breath were much too close. His prosthetic hand ground into her forearm.

"It was —"

"No lies! You will tell or you will die!" Yuri shook her violently. Emma was crying now. There was no way out of this that did not involve death. She wasn't a hero. She didn't know what else to do.

"You're right," she said. "I don't have a choice."

Emma's previously meagre powers had blossomed after the atomic age, paralleling the appearance of the first true superheroes. Emma found she could control entropy, creating order out of chaos or chaos out of order. Gross applications, like a winning poker hand, were easy. More subtle uses, such as repairing items, were harder to master. Reversing chemical processes were especially tricky, and had taken a great toll on the kitchen.

It was these fine applications that Emma counted on to save her. The familiar feeling of reaching *in* and *out* at the same time calmed her, followed by a sinking expansion of the trance state she entered when using her powers.

Here was Yuri, a nebulous flicker of chemical and electrical processes interspersed with the sharp clarity of his cybernetic enhancements. His arm was especially distinct, with its many little electromagnetic fields and mechanical pieces whirring away. Yuri had microchips in his brain and a nest of neural enhancers around his heart.

Maybe I can walk away from this and not be a murderer, thought Emma, and reversed the flow of electrons through one of Yuri's chips.

He immediately began to twitch and spasm, drooling foam down his chin. Emma removed his now-limp hands from her person and let the electrons resume their normal course. Yuri collapsed back into his side of the booth and lay there. His breathing was deep and ragged, and his eyes spoke of fear.

"I don't belong to Deimos, Yuri. I belong to myself. The woman in the picture is my grandmother, and if you ever come near me again, or if I find out that you've sold your crackpot theory to anyone else, I will do something to you worse than death. Do we understand each other?" Emma heard her own voice ring clear and somehow menacing. The tears of her terror were still drying on her cheeks. Yuri seemed thoroughly cowed despite them.

"Yes," he managed to gasp. "Demon woman. I will not trouble you again."

Emma left Flix with her head held high and a spring in her step.

Was that me? she thought. The proof of her strength was at once unnerving and deeply satisfying. *This is what Deimos means when he speaks of power. I understand him a little now. . . .*

Briefly a hero for his support of the Allies in World War II, Doctor Deimos had been imprisoned for nearly thirty years. Emma missed him. He and the bar, of which she now owned half, were the only constants that she had found in nearly two hundred and fifty years of life.

Before his downfall, Deimos had given the bar a certain reputation. Other science-villains had become regulars, and Deimos's security system and the idea of "neutral territory" had eliminated the inevitable conflicts. It became a place to do business.

As *science* gave way to *super*, Emma overheard one too many plots that later resulted in injury, death, and damage. She decided to do something about it, but her attempts to involve the police were largely unsuccessful. They had thanked her politely enough for her tips, but guaranteed no action. When pressed, the operator always said something like, "Look, lady, we already got three reports of poison gas, five probable meta robberies, and one of, uh, giant penguins — wait, make that giant *mutant* penguins — for tomorrow night. Most of these will turn out to be hoaxes. So, unless you can give us your name or where you got this 'hot tip,' we can only promise to do our best." Emma soon decided that if something were to be done, she would have to do it.

Emma never thought of it as becoming a superhero. She simply had the means and the opportunity to prevent random destruction and loss of life. After more than two centuries of helplessly watching war, disease, and human cruelty take their toll on the world, it was refreshing to wield some influence. Still, most of her interference was impersonal, either disrupting a vital device while the villain was at the bar or affecting the evil scheme from a safe distance. Very few people noticed a well-dressed middle-aged woman in the background of even the most chaotic scene.

But the thought that Yuri had discovered her activities had shaken her. Even with Deimos's security system, her remaining time on earth would be very short if word of her activities got out.

Later, at McLarney's, Emma found herself turning away from conversations she would have eavesdropped on the day before. She was slowly getting stronger, but was she strong enough to really defend herself? Going to the Ascension Institute or one of the superheroes powerful enough to help her would mean abandoning McLarney's, her friendship with Bill's descendants, everything that anchored her. She touched a picture that hung next to the bar, the original of the one that Yuri had threatened her with.

Life before her powers had been scarier, simpler, and somehow more fun.

". . . a new drug, supposed to give you a real virtual reality experience, anything you want. Leaves them breathing but brain-dead. We'll make a killing on the black market selling their organs." A greasy little man in a bad suit was displaying a vial of something clear to his equally greasy, if larger, companion.

Emma sighed. The past was the past. This was now.

She turned back to her work.

Empire City, 2003.

Empire City's finest had a long-standing policy that even murder wouldn't induce them to set foot in McLarney's, so Alice had harangued the larger science-villain into taking his ex-partner with him when he left. Fried science-villain really did smell awful, and Emma had propped the door open to the chill, late-March evening air after they left. Now she was taking advantage of the near-deserted state of the bar to play with the new stereo. In keeping with Bill McLarney's original agreement with Doctor Deimos that as little as possible be changed, the stereo had been concealed in the converted case of the old radio. Emma slid a Billie Holliday CD into the player, then stood up as a familiar, if long-absent, figure entered the bar.

Although close to one hundred, Deimos appeared to be a slender, athletic fifty. His clothes had changed cut and the hat had disappeared, but his long, dark face and quick step were largely unchanged. His choice of companion had also evolved. The two men with him resembled accountants more than gorillas, although Emma was sure that a number of unpleasant surprises lurked beneath their immaculately tailored grey suits.

As Deimos approached the bar, light glinted off of his small, round glasses and highlighted a dusting of grey hair at his temples. He dismissed his men to a nearby table and seated himself at the bar, looking around with an air of combined satisfaction and nostalgia that rapidly turned to puzzled disgust.

"What can I get for you, mister?" asked Alice.

"What is that foul stench?"

Emma felt her heart beat faster at the sound of his voice, slightly gruffer than she remembered but still familiar. She missed Bill, suddenly and with a sharp immediacy of loss that she had not felt in decades.

"Some kid got himself lit up by our security system," Emma chimed in. She figured she might as well try hiding in plain sight. "You'd think they'd have all heard that drawing a weapon in here was a bad idea by now, but . . . "

Deimos had always possessed a good evil chuckle, and he used it now to great effect.

"Fools and impostors. The genius of Deimos is timeless!"

"Thought that might be you," said Alice. "Your money's no good here tonight. My daddy would roll over in his grave if I made you pay your first night back."

After some discussion that established the fact that, yes, Alice was the current McLarney, and, yes, her mother must have been very beautiful to counteract the younger Bill's genes, Emma was dispatched to the kitchen to fetch a corned beef platter. When she served it to him, Deimos narrowed his eyes and said, "You seem extremely . . . familiar."

"My grandmother worked here with old Bill McLarney. I'm named after her. She told me all kinds of stories about you."

Emma had been about thirty-five when Deimos had met her, and was about twenty-five now. She was counting on the ten years of youth, and some creatively applied hair dye, to conceal her identity. It seemed to work.

"Remarkable. A trick of the light, but when I entered, it seemed I was seeing your grandmother all over again. A very striking woman."

"Why, thank you," she said, and escaped to serve some new arrivals.

Business picked up sharply after that, and Emma was kept too busy to worry about Deimos until the rush had died down several hours later. She did notice that he seemed quieter, his booming voice seldom ringing out over the hubbub of the crowd. She glanced his way once and caught him staring into his drink, his posture reminding her of the night he sat, sopping wet, in McLarney's kitchen after the autogyro crash.

After the rush, she sat at the bar counting her tips and mentally reviewing her crime-stopping agenda. Artificer had been in and she had buggered up as much of his hardware as she dared, and that made a good evening right there. There was a stock fraud she could foil on her way home, but the M@dd H@kker would require her to take a cab. Thank goodness he planned to release the virus at 3:00 A.M., but she would have to hurry. Villains were almost always early, a sure sign of evil in Emma's book. And she had mucked up one of the H@kker's schemes a few months back. That might be a problem; she had to be careful not to foil a villain after every time they came in and spilled their plans over a beer. They'd get suspicious. Maybe she should start a spreadsheet. . . .

"I find no joy in these times," said Deimos.

"What?" said Emma, startled out of her reverie by his quiet tone.

"My plans bring me no pleasure. I create nothing with my own hands anymore. I merely direct others. I own vast corporations. I control the men behind them. I have driven the entire scientific progress of the last fifty years from my jail cell so that I need not begin from scratch for each simple thing I need, and no one will ever know. What is the point, if no one knows? Deimos was not meant to be an administrator. Deimos was meant to rule. Which I shall, in due time. This is but an interlude before greatness!" He sighed. "But I do so miss the simple pleasures of my lab on occasion. . . ."

Deimos's habit of talk had not been blunted by the years. Emma was certain she could get him to reveal which corporations he owned and what his pet projects were. Perhaps some of the staging grounds were close enough that she could pay them a visit.

"Mutant octopi," Emma prompted.

"Precisely! To mould such a creature, see it develop . . . but time has swept on, and taken all of my old enemies with it. And my few friends." He glanced up at the picture of him, Bill, and Emma that still hung beside the bar.

"Friends pass on," said Emma with a grin, "but you of all people could always create new ones."

Deimos was a ruthless man, but not without human feeling, and Emma felt the rise of a mischievous delight at the thought of him someday discovering her secret. It was inevitable, just as it was inevitable that she would someday try to thwart one of his plans. If she was careful and clever, he might not even kill her for it. After all, Deimos was a smart man — maybe smart enough to realize that they could make each other's lives interesting for a very, very long time.

THE
FINAL
EQUATION

BY ROBIN D. LAWS

Maxwell Liberty sat in the back of a 2003 Lincoln Town Car, heading north along U.S. 59 from Houston to Livingston. He looked out the window and watched East Texas go by. Max was over a hundred years old and had been everywhere in the world on multiple occasions, East Texas included. But every time he came here, he was taken aback by how green it was. Despite the direct evidence of his eyes over a period of many decades, he nonetheless expected everything in Texas to be sandy beige desert, like in the dime novels he'd read when he was a kid. The car sped past a Holiday Inn, a Lutheran church, and a brace of barbecue restaurants, but no buttes or mesas.

Max placed his palms on the leather upholstery. It felt cool and comforting. He was riding in the Town Car's Cartier Edition. He'd requested the limo service's most unassuming vehicle and this was what they'd sent. A recurring problem — they always insisted on making a fuss. Sometimes he wished he could use a time machine or some global memory alteration device or somesuch and get his secret identity back.

He could have flown, through the sky that is, except that he wanted to arrive just like anyone else would. To rocket onto the grounds surrounded by a glowing, humming energy nimbus would only add to the carnival atmosphere. For similar reasons, he'd stowed the red cape and white tights in his briefcase. He'd chosen solemn but stylish civilian clothing: a grey worsted suit, double-breasted and custom-tailored for the inhuman perfection of his athletic frame.

The driver, whose name was Sanjay, had adjusted the rear-view mirror so he could keep glancing at Max, instead of the road. Max saw his own eerily symmetrical features reflected back at him: the grey at the temples, the dark brows, the serious lines settled in his face. Sanjay was a talker. Generally, Max dreaded the obligation to respond to drivers who liked to talk. But Sanjay didn't want to ask him about his exploits or what it was like to be the world-famous Sentinel. He wanted to explain how hard the limo business was in Houston since the Enron collapse. Sanjay asked if Max's supersociety had anything to do with bringing the company down. No, Max told him, if he remembered correctly, it was SEC filing requirements that did it.

The Town Car finally reached the prison gates. The jail stood in the middle of nowhere, but a big crowd of people had gathered around it anyhow. Reporters and their satellite trucks. Vigil keepers and their candles. Pro-penalty demonstrators, displaying photo blow-ups of the victims, mounted on placards.

His enhanced hearing picked up a reporter rehearsing her stand-up: "At midnight tonight, in this small Texas town, a costumed villain is scheduled to die. Childeric Stokes, alias the Nihilist, alias the Pain Clown, alias the Bone Sculptor, was sentenced to death by lethal injection for the torture slayings of five kidnapped day-care workers in Bailey County, Texas, four years ago. He was apprehended by Maxwell Liberty, Sentinel, who is rumoured to be on his way here to attend the execution. A noted opponent of the death penalty, some speculate that Liberty intends to use this occasion to —"

Maxwell stopped listening.

The prison was called the Polunsky Unit. The name sounded more like a management consulting firm than a correctional facility. It looked right, though: squat grey blocks, distrustful slits for windows, watchtowers on all four corners. Maxwell Liberty considered himself the world's most fervent optimist, but even he felt that prisons ought to be bad places. From foundation to roof, they should embody society's disapproval. The Polunsky Unit accomplished that goal.

Max stepped out from the car and felt the familiar whoosh of attention as heads turned toward him. TV news correspondents came at him, microphones out-thrust. Demonstrators, pro and con, waved their signs.

The first reporter to reach him was Su Mei Miller. She had the nine o'clock slot on one of the news networks. Max liked her. Even though she asked the same obvious questions the audience always wanted to hear, she managed to do it in a disarming way. Also, she had a strand of hair on the left side of her head that refused to obey her, no matter what she did to it; that was a charming flaw in a newscaster. She seemed tired. Up close, Max could see that the nubbly skin beneath her eyes had been plastered with extra make-up, to mask the telltales of exhaustion.

"Sentinel," Su Mei said, "Is your presence here meant to send a signal to the governor — a signal that you're still hoping for clemency?"

Max unleashed his pearliest smile and took the tack proven to reduce the news guys to helpless squirming. "Hello, Su Mei," he began. "How are the renovations going?"

Su Mei shifted uncomfortably on her feet. Her eyes darted to the scrum of ticked-off colleagues all around her. "Renovations?"

"Last time we talked, you said you and Ron were renovating the place up at the Hamptons. . . ."

"Oh, uh, fine. The renovations are fine."

He expected a pleading gaze from her, but all he got was dull surprise. Max was disappointed. Toying with the press was nearly the only naughty indulgence he allowed himself. He decided to knock it off.

"To answer your question, Su Mei," he said, shifting the cadence of his voice to press conference mode, "naturally, in my capacity as a private citizen, and given my longstanding objections to capital punishment, I hope that Governor Flores will exercise his clemency powers to commute the prisoner's sentence to life without possibility of parole — as I hope will happen for all twenty-three inmates on death row throughout America. But, I am not here as part of a lobbying effort. Now if you'll excuse me. . . ."

He stuck his shoulder into the crowd of reporters, causing it to part like they were the Red Sea and he was Charlton Heston. He strode to the gate and stood before the guards there. Before he could finish fishing in his pocket for his ID, they'd already buzzed him through. He didn't need identification. He was Sentinel.

From the corner of his eye, he saw movement. He turned; a broad-shouldered, middle-aged lady in a T-shirt and jeans surged at him, her brow flaring behind silver-framed glasses. She shook a sign in Max's face. There were no words on it, just a large image of a smiling young woman, her blond hair parted down the sides, blowing out the candles on her nineteenth birthday cake.

"That monster killed my niece!" the woman gasped, out of breath.

"Killing won't prove that killing is wrong!" shouted another lady, from the other side of the fray.

Max held up calming hands. He fixed the sign-carrying woman with his blue-eyed gaze. "Her name was Jenni Ansert," he said. "She was one of the ones who suffered the most, and you should know that she was extremely brave."

The woman moved back half a step. "If you were there, and saw it all, how can you come here to plead for that filthy bastard?"

"I'm not here for that, first of all. And my problem with this whole business has nothing to do with the welfare of killers." Detecting microphones in his peripheral vision, Max raised his voice. Like it or not, he was playing to an audience. "What worries me, ma'am, is what it'll do to us, if we make executions a regular part of life. I'm not a philosopher or any kind of moral authority —"

"Oh yes you are!" came a voice from the candle-carrying side.

He ignored the interruption. "I know firsthand what these psychotic murderers are like, and I don't want to be even one bit like them. You have every right to disagree with me, ma'am, but personally, I'm going to do my best not to be dragged down with them into bloodlust and hate. I think we're being tempted, and it's our duty to resist."

The lady worked her jaw at him. "An eye for an eye is what I believe."

"I want to show you the respect of continuing the discussion, but I have to go, ma'am. If you want to discuss it later, we can —" She turned her back and slipped through the crowd, muttering something. Using his superhearing, Max made out a complex string of profanities.

71

He turned back toward the facility. A chubby corrections official in a blue polyester business suit, its elbows shiny from wear, swerved to join him. The man stuck out a hand and introduced himself as Larry Garrett. His voice was a little reedy and had a catch in it, as if meeting Max made him nervous. Max gave him a modest pat on the shoulder — a little manly reassurance.

"You colleague is here waiting, in the operations centre," he said.

"Colleague?"

"Uh, yes, uh, Special Agent Charleston, he said his name was. 'Colleague,' that's the word he used, like you knew him and would be expecting him. . . ." Garrett's voice trailed up at the end of the sentence, as if it was a question.

"I see," said Sentinel. This would be Ryan Charleston, the so-called Iron General. He helmed the Order, the secret FBI offshoot established to fight metahuman crime and terror. They were colleagues, Max supposed, if not precisely friends. Charleston would have no trouble agreeing with Jenni Ansert's aunt. Eyes for eyes, simple as that. He was typical of the new crop of people coming into the scene these days, with their darker outlooks and looser limits. Whenever he was around them, Max had to reign in his impulse to lecture. It was pretty clear they thought of him as a walking relic.

He stepped up his pace and hustled into the ops centre to dispense with the requisite trading of barbs and move on to the real purpose for his visit. He was surprised to see Charleston leaning on a window sill in full combat rig, complete with quilted body armour, starred collar, and armoured epaulets. His force-sword hung at his belt. Diffused light fought its way through the dirty window pane to flatteringly highlight his granitic features.

Max considered a crack about the heads of secret organisations dressing to keep a low profile, but he had never really mastered the art of the smart-aleck comment. "Did he summon you, too?"

"Stokes? Hell no." Charleston scratched the back of his neck. "The president sent me, to inject a little balance into the coverage."

"You've given your sound bites already?"

"Frickin'-A. 'Ultimate crimes demand ultimate penalties' and 'the people of Texas have spoken, through their elected representatives.' Yada yada. Let me guess. You went for 'let's not sink to their level.'"

"Just call me Mister Broken Record."

"There aren't records anymore. We call them CDs."

"At least I didn't say 'gramophone cylinder.'"

For the third time, Max told the guards that it was all right to leave him alone with the prisoner, and finally they shut him in the cell, closing the nine-inch-thick steel door, with its heavy coat of chipped, off-green paint. Max leaned himself against the chill cinderblock wall and took a good look at Childeric Stokes. Inmate A-W083082 was sitting on the wooden bench, eyes down. He'd been freed of his manacles for the occasion, and given, as requested, a clove cigarette. Its aroma was profoundly unpleasant, and Max was grateful that he had not been gifted with a superhuman sense of smell.

In captivity, Stokes seemed smaller, almost shrunken. He was no taller than five-six, with stooped shoulders and a widening expanse of paunch hanging over his beltless prison pants. Messy fringes of side-hair ringed up around his male pattern baldness. Ancient acne scars pitted his cheeks. He shifted on the bench, trying improbably to lounge on it, giving Max his first clear view of those unsettling eyes. Their irises shone with the intense light blue of the Caribbean Sea, and they vibrated almost imperceptibly, lending him an air both manic and hypnotic.

"So," said Sentinel.

"So," said Stokes.

"You wanted to see me? I'm assuming you have some final confessions to make."

Stokes giggled. "You know what happens when you assume. You make an *ass* out of —"

Max cut him off. "I didn't come all this way for childish banter."

Stokes blew clove smoke.

"The Haight-Ashbury murders, 1970," Max said. "The victims placed in those obscene poses. The theatricality of the killings. The socio-political impact. . . . That had to be you. Surely now you'll grab at this last chance to take credit. . . ."

Stokes vibrated his oceanic eyes. "I can see hypothetically how one might say that. Coming right after Altamont, those murders brought the entire flower power peacey-weacey movement to a crashing burn, bringing about its inevitable death even sooner and more decisively than would otherwise have been. One might calculate that the despair the murders fostered led to a wave of drug addiction that caused an additional 107,544 deaths over the next seven years. And also prolonged the Vietnam conflict, long enough to destabilise Cambodia, allowing the Khmer Rouge to come to power, hence the killing fields, hence another how many deaths, Max?"

"I don't recall putting you on a first-name basis. And I don't have the figure at my fingertips."

"Approximately one-point-seven million deaths, let's say. That would be quite a dramatic result from such a small initial event, wouldn't it? A piddling twelve murders, no matter how gruesome. Why, the rewards exceed the investment by a factor of 150,000. So, hypothetically, the person who did the deed might want to take credit. If that were the purpose of this meeting, that is."

"You know I don't buy your chaos theory, social-engineering nonsense, Stokes. The flutter of a butterfly's wing in China may or may not create a storm in Oklahoma, but a sick killing spree in San Francisco certainly doesn't bring about genocide on the other side of the world, five years later."

Stokes smirked. "What I *know* is that, deep down, on those chill nights when you jolt up in bed and can't get back to sleep again, you acknowledge that every prediction I've ever given you has come true. The rest is mere bluff and denial."

"The Juarez voodoo cult murders, 1980."

Stokes twitched dismissively. "Please. You can't really think that was me."

"Multiple victims, obsessively mutilated, attracting wide news coverage —"

"I mean seriously! Amateur hour stuff! Those murders weren't about anything. They carried no meaning, had no repercussions. Take one look at Juarez and you can see it's just a bunch of coked-up cartel types freaking out on some half-baked Santeria crap they picked up down at the cantina. After all these years, Max, you've finally managed to offend me." He stood abruptly, flinging his arms wide. "But I forgive you, because we are brothers. Can I have a great big hug?"

Maxwell crossed his arms.

Stokes invaded his space. "This is what I brought you here for. Not the petty details of whose limbs I amputated where and at what time. But the grand revelation. All along, you've figured, same as everybody else, that I was just an ordinary man in a bizarre costume. When the truth is I got powers, Max, *deep powers*." With his forefinger, he jabbed repeatedly at his own left temple.

"The explosion that killed the Norman Family Singers."

"Yes, yes, that was me," said Stokes, swatting the air to drive off metaphorical gnats. He seized Max by the shoulders; Max saw that he chewed at his nails and the skin around them. "I am a prophet, Max, a prophet of two worlds. I can see the past and the future, and the purple threads of cause and effect that connect up all the history. You've no idea how long I've wanted to brag about this, but I couldn't till now, because it would wreck the effect.

"I see two worlds, Sentinel — the one we live in and an alternate, parallel one, which I'll call Earth Omega. Earth Omega is nearly like ours, with the exception that there are no superbeings. Not a one. No caped crusaders. No armour-wearers or gadgeteers or orphaned aliens. For example, on Earth Omega, when the professors tried to invigorate your crippled body with atomic energy, you did what any sane, normal person ought to do in a situation like that. You died, painfully, of radiation poisoning. The Iron General, waiting out there to see me get the needle, is just an ordinary paper-pusher at a V.A. hospital, with a string of ex-wives and a drinking problem.

"There are other differences, too. On Earth Omega, this country has had the death penalty going full bore since the mid-seventies. It's got many more than a couple dozen men parked on death row — try three and a half thousand. There's a Polunsky Unit in its Livingston, Texas; it's much bigger, and fuller.

"Question: What makes the difference? Answer: On Earth Omega, there's no you. You're not flying around in your snow-white Spandex, appearing on talk shows, embodying optimism, channelling Norman Rockwell and Jimmy Stewart. Nor are there any other *übermenschen* to make people believe in apple pie and last-minute rescues."

"You're detailing the logical constructs of a schizophrenic," Max said.

Stokes waggled a naughty-naughty finger. "Ah-ah. . . . You don't want to be saying that, 'cause that makes me not guilty by reason of mental defect. It's mitigating. Exculpatory, even. Whereas all that I have done has actually been the result of cold, precise, probability calculation. Earth Omega's real. I see it now, like one half of a double exposure, layered over this one. And for decades I've done my best to compensate for the existence of you and your friends, to make sure that all of its horrors happen here, too. The connections are easy to see, the instructions simple to follow, given my expanded consciousness."

Max took a seat on the bench. He looked at the worn soles of his shoes and made a mental note to go shopping later. "All right. How about an example?"

"You're thinking this is how you'll get me to confess and close those cases and so on. Well, here's one outside the jurisdiction. Yugoslavia. In our reality, before I intervened to harmonise with Earth Omega, the break-up of the former Yugoslav republics was destined to be a ho-hum deal. A peaceful transition to democracy, not much different than Poland's, or Czechoslovakia's. Its two superheroes, the Khazar and Mountain Eagle, paved the path of enlightenment and ethnic co-operation. Well —" he snorted out a laugh "— we can't have that.

"I looked at Earth Omega, followed the purple lines of causation, and acted. It took surprisingly little effort. Sure, there were the werewolf murders near Gorazde in '85 and '86. That was typical me. But mostly it was a matter of spreading rumours and painting graffiti on garage doors. Little things. Heightening suspicions. Ratcheting up suppressed fears. So in 1987, in Kosovo, good old Slobodan Milosevic, a man destined for obscurity in our future, became what he was on Earth Omega: the leader who started the ball of causation rolling, bringing about all that lovely civil war — the rape camps, the genocide. Khazar and Mountain Eagle even wound up killing each other in Sarajevo — oh, but you remember that."

"Yes. I was there." Max noticed that his right hand had clenched up into a fist.

"You want more examples, or should I move on to my final, imminent masterstroke?"

"You plan to kill more people?"

"Max," he giggled, "I plan to kill you. And all your superpals. It works like this. I'm the first cape to make death row. In a few hours, I'll be the first to be executed. According to my calculations, to my ineluctable lines of probability, my execution will set off a social ripple effect that will result in all-out pogrom against metamen within three generations. If I'd succeeded in my attempts to allow television cameras into the death chamber, it would be two generations, but, hell, you can't have everything. You see, despite all the heart-warming things about the human spirit you've trained the lemmings to believe, people get off on an execution. It stirs them, deep inside. Always has. And — once again, despite your example — at the core they fear us. We're freaks. We make them feel powerless. And that's dangerous, Mister Liberty. *Muy, muy dangeroso.*

"My execution, given all of the horrible things I've done, the long and ghastly list of crimes, which you are here today to further document — it, in particular, will stir the norms deeper than they've ever been stirred before. Even the saintliest bake sale lady can feel entitled to a jolt of sadistic jollies upon my demise. It'll be the first rock of crack. They'll want more capes to take a lie-down on their lethal injection tables. At first, only the deserving will die. But then standards will slide, as standards inevitably do, all the way down the slippery slope. And eventually, you and your allies will die at the hands of the very souls you've fought so hard to protect. Just as you know you can fly, I use my power of prophecy and know for a certain fact that this will occur.

"So enjoy my funeral, Max. In a way, it'll be yours, as well."

"Presuming, for the sake of argument, that you actually believe all this. Why?"

"Why what?"

"What's in it for you? Why do all that you've done?"

Childeric Stokes made a sashaying, side-to-side move, dancing slowly with himself. "Because, Max, I really, really like killing people. As many as I possibly can."

Max found the Iron General in the witness room, micromanaging chairs. The room was small, a fresh coat of eggshell paint on its cinderblock walls. The chairs were shiny new fold-ups made of chrome and rippled grey plastic. They sat in six rows of six chairs each. Charleston, his scabbard bobbing up into the air behind him, threaded through the rows picking up chair backs, making the pattern exactly even. Max held back, remaining on the threshold of the room. Noticing him, Charleston stopped what he was doing. He set the current chair down, carefully misaligning it, so that it was the only oddball in an otherwise precise arrangement.

"Okay, so it's not a nice thing, getting ready to watch a man be killed," Charleston said. He fixed his gaze on the dust-grey curtains shrouding the death chamber window. "It's not like taking out an enemy soldier in the jungle, where you don't know it's coming and it's over before you know what happened. And I could do without the whole medical procedure aspect of it. I'm a traditionalist; I'd like them to use a firing squad."

Max sat down, facing the curtain.

"But don't mistake uneasiness for doubt," Charleston went on. "You can look at me like that all you want, but this is still right and necessary. Never more so than with a man like Stokes."

"When have I ever tried to change your mind, Ryan?"

"It's not what you say. It's the way you hold your shoulders."

Max contemplated this for a moment; no good response came to mind. So he changed the subject, summing up Stokes's confession, or rant, or whatever it had been.

"Don't tell me you believe that," said Charleston.

"My brain says *no*, my gut says *yes*. Or that we can't afford to outright dismiss it, at any rate. We've both run up against a hundred crazier things that turned out to be true."

"Occam's Razor says go with the simplest explanation, which is that Stokes wants you to talk the governor out of offing him."

"Then why didn't he launch any appeals? Why did he want it televised?"

"He's come down with a last minute desire to live. Wouldn't be the first time."

Max checked his watch, an eighteen-karat white gold Breguet Classique. It was just past five-thirty — half an hour before the execution. Texas had moved its executions from midnight to 6:00 P.M. to accommodate the families. Relatives of both victims and the condemned were entitled to observe the last moments. Two corrections officers wandered into the witness room, a tall woman and a yawning man. The man moved to pull a plastic divider from the wall.

"No, no," said the woman. "I told you before — the prisoner doesn't have any friends or family coming. He won't need his half."

The male C.O. nodded and mumbled.

"You gentlemen need any taking care of?" asked the woman C.O., addressing Max.

"We're fine, thanks," Max said.

"Mister Liberty, do you think I could impose on you for a little favour?"

"Nnn?" Max replied.

She pulled a trading card, in a hard protective collector's case, from the side pocket of her regulation polyester slacks. With mid-length, laminated fingernails, she tugged it loose, handing it and a black fine-point Sharpie marker to Maxwell. An unnoticeably younger version of his face smiled jauntily up at him from the card's surface. Judging from the sideburns, the detailing on his costume, and the graphic design, the card dated from the mid-seventies. Last time he'd checked, cards of this approximate vintage sold for about fifty bucks, retail. An original American Sentinel card from the super-rare 1943 All-Fightin'-Heroes set would fetch over ten thousand.

"This for you?" he asked her.

She flushed red. "No, for my son."

Max knew the drill. No one wanted the cards personalized; it reduced the resale value. Nor did anybody want him to sign his legal name; they all wanted the scrawl to read *The Sentinel*. The strangest part about giving autographs was referring to himself with a definite article.

Max gave the woman her signed card. She waved it in the air, like it was a fan, to let the ink dry. He glanced over at Charleston; who crossed his arms and sniffed in pointed disinterest.

A low buzz of voices emanated from the corridor; Max surmised that the victims' families and press reps had been let in. He chose not to do any super-eavesdropping. Soon they appeared at the doorway, just over a dozen folks, ushered in by the warden. Max had met with him before; his name was Gonzales and he seemed to be a concerned and decent man. Today his tone was hushed, like a funeral director's.

Max's preference would have been to sit in the back row, where Charleston had stationed himself, but instead he took a position by the door, knowing that some of the people filing in would want to interact with them. For some reason each and every one of the victims' relatives reached out their hand to press his flesh, though they all had to realise he'd come out against the execution. They smiled and nodded, and some whispered thanks for capturing Stokes. His mere presence reassured people; in this situation, that was a positive. Max waited for Jenni Ansert's aunt to appear but she was not among the party.

The relatives moved quickly between the rows of seats, subtly jockeying for the back row. Moved by respect, the Iron General slipped discreetly up to the front, abandoning his prime seat. Charleston watched the witnesses reflected in the window glass as they settled themselves in, disarranging his careful placement of chair rows. Once seated, the relatives studied the toes of their shoes, or the brown water spots that spread like Rorschach tests across the ceiling tile, or kept an eye on the clock.

The five press representatives marched into the room as the rows filled in. The first three reporters, each in turn, nearly shook Max's hand, as the relatives had done. Then they remembered their professional detachment and awkwardly pulled out of the gesture. Protocol dictated that three of them — from the local *Livingston Beacon*, the *Houston Chronicle* and the Amalgamated Press — had permanent slots, guaranteed for every execution. Max didn't know the fourth one; nicotine stained his shirt-cuffs and a bolo tie with a big gnarled rock of turquoise on it swung from his collar. The fifth was Su Mei Miller. She blinked at Max as if trying to remember something.

The reporters bunched up in front of the windows; the number of chairs had been underestimated. Warden Gonzales issued hushed orders and soon the extras were provided and unfolded. Soft sobbing came from a sixtyish man in the second row, his shoulders quaking. Max took the last of the new chairs and set it up next to Charleston's.

Time crawled. The relatives coughed, or shifted in their seats. They'd already been prepared, by a prison official, in what he called a "counselling session." He'd told them what they were going to see: the gurney wheeled in, the injection of the saline solution, the last words, the downstroke of the delivery mechanism's main lever, the drifting off to sleep. They weren't given the names of the chemicals (sodium thiopental, pancuronium bromide, potassium chloride) or their functions (sedate the prisoner, stop his diaphragm, close tight his heart).

Finally the curtains parted. Stokes lay strapped on the gurney's thick blue padding, trying to tilt his head up to see his audience. The I.V.s had been attached; the saline solution would already be in him. Max's teeth clenched: Now was the bit he'd been dreading. Stokes would get to say his last words. Sentinel had no doubt that they would be exquisitely honed to deliver the maximum possible additional emotional trauma to the families.

Pressure waves rippled across Max's ear drums. The extra-human aural sensors in his brain identified them as ultrasound vibrations, at approximately ninety thousand cycles. There was a wrong sound somewhere in the room.

Max focused on the sound. It was emanating from Su Mei Miller. He pinpointed. It originated from the middle of her head. He activated his gamma vision. She lit up as a cyborg. Most of her skull had been hollowed out and filled with electronic parts. Included among them was a lens, which replaced her right eye, as well as a charged-couple device and the unmistakable plastic profile of a Hi-8 cassette. Someone had remade Su Mei into a walking video camera. Max leapt from his chair, at the same time scanning the rest of her body, seeing that her arms and torso were also robotic.

He wrapped his arms around her from behind and pulled her chair backward. Blue energy flowed from her body to his, shocking him. The smell of scorching flesh rose from Su Mei's hands. The reporter was roasting from the inside out.

"Damn it, no!" screamed Stokes from the gurney.

With surprising power, Su Mei wrenched free of Max's grip. She turned to face him.

"You couldn't have heard that!" Stokes shouted, presumably at Max. "You can't hear ultrasound above seventy-five thousand cycles!"

Your specs are out of date, Max thought. He'd been able to hear all the way up to a hundred thousand since the mid-nineties.

Su Mei clocked him with a swift punch to the jaw. It didn't hurt him, but the force was enough to turn his head a bit. Which was quite the accomplishment.

"Clear them out!" he shouted at Charleston, referring to the bystanders.

"They're clearing out fine on their own!" Charleston's power-sword buzzed free of its sheath. Su Mei whirled, nearly catching him in the throat with a whip-fast elbow shot. Charleston brought his sword down on her arm, gashing it.

Max yelled at him: "No! She's the real person, altered! Don't hurt her!"

Stokes squirmed against his restraints. Max scanned him to be sure he had no cyborg parts; he didn't. "Push the lever!" Stokes ordered, spit flecking out at the white-coated executioners. "Push the lever!"

Max dashed to the Plexiglas and shook his head at the technicians. They fled the death room, leaving the lever unpulled.

Su Mei jumped on Max's back; she weighed more than she ought to, but he was more than strong enough to retain his footing. He dropped sideways, knocking her off him. The Iron General had a Sig-Sauer in his hand, drawing a bead.

"Don't, unless those are tranquilliser bullets," Max grunted.

Blue energy crackled around Su Mei's arm as she recharged her electrical attack. Max grabbed her, spun her, and applied a choke hold from the back. He set his teeth together, felt his muscles buck and writhe as the shock surged through him, smelled his own flesh smouldering. As he knew they would, his heart withstood the assault and his lungs kept breathing. The crackling stopped; Su Mei went limp in his arms. The burns hurt, a little.

He asked directions from Warden Gonzales, then ran with Su Mei to the prison hospital. He would not need to confer with the doctors on her condition. His scan had shown that nearly eighty percent of her actual brain tissue had been removed to make room for the camera and robotic control system. The Su Mei Miller he'd known was, as a matter of practical fact, brain-dead, and had been so for some time.

By the time Liberty got to Stokes's cell, Charleston was already there. The Nihilist's lower lip had been parted in the middle, spackling blood onto his orange jump suit. Spots of it also decorated Charleston's knuckles. The Iron Duke grimaced at Max as if expecting a reproach.

"He's already given up the names of the confederates on the outside who kidnapped Su Mei and had her altered," he said.

"What can I say?" Stokes coughed. "I like it when you hit me."

"The video," Max said. "What was the plan for that? The networks wouldn't play it, not with cameras banned by the court."

The tip of Stokes's tongue investigated the degree to which a front incisor had just been loosened. "Not *at first* they wouldn't play it. Initially it'd swarm the Internet, pouring out from double-blind servers into the file-sharing stream. Forty-three percent of American broadband users would view it within two months." He stopped to blow red spit-bubbles off his lip. "Then the networks would run it, starting with Fox News, pretending they were running a story about other people showing the footage, not showing it themselves. Soon it would be right up there in the TV annals with the tape of the Rodney King beating and that water-skiing squirrel. Still not as effective as immediate live broadcast; it would only have a 1.31 multiplier effect — but still. Can beggars be choosers?"

Sentinel made a fist and jammed it into Stokes's solar plexus. The Nihilist groaned and doubled over, chin to knees. He gazed up at Max in appalled surprise.

"You, Max? From him I expect it, relish it even, but —"

Max grabbed him by the hair and stood him up straight to expose his shaking belly, then punched him there a second time. Stokes went foetal on the floor. Max let him stay there.

Stokes wheezed until his wind came back. Then he said, "You know, you'll find this the most unbelievable thing I've ever told you, but I actually feel a sense of violated morality, that you have hit me like that."

"Is that so?"

"If you are not the rock-solid paragon of quaint and beautiful values, how can I be your polar opposite?"

"You won't be anyone's polar opposite for long, dickweed." Charleston knelt to hiss into his ear. "Yeah, you've delayed it maybe a year — two, even — while we catch, try, and convict your accomplices. But then you're going right back onto that gurney. And that execution won't be televised, either."

"Please oh please, Br'er Bear, don't throw me into dat dere briar patch."

"Actually," said Max, turning his back on the prisoner, "Mister Stokes will not be executed at all."

Charleston jabbed a finger at him. "Don't give me that alternate future crap. This guy is why we have a death penalty!"

"It's not that." Max placed hands on his hips. A clichéd posture, perhaps, but, hell, he'd invented most of the really good superhero clichés in the first place and had a grandfathered claim to them. "During the altercation, I scanned him, just in case he had undetected cyborg alterations we might want to deal with. He didn't, but I found something else."

"Up yours, Liberty," the Nihilist spat.

"Dark clouds throughout the lungs. Spots on the liver. Metastatic tissue all the way up the spinal column. . . ."

"Cancer," said Charleston.

"Inoperable," Max replied.

"Good."

"We'll find out how you got the illness past the prison doctors," Max told Stokes.

"Bribes. My physician felt no qualms in taking them. Said I should die in front of the families, cancer or no cancer."

"There's an argument to be made for that," said the Iron General.

"Despite that fact, the prisoner is going to get exactly what he doesn't want. You'll die alone and unheralded here in this jail cell, Stokes. In medical segregation, at best. No vile last words to spit at mourning families. No interviews with the media. We'll see to that. And if all that talk of your execution triggering a massive anti-metahuman pogrom is true —"

"It is," Stokes interrupted. "But go ahead and disbelieve, if it suits your little mind better."

"If it's true, then your ultimate calculation has come up a big, fat zero, hasn't it?"

"Can the corny talk, Liberty. Let me rot in peace."

"Okay."

Sentinel and the Iron General strode together down the corridor toward the administrative area. Charleston's hard heels clicked on polished tile.

"So," he said to Max, after a longish silence.

"Uh-huh?"

"The last bit there, about him dying cold and alone."

"What about it?"

"Well, ya know, far be it from me and all . . ."

"How much time will you need to get from the build-up to the actual needling? Because if you're planning on taking a while, we should maybe go out and get some barbecue."

"Love to, but I gotta fly right back to D.C. So here's my question." Charleston punctuated his dialogue by leaning against the cinderblock wall. He looked at his empty right hand as if he wished there were a cigar in it. "It was good — the dying cold and alone part. Like something I'd say, except elegant. But maybe I misheard it. I mean, I wouldn't be detecting a dose of vengeance in there, would I, Mister Max Liberty?"

"No," said Max. He cleared his throat. "Only justice."

"That right?"

"The shots to the gut, on the other hand. Those were vengeance."

APOCALYPSE

BY DANIEL KSENYCH

"I'm cold. It's cold out tonight." Nemain turned up the collar of the overcoat they had lent her.

"Yes, I suppose you're not used to registering temperature like this," Mister Cray said, staring at the display on the hand-held LINC, its light painting his rugged features sea green. "A side effect of the inhibitory drugs we have you on. Johnny, could you?"

Johnny Chakra channelled his ultra-prana through the Manipura centre in his solar plexus. Slowly, the air on the hilltop warmed around them: Mister Cray, middle-aged and severe in his crisp blue suit; Johnny, in white with the seven Hindu tattwa symbols running vertically along his torso, his blond hair short and spiked; and Nemain O'Connell, clothes baggy and store-bought under the overcoat, her red hair tousled in the wind. Her features were youthful, but there was a sharpness in her eyes, like something forged. Nemain O'Connell, called the Morrigan. Nemain O'Connell the traitor.

A light on the LINC flickered. "Still reporting no presence," Cray whispered.

"They're coming," Nemain said defensively, though for a moment she imagined that they were not, that the intelligence with which she was attempting to buy her freedom was false. Perhaps DREAD had shared it with her knowing that she planned to go rogue. Perhaps she'd had fallen into a trap — the betrayer betrayed. She immediately recognized the idea as a fantasy designed to ease her conscience, which only made her feel worse. "Version Delta's sensors are only accurate up to one hundred miles, right?"

Cray didn't look up from the display. "I'm not casting doubt, Morrigan, only reporting facts."

Johnny glanced at her; his eyes seemed older than his years. She still felt cold.

In the valley below, the scientists from Horizon Labs continued with the experiment. A ring of trailers — mobile laboratories — surrounded the platform where the field would be generated. A large robotic arm extended from a terminal at the platform's edge to its centre. Hoses ran like veins along its length; they would carry the chemicals to the injection nozzles once the field was active. The particular magnetic properties of the valley combined with the precise microgravitational tides caused by the specific alignment of the moon, Mars, and Jupiter would aid in catalysing then stabilizing the resulting reaction. This was superscience. Nemain didn't understand it but she knew that DREAD was coming to steal it.

The science team had listened to Cray's threat assessment and politely refused his suggestion that they postpone the experiment. The opportunity for staging the experiment was too rare and their confidence in the Utopia Squadron's protection was absolute. When Nemain had heard that the test would go on, despite her information, she felt strangely insulted; how could the Squadron, her former enemies, inspire such faith?

The LINC flickered. "Version Delta reports incoming from the southeast. MACH 2. Johnny, if you could. . . ? And Morrigan, please follow me."

As Johnny Chakra rose into the air, invisible and silent energy radiating from his chest — the Anahata centre — Cray took Nemain by the arm and led her down the opposite side of the hill. She wouldn't see the results of her treachery against DREAD. But she had fought against the Utopia Squadron enough times to imagine what would happen.

The cell's steel walls were laced with saturnium. Besides being incredibly strong, the superalloy's unique pattern of electron decay caused a perception-dulling effect. That, in turn, aggravated the slight nausea caused by the drugs they'd given Nemain. These were feelings she had never experienced before.

The thick door hissed open and Cray entered. "At 2:05 A.M., DREAD attacked the Horizon science team in an attempt to disrupt and steal their metalchemic experiment. The strike team consisted of Titan, Parallax, and six DREADbots — exactly as you said it would. Johnny Chakra, Version Delta, and Trump Zero engaged the strike team and forced their retreat."

"Is everyone okay?" she asked, surprising herself. Her thoughts were murky and unfamiliar.

"Everyone is fine. Furthermore, Horizon Labs' metalchemic experiment was a success. Thanks to you, a profound leap has been made in the area of liquid energy paradynamics. Technological breakthroughs are expected to follow shortly."

Nemain rubbed her eyes. "Are you — is one of your telepaths doing something to my mind?"

"Morrigan, I have decided to discontinue your regimen of inhibitory drugs. And to provide you with proper quarters here on the island, in the Complex."

She managed to stand up, to look into his hard eyes. "You trust me — enough to —?"

"Not yet. But Agenda has decided that you have given us cause enough to begin trying. We wish to reciprocate your . . . effort. You also need a reason to trust us."

She held his gaze and saw only the steel of the cell reflected back at her.

The training facilities in DREADfort Three were underground. The lighting alternated randomly between pitch dark and wildly strobing colours. The sounds of gunfire and buildings collapsing were pumped through speakers embedded in the walls and floors. Everything was iron and fire and toxic, meant to simulate war. For the Morrigan it was a womb.

On the Squadron's island headquarters, in the Complex's training grounds, the sun shone or it rained, as the weather decided. Lush trees carefully pruned divided gravel and grass plots into curving spaces, fringed with flowers. The state-of-the-art physiotropic exercise equipment sat alongside sculptures and potted plants. Sometimes there was music, sometimes birdsong, sometimes silence.

"This doesn't show you what it's like to fight," Nemain had said when Cray first led her through the grounds.

"No. It shows you what you're fighting for."

As the days passed she worked hard in the grounds. The effects of the inhibitory drugs wore off. Soon she was able to add more weight to the gravipress, until its artificial gravity fields pulled at her straining legs and arms, and to increase the power of the impact cannons, until their compressed kinetic energy shells thudded painfully against her chest and shoulders. Eventually she no longer sweated when she out-ran the light pulse array laced around the track or punched through the steel braces fastened between the fluted pillars. Nemain's strength returned, and she knew that she could easily leap over the stone wall, its fitted bricks like an ancient castle, and risk the surrounding waters. To prevent this, one of the Versions was hovering over her, cloaked and watching. Or so she assumed. When she paused to rest and let her senses stretch to their superhuman range, though, she couldn't hear the telltale hum of a Version chronal battery. Perhaps the latest model had compensated for the flaw.

She always exercised alone, and no one disturbed her. Until one day, when Johnny Chakra slowly levitated down beside her while she drank from a stone-carved fountain.

"I thought you might be interested in sparring," he noted casually.

Nemain wiped her mouth with her hand. "I'm not interested in fighting. Not anymore."

"'We seek to master the martial arts not so we may use them, but so we never have to.' Caliburn said that to me once when he visited the Complex." Johnny eyed her for a moment. "Did you ever fight him?" he asked with a sly look.

"No."

Johnny smiled a friendly smile and continued to stand beside her.

"I told you," Nemain said, "I'm tired of fighting."

Johnny didn't move, but something changed in his expression.

"Don't," she said firmly. "That's your Vissudha chakra activating, for persuasion. Remember, I have fought you before."

Johnny smirked again. "Okay, okay. . . ." His look became more serious. "Nemain? Why did you —? No one's ever defected from DREAD before."

Nemain looked down at the water arcing from the fountain to the small pool below. "Okay, we'll spar. But you can't use any of your telepathy stuff."

"Fair enough."

Nemain entered the medical ward with her eyes downcast. Her hair was pulled back in a ponytail. She looked very young. The nurse glanced up from Johnny's bedside and quietly exited. His face was still swollen and bruised.

"You could at least apologize," he said wryly.

"I'm sorry," she replied, eyes still on the floor.

"Once more with feeling."

She winced.

"No," he said. "I'm sorry. That was unfair." He sighed and raised himself up against his pillow. "For what it's worth, I knew what was going to happen. Agenda told me."

Nemain looked up, confused. "But *I* don't even know what happened."

"You beat the crap out of me."

She sighed. "I know! I mean . . . not on purpose. I just . . . went red and I —"

"It's okay, Nemain. Remember, I've fought you before. And, like I said, Agenda told me what would happen."

"How did he —?"

"He is superintelligent, after all," Johnny said.

"And he still made you spar with me?"

Johnny shook his head. "It's not like that here. Agenda is our analyst. Even Cray only allows himself the informal title of 'guide.' No one *makes* anyone do anything in the Squadron. We choose. I chose."

Nemain lowered her gaze to the floor again. "So what exactly did Agenda tell you?"

Johnny absently traced a finger along one of the bio-spores suctioned to his broken arm. "That you had most likely been deep conditioned by DREAD. That they had programmed a bestiary of sorts into your limbic system — neurological recognition codes for the opponents you'd be facing in battle. In other words, us. There's probably an auto-attack cue, too. You see one of us, you attack.

"That you were able to suppress the programming when you defected is amazing. You've probably never been aware of it before because you've never had another frame of reference to compare it against. Before now."

Nemain squeezed her eyes shut and took a slow breath.

"Agenda," Johnny continued, "suspects the reaction cues are probably even more intense for members of the Guard. Sort of a murderous-rage-at-first-sight. Which made me feel oddly slighted." He shrugged. "It was all just a theory though, and I thought we needed to test it."

"Why?"

"To better learn how we could help you."

She glanced awkwardly at the monitors beside the bed. Johnny watched her with sadness in his young, wise eyes.

"So what do I do about it?" she asked.

"Well, Agenda is superintelligent, but not super superintelligent. . . . He's working on it. Hey, did you guys in DREAD know my origin story? How I got my powers?"

Nemain looked at him. "An Indian mystic known as the Yogi passed his kundalini on to you from his deathbed. All the latent abilities stored in your chakras were activated instantly."

"Yeah, that was pretty much it. Everyone thinks I got off lucky — no gruesome experiments or catastrophic accidents. No painful mutations. I bypassed the whole death–rebirth trip everyone else seems to go through to gain powers. But while the transfer seemed to happen instantly, in 4-D spacetime —" he shifted in the bed "— to me, each one of those energy centres lighting up took forever. It was excruciating. From the Mulhadara chakra up to the Sahasrara, each one threatened to incinerate me. I had to master them, one at a time. I had to suffer through them to learn from them, before I became the cool and enlightened, albeit slightly bruised guy you see today." He grinned.

Nemain's lips curved ever so slightly. "And why do you tell me this, Johnny Chakra?"

"To remind you that becoming a hero is never easy."

Agenda leaned back in his chair, smoothed his tie, then his silver-grey hair. He picked up the LINC from his desk, tapped a few keys, replaced it. He studied the Dali painting on the wall and twirled a pen in his fingers. Agenda had seven additional cortices distributed throughout the entirety of his nervous system. When he was thinking a lot he tended to fidget.

Cray entered the office, high in the tallest tower of the Complex. Agenda focused his attention on the autographed photo of himself shaking hands with Crispin Jacobs, founder of the Ascension Institute, on his desk. As he did, he performed an analysis of the handwriting as a technique to slow his thoughts to the point where he was able to converse without sounding like a junkie.

"The Morrigan," Agenda began. "She takes her name from the tri-form Celtic goddess of war. Nemain was bred and raised by DREAD to be a soldier. My best theory to date is that, while she was still in the womb, DREAD scientists somehow fused her biology with two of her analogs in near-proximity parallel realities whose physical laws are sufficiently divergent from ours so as to result in increased strength, speed, endurance, and sensory perception when translated into the materiality of this universe."

"You still haven't switched to decaf like I suggested," Cray said, deadpan.

Agenda laughed and straightened in his seat.

Cray's expression remained neutral. "I'll ask you again, Agenda: Why do you think she has come to us?"

"I still don't know."

Cray took a seat opposite Agenda. "You'll have a chance to investigate your theory of her origin."

"We're going to experiment on her?" Agenda frowned. "I'm not comfortable with that. Curious, yes — but not comfortable. She's been through so much. . . . I don't like the idea of treating her like a lab rat."

"The Morrigan requested the tests herself."

Agenda raised an eyebrow, immediately following the logic. "She doesn't know the source of her own powers. DREAD never told her."

Cray continued in his unwavering voice. "She wants us to discover the source so that we can neutralize the powers. She wants to be normal."

Agenda stood and moved to the window. The non-linear equations necessary to calculate the fractal edges of the clouds in the sky traced across his mind like graffiti. "That's not why she came," he said. "It's a recent reaction." He counted his eye-blinks to slow his thoughts. "What does the community have to say?"

"The Order wants her tried for her crimes, of course."

"The Guard supports us?"

Cray nodded. "The Guard's position is that we should continue to help her in any way we can. Obviously, she could be a very valuable source of tactical information. The Horizon incident is but a single example of the good she might do. It remains, however, her choice. So long as that is our policy, the Guard have offered any assistance they can provide."

Agenda tapped his finger against the glass. "If she does choose to undergo experimentation I'd like you to suggest to her that she also begin attending classes. Balance." He looked back to Cray. "Do you think any of the team would have a problem with that?"

Cray nodded again. "Ricky Randall in engineering and Sarah Simmons in information services. Both lost family members during separate attacks by the Morrigan in Empire City. And Doctor Elaine Evans, who was the chief AI midwife for Version Alpha —"

"Who the Morrigan destroyed during the Vulcanor Incident." Agenda sighed.

"Not to mention the numerous field agents who have done battle with her. Not all of them share Johnny's perspective."

"Best armour up the professors and get maintenance to reinforce the lecture halls then," Agenda joked weakly.

Cray didn't laugh. He stood and moved to the door, then paused.

"You never imagined a member of DREAD would defect?"

"I had hoped, just as I hope everyone may one day be saved. But, no, I never calculated the scenario."

"Do you think they did?"

"You mean, what happens when DREAD concludes that she has gone over to our side?" Agenda returned to his seat behind the desk. "You don't need my powers of omni-dimensional reasoning to field that question, Mathew. In fact, you already know the answer."

Cray nodded. "They will come for her."

The room was circular and featureless with pale, metallic walls. It was quiet.

"Welcome to the Chamber, Morrigan," Mister Cray said, the space somehow making a whisper of his voice. "The Squadron currently counts four telepaths among its members. This is where they come to practice and refine their gifts. The Chamber is electromagnetically sterile. The smell in the air is from synthetic molecules replicated from an alien plant species acquired by the Ascension Institute; they enhance permeability of the self/other psychic membrane."

Nemain took a deep breath. Her freshly showered skin felt sensitive, tingling under the white gown in which they had dressed her.

"For the telepaths," Cray continued, "this place is a laboratory. A temple. A gateway."

Neuronia stood in the Chamber's centre, her uniform a shimmering grey-blue, her face masked in white. Nemain approached the superheroine as she had been instructed, sat cross-legged on the floor, and closed her eyes. The urge to tremble, the nervousness, stirred inside her, but it slowly faded, like it was being carried away on a wind. Neuronia placed her fingers on Nemain's temples.

<Inducing trance>, she broadcast.

Cray saw Nemain wince. "What's wrong?"

<She's resisting. It's only a reflex. I'll pacify it by implanting an archetypal feeling of sanctuary.>

Nemain's fists clenched. Moments passed and she finally relaxed.

<Trance induced. Interesting. Her psyche generated a defensive threat-response to the initial implant. I had to speed-cycle through alternate feelings to find one that would allow her to open to the trance. . . .>

"Which was?"

<Conflict. Today's session will mostly consist of a survey of the Morrigan's earliest memories with DREAD. I will leave my auditory channels open in case you wish to ask me anything during the tour.>

Cray nodded and Neuronia began reading Nemain's mind. An hour passed. Cray remained motionless by the arched doorway. After another hour, he watched a tear form in Neuronia's eye and run down her mask.

The Terran Ranger stared hard into Nemain's eyes, showing only threat and desire. She wished that Nemain would say something or, better yet, lash out at her. The Ranger wasn't wearing her bio-enhancement armour but she looked no less imposing for the lack of it, her light brown skin taut over thick muscle. They stood facing each other in the corridor outside the classroom. Three other heroes and twelve Complex staff strolled down the hallway in small groups discussing the lecture, pointedly not paying attention to the silent confrontation.

Then Trump Zero appeared and interposed himself between the two women. "Did you enjoy that?" he asked Nemain. Trump was wearing the baggy, multicoloured pants from his field uniform, but his T-shirt was from a Heathens concert. His dark hair was, as ever, messy, and his boyish face seemed, as always, on the verge of a smile. "The, uh — the lecture?"

The Ranger sniffed and turned away to join the others.

Nemain watched her go, remembering their last battle, a year ago in the Amazon. She glanced at Zero, then headed in the opposite direction. He followed.

"What part of the lecture are you asking about — the two-seat radius of empty chairs around me?" she asked, when it was clear he wouldn't take the hint and leave her alone. "Or maybe the 'bladder-don't-fail-me-now' look of fear on the professor's face every time he forgot and made eye contact with me? Better yet, how about when we were on break and whatshername — Doctor Evans — she told me how I was a child killer? Or are you just referring to the general purposelessness of analysing sonnets?"

Trump grinned. "Wow. Supersarcasm. Could be a new power."

Nemain sighed as they turned the corner into a glass-panelled walkway overlooking the sheer cliff that ran along the north side of the island. Version Theta flew by over the water on a routine patrol of the Complex's perimeter.

"I'm sorry," she said.

"Not a problem. Even some of the Squad find poetry class excruciating."

"To be honest, I don't really understand it."

Trump nodded. "Yeah, the Romantics can be a little opaque. Wait till we rotate back to the Modernists. You might like them better."

"No, I mean I don't understand why you all bother studying poetry. I know Mister Cray doesn't make you. What purpose does it serve?"

Trump shrugged. They passed into a stairwell leading to the dormitories. "Bettering the world by bettering yourself. As above so below." He frowned. "Boy, that sounded like a line from a commercial. You know, one of those sports car-equals-lifestyle ones?"

Nemain stopped at the door to her floor. "No. There were no televisions in the DREADfort barracks."

"Oh."

She opened the door.

"Wait a sec," Trump said. "Um, so was there no music either? I mean, have you never been to a concert or anything like that?"

Nemain looked at him.

"I'm curious, is all," he continued, glancing at the ground, then at the door and then his hands. "Because . . . well, there's a group playing in Empire City next week — Operation. They're sort of a favourite of mine."

Nemain brushed her hair behind her ear. "I have a session in the Chamber now. I have to shower. Excuse me." The door closed behind her.

She returned to her room late that night, tired. Her mind felt sore, like Neuronia had been picking at knots deep inside her. That was certain to aggravate the nightmares she'd been having for the past week. The rash didn't help matters, either. Mister Cray had been attempting to isolate her quantum matrix, where they suspected the source of her power lay, by submerging her in metalchemic baths her skin obviously disliked.

Nemain was so caught up in ignoring the itch that seemed to leap from her brain to the middle of her back that she nearly stepped on the Operation CD carefully placed outside the door to her room.

★　★　★

Johnny Chakra watched Nemain perform the Bae Suk pattern of tae kwon do, her steps so smooth and precise they left the gravel undisturbed. She completed the form, returned to ready position, then relaxed.

"You've been in a fight," she said coldly.

"Let me guess: I took the stairs down to the yard instead of levitating, so you figured my ultra-prana must be drained."

"I can tell because you smell of battle." Her voice was sharp. She started stretching.

"Version Delta, the Sylph, and I undertook an assault on DREADfort Six. The intelligence you provided earned us a victory," Johnny said calmly, watching.

Nemain paused, but only for a moment.

"How goes the work with Mister Cray on your quantum matrix?" he asked in the same even tone.

"Fine."

"How are your classes?"

"Fine."

"What about —"

"Stop it." Nemain straightened. "Stop asking me so many questions."

Johnny took a few casual steps, as if he were considering where to go. "I suppose there's really only one question I want to have answered anyway."

Nemain shook her head, frustrated. She started practicing attack combinations, scattering gravel as she launched her kicks.

He kept talking. "No one here knows the answer yet. Even Agenda only has guesses about it — why you are here, I mean. . . ."

Roundhouse kick. Axe kick. Spinning hook kick.

"Why you came to us. . . ."

Nemain spun to face him. "Why don't you ask Neuronia to pick it out of my head?"

Johnny stood still. His voice rose slightly but remained measured. "You know that's not what she's doing with you." Nemain held his gaze, frustration and fatigue, confusion and anger surging in her eyes. He softened his voice ever so slightly. "What's wrong?"

Nemain's shoulders slumped. "Besides the fact that information I willingly gave to my enemies just resulted in my teammates being defeated?"

"I'd have preferred it if you had prefaced a couple of those terms with 'former.'"

"Oh, shut up! I'm sick of your glib, pseudo-enlightened attitude." She turned and marched toward the staircase. Johnny kept pace with her. "Leave me alone! I'm so sick —" She slowed, then stopped. "I feel so sick."

Johnny moved in front of her. "Nemain, you've been here in the Complex for weeks now. Stuck here, holed up in the heart of everything you were trained to destroy. Maybe you need a break. Some time away, doing something different. Something new."

"Maybe. Maybe I do."

Johnny smiled his warm, easy smile. "You should have accepted Trump's invite to the Operation gig last week. I hear they're amazing live."

She stared absently at the branches of a nearby tree, then closed her eyes and wrapped her arms around herself, as if she were cold.

"Listen," Johnny said, "the Sylph and I both have some down time coming. We were going to hit the mainland. A bit of a road trip. I don't know, go antiquing or something. Whatever normal people do."

She looked at him. "What about Cray? Would he let me?"

"I've already spoken with him."

Nemain smashed the door to Cray's office into pieces. She stepped through and glared at him. "You son of a bitch. You knew! You knew we'd be attacked."

Cray sat, staring calmly at her. He placed the LINC on his desk. Then the Terran Ranger, superstrong in her green and brown bio-enhancement armour, crashed into Nemain from behind. Nemain went down but was already twisting, utilizing a hybrid aikido-judo manoeuvre with which she threw the Ranger off her and through the wall.

Nemain rose, and this time Cray rose to face her.

"What were you thinking?" she growled, stepping forward.

Trump Zero materialised beside her, laid a hand on her shoulder, and suddenly they were in the cell. The teleport and instantaneous immersion in the saturnium field dizzied Nemain. In that moment, Trump Zero was out the door, which was already hissing closed behind him.

Nemain was fast, though. The door's hydraulics groaned as she clasped its edge and began prying it open. From somewhere in the Complex, Neuronia downloaded an epileptic seizure into Nemain's brain. The door hissed shut as she spasmed on the floor.

Cray was in the cell — after moments or minutes, Nemain could not say, only that enough time had passed for her body to have calmed. Agenda was with him, speaking in a controlled voice.

"Please understand, Morrigan, that the Utopia Squadron practices a non-Aristotelian logic — which is to say that we do not adhere to either/or binary dualisms."

Nemain, aching from the seizure and the battle with DREAD only hours earlier, eased into a sitting position. "It was a test, wasn't it? To see if I would . . . when they attacked."

"That's what I'm trying to explain," Agenda noted. "The incident involving you, Johnny Chakra, the Sylph, and the DREAD strike team was, in fact, many things — some of them contradictory. This is the world we strive for, where —"

Cray interjected, "On topic, Agenda."

"Oh . . . yes. You are correct, Morrigan, when you say it was a test. It was a necessary means of ensuring you would not revert to your conditioned behaviour during an encounter with your former allies. And it —"

"You bastards," she said softly. "How could you be certain? I mean, what if I had attacked Johnny, or —?"

"You didn't," Cray said sharply.

"And it was a countermeasure," Agenda said. "We had to assume that DREAD would discover or deduce that you had defected, and that they would make an effort to either retrieve or terminate their lost asset. It was our decision to provide them with an opportunity to do so — one that would not invite an attack on the Complex and would dissuade them from further attempts. After the damage you did to Titan, the Node, and the DREADbot battalion, I'm sure they'll be wary of —"

"But you couldn't have known what would happen. Even with your stupid superintelligence. Not for certain. . . ."

"Yes, quite." Agenda straightened his tie.

Cray glanced at Agenda, then back to Nemain. "The Utopia Squadron does not seek to control the future, only explore it."

Nemain rubbed her eyes, ran a hand through her hair. Agenda stepped closer to her and knelt down. He offered her a handkerchief, and she realized that her nose was bleeding, perhaps from the impact with the Terran Ranger. She pressed the cloth to her face and looked up. Johnny was standing at the door, his uniform scorched from DREADbot pulse weapons. Cray gestured for him to leave. He looked concerned, but turned and went.

"Nemain," Agenda said, the edginess of hyper-thoughts gone from his voice. "It was a test *and* a countermeasure *and*, we hope, a form of medicine."

Nemain looked away.

The two men left. The door remained open.

<Very good, Nemain. Very good.>

Minutes passed in the silence of the Chamber.

<Mister Cray, she's letting me go deeper than before. . . . There are openings, small fissures. . . . What should I —?>

"Proceed, Neuronia."

She stood over Nemain, her hands touching the young woman's forehead and chin. It reminded Cray of the Tarot card Fortitude.

<It's music. The openings are made of music.>

"Let me hear it." Neuronia broadcast the songs, and he knew them; he'd been forced to tell Zero to turn down his music enough times to recognize the young hero's favourite band. "Follow them."

<I'm tracking them. . . . It's like hunting — like —>

The reference to hunting made Cray flash on a memory of fishing with his father, the Iron Duke's attack still years away, his parents both still alive.

<Okay, I'm almost — my god. . . .>

"Show me, Neuronia."

And she drew him in, inside Nemain's mind, and he gasped. Battlefields churned into and around each other, slick with blood, swarming with crows, war devouring and excreting itself, an Escherian Ragnarok. The corpse of Slipstream, his bones shattered to dust, Red Phoenix impaled on her sword, Sentinel hanging from an iron gallows. Everything bound with a fractal pattern of chains — DNA chains or veins or dendrites. Cray had a brief thought, an inspiration about her quantum matrix. Then he was choking. There was smoke everywhere, suddenly obscuring and infecting. *What* —? he thought, and Neuronia answered.

<Her twofold guilt. It clouds the damage done by her and to her.>

Neuronia's thoughts became like a wind, but they could not move the smoke, only Cray. It carried him up and out, beyond Nemain's psyche. Then he was in the Chamber.

Cray watched the tears form, as he had many times during these sessions. Only this time it was Nemain herself who was crying them.

Nemain pushed back the covers and sat on the edge of the bed. She went to the bathroom, washed her face and brushed her teeth. She stared into the mirror.

When she arrived at the lab for the day's bath she found the equipment powered down. None of the technicians were present, only Mister Cray.

"We will not be proceeding with the experiments." He spoke in the same hard voice he had used with her since she first contacted him. That terrifying phone call, so long ago.

"Why not?

"We have sufficient data."

Nemain pursed her lips. "For what?"

"To remove your superpowers." She stood very still. Cray continued. "I'm embarrassed to say that the process has only taken so long due to a rather Aristotelian assumption on my part. Or Cartesian, to be precise. I was directing the technicians to focus on the quantum bonding that was anchoring your parallel selves to each other. This attention to your body left an incomplete picture. The final component is in your mind."

Nemain closed her eyes. "I don't understand."

"It is my belief that the fusion with your alternate selves was, beyond the material process initiated by DREAD, a choice. Made by you. Agenda concurs."

"But . . ." The lab was quiet with all the machines shut down. "I was born this way. . . ."

"You made this choice pre-natally. The option was made available by DREAD science, but you — perhaps even the two alternates, as well — chose to accept the bond. To acquire superpowers."

Nemain felt light-headed. Perhaps it was a lingering association she'd formed with the metalchemic baths, which stood nearby. She inhaled to steady herself. "Why? I mean, what does this mean?"

"We have the science to release the bond — if you choose to let it go."

It was their first day studying poetry again after a series of workshops on engineering. Nemain was certain she could feel Ricky Randall staring at the back of her head. Her hands felt heavy, her pen moved stiffly as she copied down the professor's words.

". . . to consider a very ancient type of poetry called an 'apocalypse.' The most well-known example of this style is the *Book of Revelations*. It's so well-known, in fact, that the formal term and the idea of the end of the world, specifically Christian eschatology, have become inextricably linked. An apocalypse however is technically a poem that describes the revelation of a mystery. 'The Apocalypse of St. John' is, therefore, only one —"

Nemain excused herself. There was a throbbing deep inside her head.

Walking past the training grounds, she saw the Terran Ranger taking part in combat drills with Version Delta. Nemain immediately analysed the Version's firing pattern and plotted a trajectory of acrobatics that would allow the Ranger to evade the missile swarm and land a destabilizing blow against Delta. Simultaneously she calculated which martial arts style would be most effective against the current tactical configuration of the Ranger's armour: Drunken God. Nemain felt a wave of nausea come over her, as if the entire island were lurching. She thought briefly of Agenda and felt suddenly sad. Then there was no thought, only sadness. She rushed to her room.

Hours later, the moon shone over the water. After knocking and knocking again, Trump Zero opened the door to her room. Nemain was curled in a foetal position on her bed, crying in the dark. Her uniform, black with red patterns, splashes and streaks like blood, lay on the floor. She was clutching the black mask tightly. He hadn't seen the costume since the day she was escorted into the Complex by Cray, Johnny Chakra, Prime, Neuronia, and four of the Versions. He remembered being surprised when she took of her mask that they were about the same age.

She didn't move, except for a shuddering in her shoulders. He draped the Operation T-shirt he had bought for her over the back of a chair.

Trump Zero tapped his chaotic flux powers, like stepping off a cliff in his mind. He hoped for empathy, to soothe her heart. Or dreaming, to send her peaceful visions. Even hypnosis, to lead her to rest. The cards shuffled and the spread was revealed. Telekinesis. He could make do.

From across the room he touched POWER and PLAY on her stereo. "Beholden," the first song on the Operation CD, started to play. He whispered her name, and she looked up, her eyes red and raw. She didn't flinch or tense, so he reached out with his mind, like arms strong and warm, and lifted her up. The door to the balcony slid open. They rose, both of them, gently, drifting out into the cool night air. She looked at him. Out over the water, a second liquid night. And he took her in his arms, to the music spilling out of her room, and danced with her.

"Noo Media" played. Then "Welcome to the Culture." They turned together in the sky. "The N.E.O." played.

"How do you. . . ?" she asked, her voice small, her head against his shoulder. "We — DREAD never understood how your powers worked."

Zero smiled. "They manifest transpardigmatically. That's what Agenda calls it. It just means that they can be more than one thing and come from more than one place. Sometimes it's like I'm channelling energy. Sometimes it's like a genetic mutation. Sometimes it's like calling on spirits." She relaxed against him. The breeze teased her hair.

"That's cool."

"Sometimes it's difficult. Frustrating. But, yeah, I think it's pretty cool. Agenda says it makes me an excellent representative of the Utopia Squadron's philosophy. Really, though, would you want to be part of a movement that I was the poster-boy for?"

She giggled softly.

After "Homework" and "It Came From Sideways," Nemain fell asleep and he carried her to her bed.

Nemain pushed back the covers and sat on the edge of the bed. She went to the bathroom, washed her face and brushed her teeth. She stared into the mirror. She changed her clothes.

There was a knock at her door. She opened it and he was standing there. The eagle on his chest reminded her of a statue, a marble angel, that she once saw during an attack on Moscow.

"Hello, Morrigan."

"Hello, Sentinel."

"Call me Max."

"Oh. Okay. My name is Nemain." His cape rippled, tracing the outline of a breeze blowing from the balcony. "Please come in. I'm sorry for the mess."

Standing inside her room, he turned to face her. To look at her. There was a moment of stillness. Then, "Thank you, Nemain."

"What do you mean?" she asked. "Thank you for what?"

He smiled at her.

"Oh. You're welcome."

She saw something in his eyes then, or imagined she saw it. Something beyond the strength and the vigilance, beyond even the kindness. Something never captured in any photograph or portrait, or any video footage. A fatigue. A weariness. And she imagined that he was allowing her to see it, that he was revealing it to her, for her, so that they might share an understanding.

He glanced at her shirt. "I think their second album is my favourite. 'Arbitrary Burning' gets me every time I hear it."

Nemain looked down at the band logo across her chest, then back up, surprised and smiling. "I only have a copy of *Governed*. I think 'Welcome to the Culture' is my favourite song." She shook her head, a little disbelievingly.

He smiled again, a different smile. "I know — what's an old guy like me doing listening to Operation? Trump played them for Slipstream once and that was it; for months we couldn't go a day at the Tower without hearing them. I got hooked. I can lend you a copy of *Cycle* if you'd like."

They continued talking. Hours passed. She told him about poetry class and how she thought the Romantics were her favourite. They compared the Complex's and Olympian Tower's exercise equipment. He said that Mother Raven was looking forward to meeting her because their totem animals were so closely related, the raven and the crow. She told him about how she used to imagine that she had two sisters, when she was young, and that she would make up games with them. He told her about the first time he met Mister Cray and about the corny costume Cray used to wear. When she asked what Cray's superpower was, he only winked conspiratorially.

As the sun was setting, he looked at her and smiled again. "I have to go now."

His voice, she decided, made her think of rain. She felt like each word had the power to wash her away, so that she would dissolve and fade into the earth.

"Thanks for stopping by, Max."

"It was really nice to meet you," he said as he moved to the door.

"Likewise."

He stepped into the hallway.

"Um, Max?"

"Yes?"

"You never — all today, we talked — but you never asked me why I defected, why I came here."

He looked thoughtful. "It never occurred to me to ask why someone would do the right thing." He shrugged. "It seems obvious."

She nodded. And he left.

Mister Cray and Nemain stood on the hilltop looking out over the valley, colourful in the sunlight.

"It's a nice day today," she said. Nemain wasn't sure if it had been a long time or only a short one since that night here. She turned to look at Cray and the colours of the valley seemed to gather briefly in his eyes. She had the sudden feeling that she was still learning, that there was still so much yet to learn. She looked back to the rising earth beneath them. "How does it go? 'Ay, many flowering islands lie in the waters of wide agony . . .'"

Cray's brow furrowed. There was silence and wind for a time.

Then he asked her the question.

And she answered: "Yes, Mister Cray. I would like to join the Utopia Squadron."

He looked at her and smiled. She looked down shyly.

"I wonder though," she asked, "if I could maybe get a new uniform?"

Cray produced a LINC from inside his coat, touched the keypad, and handed it to her. She stared at the sketch on the screen.

"It's something I worked up shortly after you came to the Complex."

"It's . . . wow. It's really —" She grinned at him. "Beautiful. It's beautiful."

Cray offered her his arm, and they walked together down the hill.

"So, you've taken to Shelley." He cleared his throat. "'Through the broken mist they sail, And the vapours cloven and gleaming follow down the dark steep streaming . . .'"

And Nemain couldn't stop smiling, new and soft. "'Till all is bright, and clear, and still, round the solitary hill.'"

THE MAN IN THE WALL

BY ED GREENWOOD

The klaxons and the bells both went off this time, so the MTU bluehelms responded, too, pelting down the stairs with guns at the ready, right behind Horth's police detail. Heavy boots thundered along the corridor . . . slowed . . . came to a stop.

Duty Guard Samson Willdon was standing alone in the B Block detention hall, looking bewildered and angry. His gun was in his hand.

"Well?" Sergeant Horth snarled, looking around for trouble. This was where drifters and street thugs were brought, not metahumans or suspected murderers, so — where was the riot?

Willdon stabbed a finger at the cell he stood beside. "The Lurker. He was . . ."

"He what? 'Was'? He went and died on you?"

"N-No. He's sitting in there now. But he wasn't when I made my rounds! So I rang the alarm. . . ."

Silently the MTU bluehelms stepped around Horth and took up stances facing the cell door, fanning out to gain clear fields of fire. One of them lowered his gun to aim at the prisoner, and a soft, frightened curse came from the cell's depths.

Horth jerked his head in a signal, and the other two policemen rushed forward, peered in at the cowering prisoner, then hauled on the bars of the cell door, top and bottom, finding them as firm as they should be. They shook their heads grimly and stepped back, looking at Willdon.

The sergeant lifted an eyebrow, stalked forward, and peered into the cell. An old man huddled in one corner of a bare cot, cowering. Horth glared into the frightened eyes of the informant they'd codenamed 'the Lurker.' The man shuddered and turned his head away.

Horth fixed the guard with a cold look. "He looks pretty damned solid to me. And harmless."

"He was *gone!* I swear it! Gone — the cell was empty! I shone the blinder into every corner, not just my belt light! Ceiling, too! He wasn't in there!"

The three cops glared at Willdon. The full-face helms of the MTU officers turned to look at the guard, too.

Duty Guard Willdon glared right back. "And, no, I'm not drunk, I don't 'see things,' and I'm certainly not craving attention. He *was . . . not . . . there*. I'm telling you, and I'll swear it before a judge!"

"Get a zapper," one of the MTU men said suddenly to the other — who jogged off down the corridor without a word.

Horth's head jerked around. "You're not serious?"

"Better safe than sorry. We'll take him from here."

Horth shook his head in disbelief. Then he squinted into the cell again. "Well, okay. But if *that's* a metahuman, I'll eat my hat."

The helmed head regarded him expressionlessly, but the voice from within it sounded very dry. "Shred it first — and fried in butter's better than with ketchup."

Detective Raemer was one of the best. Even with his large, heavy gun clearly visible in its shoulder holster, he managed to seem gentle and friendly in his shirt sleeves, as he held out an open pack of smokes toward the prisoner. "D'you know why your arrest was ordered?"

The Lurker waved them away. "No," he said bitterly. "No, I don't. I've always helped the police." He kept his gaze on Raemer's face, ignoring the MTU bluehelms in full battle armour ranged along the other wall.

Raemer smiled encouragingly. "That's right. You told us names, places, what was going down before it happened, who boasted after the fact. Everything."

"Everything," the Lurker echoed. "And for this, you locked me up."

Raemer nodded. "Now, I want you to know that a lot of the boys were unhappy about that — are still unhappy about that. They told Ridgefield what a help you've always been, but Ridgefield told them he already knew that. I know he did, because I saw your file on his desk. Five inches thick, Morton — five *inches*. That's a lot of help. So I asked Ridgefield, and I wasn't gentle about it. I yelled."

He took a cigarette and thrust it into his mouth, unlit, letting it wave and dangle as he spoke. "And you know what he said to me?"

The Lurker just shook his head, face an angry mask.

"Of course you don't. But can you guess?"

The Lurker shook his head again, barely moving it this time.

Raemer sighed and sprang up from his seat to pace around the room. "He said to me, 'Raemer,' he said —"

The detective spun around to face the old man in handcuffs, and pointed at him. "'That Lurker guy is *always right*. Whenever we says he can prove something, it turns out he has the right stuff. So how does he do it? *How can he possibly know about all these crimes if he isn't mixed up in them?*'"

Silence fell, so profound that it almost seemed as if the row of bluehelms had stopped breathing. The two men stared at each other. Raemer lifted his eyebrows together, almost comically, in a silent question.

"So that's it?" the prisoner said slowly. "You threw me in here to rot for a week because one cop — one *deputy chief of police* — is so cynical and suspicious that he can't believe a citizen of Empire City just wants to help?" He shook his head. "I guess it's time for Deputy Chief Ridgefield to retire — and the rest of you to remember my constitutional rights."

For the first time, he turned slowly to survey the line of bluehelms. Their faces were concealed behind plastic shields, but their stance still cast them as professionally distant and dour. "Or have we finally become a police state, with the Constitution quietly discarded in favour of something more *convenient*?"

Raemer sighed and sat down again, wheeling his chair over close to the Lurker's. "Mister Morton, even you have to admit that knowing that much about crime in this city is pretty incredible — even suspicious, hey? Now, is there something you're not telling us?"

"No. I've told you five inches worth so far, remember?"

Raemer leaned forward. "Mister Morton," he asked gravely, "are you a metahuman?"

The Lurker blinked. Then he leaned forward as much as the cuffs would allow, until his nose was only inches away from Raemer's. "No."

There was a faint, quickly repressed chuckle from somewhere along the line of bluehelms.

The detective sat frozen for a moment, then asked briskly, "And do you have access to any device, or 'magic,' or friendly aid that can do things out of the ordinary?"

The old man leaned back in his chair, nodded a little wearily, and said, "Yes."

"*Hah!* Why didn't you tell us this before?"

"You never asked," the Lurker snapped. "Four bulls just threw me into that cell and slammed the door. When I asked them why, they told me, 'You know.' But I didn't, and I still don't. Not really."

The detective sat back and spread his hairy arms in contrition. "Mister Morton, I'm sorry. Now, does this device have anything to do with you disappearing from your cell a few hours ago?"

The old man regarded him severely. "I did *not* leave my cell."

"But the duty guard — a veteran, well-respected police officer who's seen a lot, mind you — couldn't see you in there, anywhere. We know from the surveillance tape that he didn't fall asleep, and that he did just what he told us he did to check on your whereabouts. So . . . can you turn invisible?"

Morton smiled wryly. "No."

"Well, what can you do?"

The old man turned to look at the row of MTU men. "My answer to that depends on what really happens to people who can — do special things. Do you lock them up? Quietly 'experiment' on them? Brainwash them?"

No one seemed in a hurry to answer.

"Well, what?"

Raemer sighed. "This is Empire City, Mister Morton. You live here. You watch the news, see the papers. Sentinel, Caliburn, Red Phoenix . . . whaddya *you* think we do with them? Let me guess — we lock them up and let them out on slow news days to do exactly as they're told, hey?"

"Any of you Marvels officers a captain?" the Lurker asked quietly. "Will any of you — are any of you *allowed* — to answer me, fully and honestly, about this?"

After a silent moment, one of the bluehelms stepped forward, neither shouldering his gun nor raising his visor, and said, "Criminals who have powers get restrained and sedated, yes. So do rampaging beasts who can do a lot of harm . . . or folks who behave like that. You're not in either category, Mister Morton — yet. Obstruct law officers in matters of justice — for example, refusing to answer questions on matters vital to the peace and security of Empire City — and you will be recategorized."

The old man in the handcuffs sat very still for a moment, then sighed and said, "You're recording this."

It was not a question, but Raemer nodded in silent confirmation. The old man let out his breath explosively and hunched down in the chair. "I don't want to be some fool in tights on the news. I don't want to be dead, either, or see my face on television. If that happens, I soon will be dead — or won't be able to . . . do what I do, to give you those inches of 'help' any more."

"We can't make any deals at this stage, Mister Morton," Raemer said. "I think you realize that."

"Right. Okay. So listen." The Lurker straightened up slowly, drew in a deep breath, and announced, "I can hide in walls. You people call me the Lurker, but I prefer to call myself the Man in the Wall."

"Hide how, exactly?"

"I can, uh, meld with brick and mortar — walk into them, and around in them, and hear and see out of them like I was looking out a tinted shower curtain. So I spend a lot of time in hiding, in alleyways. I overhear deals, see shootings . . . things. I come back and report to you. No one sees me, no one knows I'm there, no one knows what I look like. Screw that up, and you lose me. Hell, *I* lose me. The moment the criminals figure out I exist, I'm dead."

"And how did you learn to hide in walls, or get started doing it, or whatever?"

The old man looked at the row of MTU bluehelms again and said, "Get yourselves some chairs. There's a story. . . ."

None of them moved.

The old man sighed, bowed his head. "I'm old. I live alone with my books and the dust and lots of baked beans and whatever's on special — but once I was as young and as much the potential king of the world as any other young man with dreams. Especially in Empire City. Heh. Little Johnny Morton. I lived in a little tangle of streets folks called Sunshine Corners."

Raemer frowned, but one of the bluehelms nodded. The old man looked up at him. "Do you know why it was called that?"

The bluehelm said nothing. After a moment, Raemer said quietly, "Tell us, Mister Morton."

The old man's head snapped around. He looked at the detective with something that might have been a smile lurking behind a muscle in his cheek, and sat a little straighter. "It was called that," he said, "because none of the gangs could get a foothold there. Oh, they raced through it, and had their fights, and all that — but whenever they tried to set up rackets, or shake someone down, the cops got them. It was as if they knew about the crime already, and were just waiting. As if . . . as if a Lurker was whispering to the cops."

Not a policeman moved or spoke. They might have been so many statues leaning forward, staring. The old man smiled.

"And one was. We kids knew it, we who played in the streets and alleys — because we saw him, now and then, just for an instant, stepping out of one wall and into the next. We called him 'the Wall Man.' He wore a dark costume, close-fitting like an acrobat's, with a half-mask. And gloves. Except for his mouth and chin, we never saw his face. We didn't know who he really was."

Mister Morton licked his lips, and said, "Raemer? Can I have some water? Please?"

The detective shook himself like a man coming out of a dream. He went out to the coffee machine and filled someone's chipped coffee mug from the waiting carafe full of water, then came back and handed it the old man — who sat, helpless, looking at the cup.

Raemer reached for the keys at his belt, then slowly drew his hand back, shook his head, and took back the mug. He raised it to Morton's lips so the old man could drink.

The Lurker smiled bitterly. "That's enough, thanks." He cleared his throat. "So along came the day when some gang boss on the run got the bright idea that a classroom filled with kids is a ready-made supply of little hostages. A big man in a suit, red-faced and not much hair left, three chins — he came in yelling and waving a tommy gun, and herded us and Miss Mitchell into a windowless classroom. Then he took Mister Peldown, the principal, to the front door and yelled at the cops to keep back or he'd shoot us in the head, one by one, and push our bodies out. To prove he meant it, he put his gun to old Peldown's ear, pulled the trigger right there in front of them, and ducked back inside. The cops believed him after that."

Raemer offered the mug again. Morton drank, and said, "And then the Man In the Wall came. . . ."

"Johnny." The voice was warm and deep in his ear — as solid and as reassuring as the hand that suddenly held his arm. "*Please* keep quiet."

Johnny Morton swallowed. "Y-Yes."

"Thanks. You know who I am?"

Johnny could see the masked face and the dark glove on the hand that held him. And since the boy was pressed back against the brick classroom wall, with no space behind him in which anyone could stand, the answer was obvious.

"The . . . Wall Man."

In the room outside, the man with the gun shouted something angry at the police, and unleashed a burst of bullets. The cops shouted back, but they didn't return fire.

"That's right."

Other kids were turning to look now, and going wide-eyed. Lost in her sobbing, Miss Mitchell hadn't noticed the masked man in the dark skinlike suit as he stepped out of the wall, crouched among the children, and asked, "Now, did any of you notice if that man has a metal box, about the size of a book, with him? A magazine of bullets for that gun of his? Or a round, thick thing of metal about so big?"

There was another rat-tat-tat of bullets from the mobster's gun, louder and closer. Doubtfully, some kids shook their heads. Miss Mitchell turned her head, saw the Wall Man — and screamed.

He put a finger to his lips warningly. In the same instant, the mobster roared from the next room, "*Shaddup*, lady! Or I'll shut you up for good!"

Miss Mitchell turned ashen and almost fell. Dark-gloved hands caught her and lowered her to sit on the floor among the children.

The tommy gun roared again outside.

"W-Who are you?" the teacher whispered.

"I call myself Rampart, the Human Wall, ma'am. I can walk into — *into*, and through — walls."

"Then —" Miss Mitchell shook her head in disbelief, white to the lips with fear. "Then you can get us out of here?"

The masked man shook his head grimly. "I can go through walls. Using the extra button on my costume, one of you could go with me . . . but if you do it wrong, you'll die. Instantly, and more horribly than —" He nodded his head at the roar of the tommy gun just outside. "And since I only have one extra button, and there's a lot more of you than that, we'll just have to hope our friend out there is running low on bullets. . . ."

Miss Mitchell swallowed, but it was Johnny who asked it first: "Mister Rampart, what're you gonna *do?*"

The masked man smiled thinly. "These buttons of mine can do something else, Johnny. They can make my costume as hard as a brick wall. But that only lasts for a few seconds, before they burn out. I'm just going to have to hope that I can take out that thug before my time's up." He rose out of his crouch and added, "If I don't, my time really *will* be up."

"But — but you'll be *killed!*" Miss Mitchell clawed at his leg. "You can't —"

Rampart smiled down at her, at them all. "There's no one else to do this, is there?"

Johnny was trembling so hard that he could hardly get the words out, but he managed to say, "T-There's me. There's all of us. We could fight him, all of us together. . . ."

His voice trailed away as he saw the white-faced stares of the other kids and pictured what would happen to them if they tried to take on the mobster.

"I'm gonna start killing the kids!" the mobster bellowed, firing a single bullet from the hallway into the classroom. It passed over everyone's head and shattered the blackboard with a loud crack. "Back away, coppers! This is your last chance!"

There was a moment of silence, some shouts, and the police finally began firing back. Bullets shattered the windows in the hallway outside the classroom. Some found their way through the open door and chewed up the desks at the front of the room. The mobster snarled something, fired back in short bursts, and twice shouted triumphantly, "Ha!"

Then his gun stopped spitting lead. He pulled the trigger, but only a loud clacking sound resulted. He cursed.

The Human Wall spun around and stalked eagerly toward the door — and then froze as something empty and metallic clattered to the floor. A moment later, the clanks and clacks of something else metal being rammed into place were heard, and fresh gunfire began.

He turned and smiled crookedly at Class 4-B. "It seems he had a spare magazine after all. Goodbye, kids. Farewell, ma'am. This is going to get messy. I'm going to try to shove him up to a window, where the police can see him — and shoot him. Kids, keep out of this. Everyone lie down on the floor, right now."

Under his gaze, the children did as he ordered — some terrified, most eagerly, and a few reluctantly. Johnny raised his hand, and the teacher just sat staring at the dark-garbed man.

"I could —" Johnny blurted. "I could —" And then his eyes filled with tears. He realized that he didn't know what he could do.

Rampart gave him a warm smile, and nodded in the same way that Mister Peldown did, when thanking or praising someone. He gestured at the floor, and Johnny got down onto it, feeling numb.

"You, too, ma'am," Rampart said.

Miss Mitchell shook her head. "You're . . . you're just going to go out there and get killed."

Rampart shrugged. "We all have to die some day."

"But you could go right back through that wall, and be safe!"

The Human Wall knelt down facing her. "And read in the papers about you and your kids getting hurt? Spend the rest of my days walking the streets of Empire City knowing that I could have done something about it, but didn't? No, ma'am. Never. These kids . . . these kids are our future . . . and you know something? I don't think we can spare a single one."

He glanced at the wall and added thoughtfully, "But thank you for reminding me about going through walls." He knelt down beside the children and murmured, "Everybody crawl over to the walls — *slowly*. Don't hit any chairs, and spread out. Don't end up lying close to anybody else."

The kids stared at him, and he smiled and waved his hand gently, until first one and then another started to crawl. When they were all moving, he crawled right in front of Johnny, who mumbled, "Maybe I could —" But that helpful suggestion went unfinished, too.

Everyone else had their heads down, their faces buried, when Rampart took hold of the lower button on his uniform and pulled, hard. The button came free. With snake-swift speed, he slapped it into Johnny's hand and closed the boy's fingers around it.

"You're a good boy, Johnny," he whispered. "Keep this for me. Someday, I want you to wear it for me, or find somebody who's the right one to wear it. Someone who'll keep Empire City a good place to live, help the poor and the weak in Sunshine Corners."

Johnny clenched his sweaty fingers around the button and tried to say something, but tears were making everything starry-bright now, and there seemed to be something in his throat. . . .

The Man In the Wall rose in a sudden, fluid movement and strode toward the door — where a deafening storm of gunfire now raged.

He glanced over his shoulder to look at Johnny. "A good life is one where you make the right choices."

And then he turned and raced out the door — into the thunderous barrage of gunfire, a cacophony that Johnny heard in his dreams and quiet moments, down all his days.

"I think he was already dead by the time he rammed the mobster up against the window," Morton said wearily. "But the cops shot them both full of holes. They never did find out his real name."

The dry old voice finished speaking, and the silence returned.

It hung heavy in the room for what seemed a very long time before one of the bluehelms stirred. "Let him go," the MTU man said, and two others nodded.

"Yeah," a fourth agreed, voice almost angry. "Let the man go."

All along the line, the guns came down.

Detective Raemer got up slowly and said in a rough voice, "Deputy Chief Ridgefield made it clear to me that he has the final say in this. He's been listening to us; he's heard your story. Uh . . . everybody wait here."

And without looking at anyone in the room, he turned on his heel and strode out.

The silence was uncomfortable, and it stretched. And stretched. Until finally a bluehelm slid back a wrist cuff to check his chrono-band, shook his head silently, and looked at the man next to him. Someone else cursed softly. The Lurker just sat in the chair, looking at the floor.

Two more bluehelms had checked their wrists, and one even stared longingly at the exposed tip of a cigarette before slapping a flap closed over it, before Raemer returned.

He came in smiling uncertainly and fumbling at the keys on his belt. "Uh, Mister Morton, Ridg — Deputy Chief Ridgefield sends his apologies. I'm sorry you've had to spend so much time . . . uh, assisting us, and —"

Another, larger man came into the room behind the detective. "*I'm* sorry, Mister Morton. I'm Ridgefield, and the mistake was mine. I'm sorry I had you picked up, and sorrier to have kept you waiting."

The old man in the chair looked up as Raemer unlocked the cuffs from his wrists. "That's all right. I'm used to waiting. I've been waiting all these years for the right person to give Rampart's button to."

Raemer cleared his throat. "I'd just like to add my apology to the deputy chief's. I think we're all sorry about this mistake of ours, and . . . well, you're free to go."

Johnny Morton got up, rubbing at the marks the cuffs had left on his wrists and wincing. "Thanks."

He took a few slow, unsteady steps in the direction Raemer was indicating, then looked back at all of the lawmen and said slowly, "I'm getting too old for this. Let me know if any of you find the right guy to wear the button. I'll gladly hand it over."

Deputy Chief Ridgefield cleared his throat. "Mister Morton, I think your search should have ended some time ago. The right person *is* wearing the button, and has been since Rampart put it in your hand."

Ion
Shells

by Steven Harper

Neil Fade picked up the bucket, tapped his wristband, and walked through the closed vault door. The door was dense, and Neil felt a moment of resistance. Then he was inside. Neil dephased and set his bucket down with a sloshy thump so he could look around.

The Empire University lab vault was big enough to echo, and the air smelled of ozone. Rows and rows of locked storage compartments lined the walls. Dim red lights provided meagre illumination that reflected off a highly polished marble floor. The upside-down reflection showed a young man of average height wearing a brown trench coat, khaki slacks, and a brown fedora pulled low. Bogey gone cat burglar.

Neil spared a glance at the vault ceiling. The security cameras were still there, but they were dead, thanks to a side trip to — through — security. While shutting off the cameras, he had noticed that the sprinkler system had been deactivated. He had turned that back on, and the thought brought a little smile to his face.

Neil crossed the vault floor and slipped a hand into his pocket. Although it looked like he was reaching into his coat, he was actually digging into the hip pocket of his jeans. The trench coat, hat, and khakis were a shell of reshaped photons, insubstantial as air. Neil did, however, take the precaution of wearing a simple domino mask, a real one, in case something interfered with his powers. No sense in being stupid.

After a moment's fishing, Neil produced a paper packet and a card with a number scribbled on it. Bucket and papers in hand, Neil searched the vault's perimeter until he found a compartment that matched the number on the card. He set the bucket on the floor and dropped the packet into the water.

A hand landed on his shoulder. Neil stiffened. The gloved fingers sparked slightly, and Neil's skin tingled.

"This is where I say something about coming quietly," said a tenor voice.

"And where I say something about you and your horse," Neil replied without turning around. "You know I can get away any time I want."

"You want that component. I figure you'll stick around."

Neil licked his lips. His heart was pounding. If he got arrested, his shell would come down, his life would be over. Then he grinned. This was almost better than sex. Neil turned around, stepping out of the unresisting grip.

The man standing behind was an inch taller than Neil, with white-blond hair and sky-blue eyes. He looked to be in his late twenties, just like Neil. Sparks leapt and danced around him like blue fireflies. The man's blue-and-white costume showed off lean, chiselled muscles even as a mask hid the upper half of an undeniably handsome face.

"Trickster," the man said.

"Ion," Neil replied. "Going to arrest me?"

Sparks snapped across Ion's gloves as he raised his hands. "It had crossed my —"

The bucket lurched as the water penetrated the paper packet and hit the chemicals inside. A cloud of black smoke gushed upward like a genie. Neil slapped his wristband and phased as cold water sprayed down from the ceiling. Arcs of electricity crackled down Ion's body in a sizzling wash, and he fell twitching to the marble floor.

While Ion was thus distracted, Neil reached through the compartment door with one hand and touched his wrist with the other. With a few expert taps, he solidified his fingers and felt around until he touched a hard object the size of an engagement ring box. He picked it up, phased his fingers again, and pulled the box through the compartment door. Then he turned back to Ion.

The hero had stopped twitching, though he was clearly not at his best. He propped himself in a shaky sitting position against the vault wall. A bit of guilt twinged at Neil. He should vanish through the wall, but Ion looked so unhappy, Neil couldn't leave him alone. For a moment, Neil was fifteen again. Dad had gone through another fifth and had "a little conversation" with Jeff, Neil's brother. Neil had learned to yell and cry right away — Dad kept hitting until you did — but Jeff always pulled into himself like a turtle. When it was over, Jeff would hobble into the bedroom, lay on his sagging mattress, and look at Neil with an expression of bewildered pain just like the one Ion wore.

"I'm sorry." Neil hunkered down next to Ion. Water continued to pour through him. "You're a decent enough guy and I didn't want to hurt you."

"You reactivated the sprinkler system," Ion slurred. "You knew I was here. How?"

You smell like ozone, Neil thought, but kept his mouth shut. Some people revealed their plans when the hero was helpless, but not Neil. Why did villains always shoot their mouths off, anyway? Maybe it was a loneliness thing. God knew Neil didn't have anyone to talk to, though he wasn't a supervillain. Supervillains wanted to conquer the world. Neil wanted to retire to a nice, quiet mansion in Cancun.

"How did you know *I* was going to be here?" Neil countered.

"Anonymous tip," Ion said. "Look, can you do something about the water? You already know I'm not going to get my powers back until I'm dry, and that's not going to happen while I'm sitting in a puddle."

Without thinking, Neil flicked a gesture at the sprinkler valve above them and a laser beam flashed from his palm. The valve melted shut and the water cut off, though other sprinklers continued to shower the rest of the vault. A second later, Neil realized what he had done. Anger flared.

"That was a shitty thing to do," he snarled.

Ion blinked at him. "What?"

"You —" Neil clamped his lips shut. Maybe Ion had been trying to trick him into showing what kind of powers he had, and maybe he hadn't. Either way, the more he talked about it, the more he gave away. Talk, talk, talk. God, he was turning into one of those idiot villains.

"Nothing," he said instead. "Look, I've got to go."

"Where you headed?" Ion asked. His face was the picture of innocence, and Neil's earlier anger vanished in a bubble of amusement.

"Blatant," Neil laughed. "But you get points for trying, friend."

"How many points to win the game?"

"Sorry, I've bribed the referee."

Neil dephased and patted Ion's shoulder with mock condescension. His hand tingled at the touch, and he pulled away, confused. Ion's powers were gone, washed away by the water. So why —?

The vault door made a series of *thunk* noises as the internal bars slid aside. Neil blinked at it, then smiled with genuine admiration. "You were stalling me," he said. "Pretty smart."

"High praise from a trickster," Ion said. "Look, you seem to be a solid guy. Intelligent, too. Why not stick around? I've got contacts with the Guard. We could use someone like you on our side."

Neil snorted. "Yeah, sure. I'll head straight over to the Olympian Tower. They'll welcome me with open arms and happy leg irons."

"I'm serious," Ion said. "You're a nice guy."

"You think I'm nice?" Neil said. The idea pleased him somehow. The final bar inside the door thumped aside. "What makes you think I'm nice?"

"You haven't hurt anybody that I know of," Ion said. "You only steal. Besides that, one day after each one of your robberies, the Starbright Memorial Shelter gets a big bag of money. Coincidence?"

Neil remained silent.

"Listen," Ion said, "Sentinel's got pull. He could arrange for a probationary period while you train with the Guard. You could do some good instead of sneaking around all the time. People need your help — and not just abused women and kids. Think of it — no more cops or metas chasing after you, no more looking over your shoulder, no more —"

"Money," Neil finished. The vault door swung slowly open. "Saving the world has a cruddy pension program."

"Does money love you back?"

Neil's face hardened. "This is where I say something about loving to stay and chat, even though I can't," he said as a dozen armoured and helmeted operatives from the Marvels Tactical Unit poured into the vault. "See you."

He snapped his fingers and bent the light. Instantly the vault plunged into darkness. Blindness was the sucky part about invisibility. To compensate, Neil shifted his vision to infrared, and the room popped back into view.

The MTU operatives had spread out through the vault, half-heartedly training weapons in a dozen useless directions. Neil phased to avoid getting bumped, and watched everything with a wide, silent grin.

"Sorry we didn't get here earlier," said one of the operatives as he helped Ion to his feet. "How did he get away?"

"Looks like Trickster can teleport," Ion sighed. "That explains how he gets in and out of locked vaults. Anyone got a towel? Shit."

Neil bit his lip to keep from laughing. So heroes *did* swear. That was somehow comforting. Neil found himself liking Ion a great deal.

Ion and the MTU headed for the door. Deciding it would be fun to see what happened next, Neil followed them out of the vault, through the Empire University electronics lab, and out of the building. Ion cut a fine figure, a muscular streak of blue and white among dull, armoured cops.

"Doctor Suzuki's going to be pissed," Ion said as the group reached the sidewalk. It was dark outside. Two MTU transports were parked at the curb, and Neil was impressed at the amount of firepower he rated. "I should have zapped Trickster the moment I had the chance, but no, I had to talk first."

"What was he after?" asked one of the operatives from behind his faceplate.

"Suzuki's perfected an organic computer chip," Ion said. "It's supposed to allow easy neural interface between a human and a computer."

Neil touched the bulge in his pocket. So that's what the gadget was for. Then a tickle caught in his throat and he coughed. Ion's head came around.

"What was that?" he demanded.

Neil didn't wait. He dropped straight through the sidewalk into the steam tunnels beneath the university. With a light laugh, he trotted away.

"You have it, then?"

Neil opened his palm with a flourish, displaying the component box as if it were an India ruby. Currently Neil wore the shell of a college frat boy, complete with Empire University sweatshirt and moussed blond hair. Neil actually had dark brown hair and green eyes set into pointed, foxy features. It was a face he never showed in public.

The man sitting on the other side of the Starbucks table was a dumpy landslide of a human being, balding and thick-lipped. He spoke with an accent Neil couldn't place. The man reached out to take the box, but Neil closed his fist.

"The other half?" he said.

In answer, the man pushed a satchel toward him with one foot. Behind them, the milk steamer hissed and gurgled as if someone were strangling an anaconda. Every table in the coffee house was occupied, and a dozen-odd more patrons — a mix of college students and faculty members — waited patiently in line.

Neil flicked the satchel open and glanced inside. Green sheaves of bills looked back at him. Lots of sheaves.

"You've never tipped before," Neil said. "What's with the pay increase?"

The man pocketed the box and said, "It's the advance for another job. Do you have interest?"

"Always," Neil said. "There's this lifestyle I'm dying to live up to."

"The Ascension Institute has created an incubation machine under the supervision of Doctor Devinder Singh," the man said. "His laboratory is on the fourth floor of the institute's south tower, and the incubator plans are stored in his computer. I wish to have a copy."

"Sure. Three days?" That would give Neil a day to invisibly watch over Singh's shoulder and get his access codes, a day to steal the files, and a day just in case.

"Three days. I await with eagerness."

Neil leaned over to pick up the satchel. As he did so, he caught a glimpse of his reflection in the coffee house's front window. With a start, he realized he looked rather like Ion. Had he done that on purpose? Neil shoved the thought away and turned back to the landslide man.

"There's a complication," he said. "I'm sure you know about it."

"The hero Ion."

"He said he received an anonymous tip about me. You got a leak in your organization?"

The landslide man shrugged. "I doubt it."

"I don't," Neil snapped. "Ion is —" *a nice guy* "— a damned nuisance. I don't talk to anyone about my work. Ever. That means the leak's coming from your end. If Ion shows up again, the price doubles. Got it?"

"No. Your fee already takes into account the possibility that you might encounter metahumans."

"My fee is for breaking security. Metas are extra."

The man leaned forward, a mountain ready to shed an avalanche. "We agreed upon a price."

"I'm renegotiating."

"No."

Neil shrugged and picked up the satchel. "Then steal your own plans." He pulled a handful of bound money packets from the satchel and laid them on the table.

"What are you doing?" the man hissed.

"I'm not taking the next job, so I owe you the advance. How much is it again?"

Customers turned to stare. The landslide man snatched up the cash and stuffed it back into the satchel. "Are you insane? We are in public."

"It's not my money. Take it."

"I —" A line of sweat broke out on the man's forehead. "I will track down the leak. If Ion interferes, you will receive double your fee."

The landslide man heaved himself out of the chair and trudged toward the door. Neil took the satchel into the men's room, waited until he was alone, and changed his shell into a round-faced, overweight office manager type. He went to the payphone near the back door and dialled.

"Guard hotline," said a voice at the other end. "How may I help you?"

"Trickster will hit the Ascension Institute in two days," Neil said, and hung up. Then he left the coffee house and headed for the Lady Starbright Memorial Shelter.

"I can't believe you fell for the water-bucket-over-the-door trick," Neil said. He slid the newly burned CD into his jeans pocket and knelt next to Ion, who was lying on the research lab floor. "Guess I'm not such a nice guy after all."

Ion looked up at Neil miserably, and Neil felt a twinge of sympathy. The water was cold, and it couldn't be fun to sit in a puddle with muscles weak as spaghetti. Neil felt like a bully.

"I'm a shit," he said, and was surprised at how much he meant it.

"Actually, you're a refreshing change," Ion said wryly. With obvious effort, he rolled away from the puddle. "Alice, Queen of Hearts, would have cut my throat."

"So how do you stay clean if you can't touch water?"

"Your little bucket caught me off guard. It doesn't bother me so much if I'm ready for it. But you should see what happens to me in a Jacuzzi."

Neil firmly pushed the accompanying mental picture aside. "So when does the MTU show up?" he asked.

"I didn't call them," Ion replied. His blue eyes were perfectly calm, and Neil found himself staring into them. "I wanted a chance to talk."

Neil backed away. A strange feeling gathered in his stomach. "Talk?"

"I saw Sentinel. He said my word was good with him, and he'd back a conditional pardon."

"That lie again?"

"No lie. All charges will be dropped if you return the stuff you stole or give up the cash you got for it, then go through a probationary period under my supervision. What do you say?"

For an irrational moment, Neil imagined himself sharing a Village apartment with Ion. He blushed, then felt angry at Ion for embarrassing him.

"Why do you keep hounding me?" Neil burst out. "There are other metas who are a lot worse. Rain Killer is wanted for murder. Janus goes after masks. I just steal."

"Janus isn't worth saving," Ion said. "You are."

"I'm not worth shit!" Neil snarled. He squatted in front of Ion and shook him by the shoulders. "Why can't you just —"

Ion's shoulders were dry. Startled, Neil locked eyes with Ion for a split second before the jolt thundered through his body like a charging sumo wrestler. The shock flung him backward and his shell flickered out. Neil lay gasping on the floor. A burning sensation at his wrist told him that his wristband had shorted out, too.

Ion's masked face poked itself into Neil's range of vision. For a horrible moment, Neil thought Ion would see his real face. Then he remembered the mask he wore under the shell.

"I knew you'd have something ready for me," Ion said gently. "So I put up my force field before I walked in."

"You were faking," Neil slurred.

"Nice to know I can trick a trickster. What happened to your hat and coat?"

Neil just stared at him, trying to recover. His muscles refused to respond, though his mind still worked. He tried to gather the photons, shape the light. Couldn't.

"And don't teleport again," Ion continued. "The A.I. set up a quantum drain around this entire floor. If you try to pop through it, you'll scatter a mess of Trickster-type atoms up and down the eastern seaboard. No lasers, either, or I'll zap you."

"You AC or DC?" Neil managed. He tried the photons again, and this time they moved at his command.

"Wouldn't *you* like to know," Ion laughed. "But seriously, the offer's still open. No cops, no MTU, no jail. Just probation and a pardon. You in? It's either that or prison."

Neil spun another shell, this one a perfect duplicate of himself. He flipped into invisibility, readjusted his vision, and made the shell sit up.

"My teleport powers aren't quantum based," Neil said, lip-syncing the shell. Then the shell snapped its fingers and disappeared, leaving Neil lying invisible on the floor.

"Dammit," Ion said, and there was real disappointment in his voice. He sighed and ran a hand through white-blond hair, then tapped his ear.

"You there, Sentinel?" he said, and Neil realized he had some kind of communicator. Ion paused, listening. "No, he got clean away. I'm sorry, sir." Pause. "The problem is, he thinks the offer isn't genuine. The governor didn't put a time limit on the pardon, did he?"

Neil's mouth fell open. So Ion hadn't been lying after all. A strange, warm feeling suffused him.

"Okay. Did Caliburn sniff around the consulate? Cool. What did he find out?" Another pause. "I'll be goddamned. Thank you, sir. Yeah, I'll keep trying with Trickster. Ion out."

He walked out of the lab. Neil checked his wristband. It was still non-functional. His brother Jeff had invented it last year after Neil had offhandedly remarked that it would be a lot easier to get in and out of locked rooms if he could walk through walls. The remark had apparently caught Jeff in one of his more lucid moments, because a month of feverish work later he had presented Neil with the wristband. The controls were actually quite simple, and Neil's photons easily fed it the huge amounts of power it required. A small army of nanobots repaired and maintained the device. Unfortunately, the nanos hadn't quite recovered from Ion's shock, and the wristband didn't respond to Neil's tap. He would have to get out of the lab in invisible, but solid form.

Keeping as quiet as he could, Neil crept after Ion. They passed several security checkpoints, and the guards, who all seemed to know Ion, invariably asked if his "investigation" had turned up anything. Ion replied in the same rueful negative. Neil made invisible faces at the guards as they passed and stifled silly laughter. It always gave him such a rush to pull the wool.

Eventually Ion reached the street. Neil shifted his vision into the ultraviolet range, which, for reasons Neil hadn't yet been able to fathom, allowed him to see colour. The silvery A.I. twin towers rose into the night, and lines of street lamps cast yellow light over the sidewalk. Warm July air clung to Neil like a muggy blanket.

The Ascension Institute and Empire University bordered the Village, and Neil, who had half a dozen residences scattered around Empire City, owned a nearby apartment building under a false name. He could be home in a couple of minutes. But Neil wondered where Ion lived, and that thought was immediately followed by an obvious conclusion:

Why not find out?

Ion looked up and down the street. It was two o'clock in the morning, and the area was devoid of traffic. Neil waited. After a moment, Ion trotted across the street to a block of office buildings and dodged into an alley. Neil followed, heart jumping around the back of his throat.

The alley was dark, and a faint smell of garbage wafted from a dumpster. Ion glanced around to make certain no one was looking, then clapped his hands once. An electric *snap* cracked the air, and Ion's costume vanished. Instead, he wore ordinary blue sweats, a white T-shirt, and tennis shoes. His hair was darker, too, though still blond, and his face — which Neil didn't recognize — was even more handsome without the mask. That earlier odd feeling swelled in Neil's chest.

Ion left the alley and jogged lightly up the street, looking for all the world like a yuppie out for a late-night run. Neil followed. To his astonishment, Ion entered a brick apartment building only a block from Neil's. Neil didn't go in for fear Ion would hear him in the enclosed foyer, but he peered through the door's window and saw the man pull a handful of mail from box A2. It seemed so ordinary, a regular man picking up his regular mail. Ion took the first-floor hallway to the rear of the building. Neil dashed around back to a small paved courtyard where fragrant flowers sat imprisoned in brick planters. Lights came on in one of the lower windows, though the blinds were drawn. Neil's heart beat faster. He had learned everything he could. He should go home now. He should get some sleep.

He stood and watched the window until the light went out.

★   ★   ★

A while later, Neil entered his own apartment. It was large and airy, with sparse furniture and intricate wall hangings instead of pictures. Jeff's bed was empty, so Neil went down to the basement. It was filled with individual locked storage bins for the other residents. Neil passed these by and pressed his hand against a cinder block on the back wall. The hidden scanner checked his palmprint and a hidden door slid open. Neil went through, allowing it to close behind him.

Jeff's lab was extensive, crammed with powerful computers and intricate equipment. The man himself was standing in front of a white board scribbling furiously with a dry-erase marker. He was taller than Neil, but they shared the same brown hair and green eyes. The board was covered with numbers and symbols that made no sense to Neil.

"Jeff?" Neil asked. "Did you eat supper?"

"Uh huh." He continued to scribble.

Neil thought a moment. "Did you eat supper *today*?"

"Yes. I lost fourteen gluons, too. The cat got them. Or was it the wimps? No, wimps don't interact with much. They get stuck in electron shells. . . ."

Neil chewed his lower lip and leaned against a counter. Jeff had always been a little sub-orbital, but after Dad had . . . died, he'd gone total space case. He missed the old Jeff, the one that would plot with him, climb trees with him, race bikes with him. Dodge Dad with him. Now all he did was play Invento-Man and talk bullshit.

"I opened the cat box," Jeff continued. "The probability cloud flew out, so I shut it again. I think only hope was left."

Suddenly Neil was seized with a desire to *talk* to someone, someone who would listen to him. Someone who knew what it was like to have freak-o powers that sometimes went wrong and . . . did things by accident.

"I'm sorry, Jeff," he whispered. "I didn't mean to kill him."

"Dad had a pipe wrench," Jeff said matter-of-factly, still writing. "He opened the box, and the cat killed him. Maybe you should try it. The cat likes you."

Neil didn't know whether Jeff was having a lucid moment or not. And he was abruptly too tired to care. He turned and fled the lab.

Late the next morning, Neil stood in front of Ion's apartment door. It loomed before him like a bank vault. He took a deep breath and phased through it.

Kitchen. Late morning sunlight pouring in through the window. Coffee machine filling a carafe with rich-smelling coffee. Shower running in the bathroom. Mail on the counter. Neil rifled quickly through the latter. Everything was addressed to Grant O'Dell. So that was Ion's real name. It felt intimate, knowing this about him.

Neil took a quick tour. Small place, but nice enough. Fridge with lots of takeout leftovers. Living room with the requisite enormous TV, shelf full of action movies and, oddly, *Fried Green Tomatoes*. Several books on electricity.

In the bathroom, the shower continued to run, and Neil wandered through the apartment, solid and visible inside his Bogey shell. Single bedroom, double bed. TV/VCR combo on the lone dresser, box of condoms and bottle of lube in the night table drawer. No porn videos, but they were probably tucked out of sight somewhere. Neil had yet to rifle a guy's bedroom without finding porn. He wondered what kind Ion — Grant — liked. He was about to do a more careful search to find out —

"You AC or DC?"

— when the shower shut off. Neil sat on the bed and ran sweaty palms over his jeans. He should get the hell out. Confrontation wasn't his style. It was easier to run away.

"You should open the box. The cat likes you."

God, why was he so nervous? He had the drop on Grant O'Dell. Neil's shell was carefully in place, he was wearing his usual mask beneath it, and his wristband was functioning perfectly. He should be totally calm.

Problem was, Neil didn't know how Grant would react. Neil could hope and fantasize all he liked about having a friend, but once Grant walked through the door, the box would be open, the probabilities resolved.

Grant O'Dell walked into the bedroom, large towel knotted around his waist, small one drying blond hair. Water glistened on his bare skin, and his muscles moved with supple strength when he walked. He looked so normal. Your normal, everyday —

beautiful

— guy.

"Every time we meet, you're soaking wet," Neil said. "I'm starting to think it's a fetish."

Grant jumped and dropped the small towel. Panic flashed across his face. Neil felt suddenly stupid.

"Who are you?" Grant demanded, pretending ignorance. It would have sounded more realistic if his voice hadn't cracked. "What the hell are you doing in my room?"

Neil's heart sank. "It's okay," he said. "I just . . . I followed you home last night and thought we might — I didn't mean to — oh, shit. I'm scaring you. I'm sorry, Ion — Grant — whatever. . . ."

Grant licked his lips and glanced around. "I don't know what you're — I'm not —" He sighed. "Hell. Okay, you know who I am. What are you planning?"

"Nothing," Neil said weakly. "I just want to talk."

"What about?" His tone was belligerent.

Neil cast about for something to say. This was stupid. What had he expected, that Ion would greet him with open arms?

"I'm sorry," he said again. "I'll leave you alone. You won't hear from me again, I promise."

He got up, and realized that Grant was blocking the only door. Neil would have to turn invisible and phase through the wall, creating the illusion he had teleported again. He raised a hand to snap his fingers as he always did, then felt a wave of disgust. What had seemed a clever trick before now seemed trite and childish, a stupid shell game.

"Wait!" Grant said, still clutching the towel around his waist.

Neil paused. "What?"

Grant licked his lips again. He seemed to be working up courage. "Stick around. I've got coffee in the kitchen."

Every instinct Neil had screamed at him to refuse, to vanish as he always did.

"Sure," he heard himself say. "Why not?"

"So, how did you get your powers?" Grant asked from across the tiny table. "Aliens," Neil lied automatically.

Grant gave him a hard look, and Neil shifted in his chair. Grant's kitchen, with its yellow walls and warm smells of toast and coffee, was throwing him off-kilter. So was Grant. The only times Neil had talked to him was when the other man lay helpless in a pool of water. Right now, however, Grant was perfectly dry and dressed in sweats and a ribbed T-shirt. His strong hands were wrapped around a coffee mug with a *Far Side* cartoon on it. Neil's mouth was dry, and he was afraid to pick up his own mug, his hands were shaking so badly. He was living a daydream made reality, and he didn't know how to react. Grant continued to look at him.

"Sorry," Neil said finally. "I have to lie to survive. I actually don't know where I got my powers from. They just . . . showed up."

"You manipulate light," Grant said.

Neil froze. He checked his shell. The trench coat and hat were still in place. "How —?"

"Your appearance changes, your clothes don't rustle, and your hands shoot lasers. Doctor Singh tells me *all* teleportation is quantum based and you shouldn't have been able to pop away last night. Logic says you never left, which points to invisibility. Light control. Though it doesn't explain how you get in and out of locked vaults."

"There needs to be some mystery about me," Neil said weakly. "So how'd you get *your* powers?"

Grant allowed the change of subject. "You're going to laugh."

"I won't be laughing at you," Neil promised. "I'll be laughing with you."

"You know those blinking lights on top of cell phone towers and broadcast antennas? I used to be the replacement guy."

"You climbed all the way up there to replace light bulbs?" Neil asked, aghast. "Cripes!"

"Someone has to." Grant sipped his coffee. "Besides, I like heights. You can see the whole world, and birds fly under you. . . . Anyway, a freak storm blew in and —"

"Lightning struck," Neil finished. "You were right — I'm going to laugh at you."

"No lightning." Grant stirred a little more sugar into his cup. "I was trying to get down when I slipped and my safety belt gave way. Some high-tension wires broke my fall."

"Oh." Neil shuddered. "I'm surprised you didn't become Acrophobia Man."

"I learned something about the jobs you pulled," Grant said abruptly. "Do you know who you're working for?"

"I never ask," Neil said, feeling defensive. "Occupational ethics."

"Caliburn did some checking for me. Seems there are rumours that Kreuzritter — you know, the guy who rules Thule — has been perfecting metahuman cloning. He ran into equipment problems, though. Quick for-instance: He needs a way to transfer memories from a metahuman to a clone via computer. A certain chip might do that. Know of one? He also needs an incubation chamber that can withstand the pressure of force-growing a metahuman to adulthood in days instead of decades. Know of one?"

The CD in Neil's pocket suddenly felt very heavy.

"Once he gets everything he needs, he'll clone an army of metahumans, his version of the perfect Aryan race. Guess what he'll do with that army."

"This has nothing to do with me," Neil said.

"It'll have to do with the whole freaking world," Grant said intently. "Did you hand over the plans you stole?"

Make me a better offer, Neil thought, and glanced down at his mug. "I seem to do a lot of business over coffee, don't I?"

"What? Trickster, I don't have time for —"

"Call me Neil," Neil blurted out, then bit his lip.

"Neil, then." Grant reached across the table. His hand went through the trench coat shell and touched Neil's wrist. It didn't even occur to Neil to pull away. Grant's blue eyes held Neil's gaze. "Help us, Neil. Please. People will die if Kreuzritter pulls this off. Could you live with that?"

Suddenly Neil was back in the filthy, thin-walled trailer in New Jersey. He was seventeen and his father lay dead on the floor. The blue tattoos on Dad's arms stood out stark against pale skin. A pipe wrench lay next to him, alongside a big chunk of plaster that had been gouged from the wall because Neil had ducked. The smell of laser-cooked meat hung in the air. Jeff stared at the scene from the corner. Neil felt the fear, loneliness, and self-loathing engulf him all over again.

"Neil?" Grant said.

Neil swallowed hard and stood up. Grant scrambled to follow suit. "What's wrong?" he asked anxiously.

In answer, Neil held out his arms. He trembled, as if he were going to be crucified. "Can you open the box?" he asked.

Grant stared at him for a long moment, then stepped forward and put gentle hands on Neil's shoulders. Wherever he touched, the shell dissolved. Grant slid hands light as feathers over Neil's arms, chest, stomach, legs, and back. Grant's touch revealed jeans, tennis shoes, a black T-shirt. Neil felt naked. His skin shivered, but he didn't pull away.

Grant saved Neil's head for last. He ran his hands through Neil's hair, and the hat disappeared. Only the mask remained. Grant discovered it was real, hesitated, then slid his fingers beneath it, pushing it up and off. It dropped to the floor like a dying butterfly. Shaking with anticipation and fear, Neil closed his eyes, feeling Grant's large fingers drift across his open face. Then the touch ended. Neil opened his eyes.

"This is where I say something about you being beautiful," Grant said, and kissed him. Neil froze for a moment, then kissed back. Their arms went around each other, and Neil pressed hard against Grant, wanting to fuse with him, slide through him. Neil couldn't breathe, didn't want to.

When at last they parted, Neil said, "I have to go."

"Where?" Grant was breathing hard.

"To see a man about a plan."

"What are you going to tell him?"

In answer, Neil reached into his pocket, pulled out the CD, and broke it in two. Grant grinned.

"Want me to come with you?" he said.

Neil shook his head. "I'll meet you later." And just for effect, he vanished.

The sounds and smells of the coffee house swirled around Neil and the landslide man at their regular table. Neil wore the short, round man for his shell.

"The incubator?" the landslide man asked.

"Sorry — Ion blew it for me. I guess you'll want your fee back."

The landslide man's lumpy face hardened. "I do not want the fee. I want the plans."

"Nothing I can do. Now that the A.I. knows someone is after the project, they've linked the access to DNA scan. Even I can't get past that."

"And for this lie to me, you receive a pardon."

Neil froze inside his shell. "A pardon?"

"I have eyes in the governor's office." The landslide man's gaze glittered. "The details of your deal are known to me. Just as I know Ion arranged it."

"Ion offered me a deal, yes, but I haven't agreed," Neil said. He started to move his hands from the table, intending to tap his wristband and phase. But the landslide man's lumpy fingers flashed across the table to grab Neil's wrist in a grotesque parody of Grant's gentle grasp.

"Liar," the landslide man hissed. "Ion called the governor's office this morning. Apparently the two of you talked extensively and you're a team now."

Anger knotted in Neil's stomach. Grant was reading a lot into one kiss. Okay, Neil was half in love with him —

Only half?

— but that didn't mean Grant spoke for him.

"We're not a team," Neil said.

A hot, terrible pressure engulfed Neil's arm above his wristband. He looked down. The landslide man's hand had melted into a muddy ooze that was crawling toward Neil's shoulder. With a shout, he kicked backward, trying to pull free. Table and chair went flying, but Neil's arm remained stuck fast. Heat bit his skin. The landslide man lurched to his feet without letting go. His face dissolved like lava, leaving two empty eye sockets and a gooey, open mouth. Screaming coffee shop customers stampeded for the exit. Neil went to his knees, and the landslide man loomed over him.

"Then you'll die alone," bubbled the landslide man in a thick, liquid voice.

Neil forced himself to ignore the burning pain. Photons rushed around him, focused into a laser beam that flashed from his free hand. It burned a hole straight through the thing's chest. The hole oozed shut, and the landslide man chuckled in remorseless glee. The molten mud reached Neil's neck, his face. Desperately, Neil concentrated again. He vanished into invisibility while the coffee shop was struck by a dizzying swirl of colour and light, which he hoped would put his attacker off-balance, force him to let go. But the landslide man simply laughed again.

"I can feel where you are," he bubbled. "Would you like a kiss?"

The ooze covered Neil's mouth and nose. He couldn't breathe. There had to be something he could try, one more trick. The coffee shop popped back into normality, and through the door strode a tall man in medieval armour and a red cloak. His helmet gleamed.

"My Lord Kreuzritter," said the landslide man in surprise. "What is this?"

Neil's lungs screamed for air, a scrap or molecule. His heart pounded and his vision dimmed. He clawed ineffectually at his mouth and nose with his free hand, but the hot mud stuck fast.

Kreuzritter made an imperious gesture, ordering the landslide man outside.

"My lord?" said the landslide man.

Neil's world flickered, and he lost concentration. The Kreuzritter hologram wavered. The landslide man blinked sloppy eyes, then laughed like acid. "A fine try, Trickster. But soon you will be dead."

And then Grant, dressed as Ion, rose up behind the landslide man and slapped his hands on the thing's temples. Electricity snapped and sparked. Neil dimly heard a horrible scream before he dropped into the dark.

★　★　★

"I'm sorry I didn't get here sooner," Grant murmured. "You said something about doing business over coffee, but there are a lot of coffee houses in the Village. Eventually I just followed the screams. How do you feel?"

Neil checked. He was sitting on the floor, propped upright against the coffee house counter. Broken furniture littered the place, and smells of hot earth and cold coffee hung in the air. An enormous pile of mud occupied the centre of the mess. Light pain burned up Neil's arm and face, but nothing seemed to be broken. Sweet oxygen filled his lungs with every breath.

"I'm all right," Neil said. "Maybe a little singed. God. That was awful."

To his horror, tears filled his eyes and he turned his head away so Ion wouldn't see. And then Ion's arms were around him. Neil let himself be held for a long moment.

"When the MTU comes," Grant said into Neil's hair, "you're coming with me, right?"

Neil's earlier anger returned, and it tried to mingle with Grant's embrace. Neil felt split down the middle. He closed his eyes and hung suspended between choices for a long moment.

"No," he said finally.

Ion sat back on his heels, looking hurt and puzzled. "Why? Neil, I want to be with you — to help you."

"That's what it's all about," Neil said wryly. "You want to rescue the world, rescue me. You rescued me from the mud guy and now you want to rescue me from myself. But *I* need to rescue myself, Grant. Please understand."

MTU sirens filled the street, and vehicles screeched to a stop outside. Grant's masked face looked unhappy. His expression tore at Neil's heart, but Neil refused to give in. Booted feet hit the pavement near the front of the ruined shop. Neil started to gather photons into a trench coat shell, but Grant touched his unburned shoulder.

"You can't close the box again," he said.

Neil knew he was right. The shell flickered out, leaving just Neil.

"This is where I say something about not giving up on you," Grant said.

"And this is where I say I'm glad," Neil replied, and meant it. "One more trick. . . ."

He leaned over and gave Grant O'Dell one long kiss.

Then he vanished.

STORMCLOUD RISING

BY JIM C. HINES

I pulled the note from my pocket while Fazura investigated the entrance to the old silver mine. In barely legible loops and whorls of purple ink, our daughter Kira had written: *I have to go to the Virus's lab. Please don't be angry. Love, Kira.*

"There are footprints in the dust," said Fazura. A Sudanese accent turned her cool voice to music.

Another man would have seen only Phantom. She was the ghost in the darkness, the avenging spirit against whom bullets and barriers were equally futile. She had protected Las Vegas and much of Nevada for fifteen years, armed only with her trademark fighting sticks.

She was also my wife, and I knew that she was as frightened as I was.

She extended her sticks, twin cylinders of clear, unbreakable plastic, which she used to pry the boards away from the entrance. When the old nails refused to budge, she stepped back, balanced herself on the balls of her feet, and brought both sticks crashing through the wood. The sticks were invisible at that speed. It was as though the boards exploded from the movement of her hands alone. Fazura twirled each stick, shaking off fragments of wood, then slid them into the parallel sheaths across her back.

A few feet beyond the splintered boards, a steel door blocked the square tunnel. A gleaming lock and keypad sat on the right side of the door, unchanged since I — since *Stormcloud* — had sealed the lab years before.

I pulled a heavy black flashlight from my belt. Kira's footprints clustered at the lock. I knelt closer. "How did she know the combination?"

Fazura shrugged. "Her gifts are untrained, but powerful. If she had a vision of herself gaining entrance, she could have seen the code."

"How much of a head start does she have?" I asked as I punched in the twelve-digit code. I could feel the pulse of the generator buried deep in the rock, strong enough to power the lock for another century. The electricity flowed through my veins, an echo of powers I no longer used.

"The principal said she didn't show up at school."

I gave the keypad a savage jab, and the door slid soundlessly to one side. "This is why I gave up being Stormcloud. She's still a child." The fight was as old as Kira. "She should be safe at home, not breaking into the Virus's lab, pretending to be a superhero like her mom."

"You would rather teach her to turn her back on pain and suffering? To ignore her responsibilities and allow others to shoulder the burden of protecting the people?"

"*Kira* is our responsibility. I wanted to protect *her*, to save her from the nights spent lying awake, wondering how badly hurt you'll be when you come home. To save her from the fear that one day some psychopath would take you away from us for good."

She held up her hand, then pointed toward a man jogging up the road behind us. We waited until he reached the entrance, where the setting sun silhouetted his large frame.

"Evening," I said cautiously. One hand still held the flashlight. The other rested on my black semi-automatic. Standard issue for Nevada state police. Despite my wife's jabs, I hadn't entirely abandoned my duties to the people.

"Howdy, Officer," he said, sounding out of breath and somehow *off*. Distracted somehow. I still couldn't see his face. "I was out hiking, and I saw you nosing around. This is a dangerous place. They say it's contaminated. You should take your friend and go home." He turned his head, searching for my wife. "Where'd she go, anyway?"

I kept my face neutral. "Who?"

He hesitated, then shrugged his meaty shoulders. "All I'm saying is, this place ain't safe. You'd be wise to get home. No sense taking chances, Officer. . . ?"

"Fiedler. Russ Fiedler. And you know an awful lot for a hiker. What's your story?"

"My name's Iman. I'm just saying it's dangerous around here."

"And I don't see you running home, Iman. Besides, they say Stormcloud sealed this place good and tight."

He stepped closer, giving me my first good look at him. His tan skin was covered in sweat, and his eyes twitched constantly, reminding me of a jackrabbit alert for predators. "Sorry. I gotta take you out of here."

"I'm afraid not, friend."

He moved faster than I expected. I barely had time to block the first punch with my flashlight. My wrist went numb from the impact, and he swung again.

I ducked and rolled away. I saw Fazura emerge from the tunnel wall behind him, sticks ready. Iman followed my gaze. When he spotted her, he pulled an odd-looking gun from his pocket.

He fired before I could get to him. The gun made a quiet *puff*, and a small projectile shot through my wife and ricocheted off the stone behind her.

Fazura and I struck together. One of her sticks smashed the gun from his hand while the other slammed against his neck. I kicked him in the thigh. The instant my foot touched him, electricity shot from my body into his. He twirled to the ground and didn't move.

I spun toward my wife. "Are you okay?"

Fazura was already retrieving a small dart from the dirt. "I hadn't yet materialised," she said.

I shone my light on the dart. A tiny steel cylinder was mounted behind a Teflon-coated needle.

On impulse, I turned to Iman and stripped his shirt away. It took less than a minute to find what I sought: a small red pinprick on his left shoulder.

"I thought the Virus died in your last encounter," Fazura said.

"So did I." We looked into the tunnel. Somewhere in the darkness, Kira was making her way toward one of the most dangerous criminals I had ever fought.

I whipped a plastic cord from my belt and used it to bind Iman's hands and legs. I hadn't given him much of a shock, and his pulse was steady. He would be fine.

Without another word, Fazura and I headed into the darkness.

"The two of you will never have children."

The pronouncement had come fifteen years ago, as Doctor M, a mystic healer from Empire City, sat with us in the sweltering heat of his run-down apartment. The place smelled like bad coffee. Punk rock blasted from ceiling-mounted speakers. Doctor M said the music helped him commune with the spirits.

"Thank you for trying," I said. I turned to Fazura, who offered a shaky smile. "It's not like we expected anything else."

As a child, I had spent my free time exploring the desert. Back then, the government was testing A-bombs and other weapons, including a cannon designed to shoot a focused beam of bioelectrical energy. The idea was to create a weapon that would kill living things without damaging their surroundings.

It didn't work. The explosion wiped out the lab and every living thing in a one-mile radius. Everything but me. I survived, but not a single strand of DNA was left unchanged.

"Is it just me?" I hadn't wanted to ask. But if Fazura could still have a child with another man . . . I had to know. "Is Fazura . . . could she —?"

Doctor M shook his head. "Neither of you are entirely human."

Fazura's hand interlaced with mine. Nobody knew the origins of her powers. She had been among a group of Sudanese girls I rescued from slavery in Reno. Her gifts would have allowed her to escape, but she was new to America and hadn't known where to go for help. So she had remained with her companions, enduring their fate rather than abandoning them. When I arrived, she fought by my side against the slavers. Exhausted and half-starved, she refused to leave until every last girl was free.

I squeezed my wife's hand, and we turned to go. "Thank you," I said again.

"I'm sorry, Russ," Doctor M offered.

Kira Elizabeth Fiedler was born two years later. Doctor M delivered her himself, all the while protesting the impossibility of it. He was still grumbling when Kira peed all over his scrubs.

At the time, Kira had appeared to be a normal human baby.

The batteries in my flashlight had died back in '92. I had never bothered to replace them. Instead, a steady current flowed through my palm and into the bulb, producing a white beam that illuminated the wood-planked walls around us.

"Do you remember how to reach his laboratory?" Fazura asked.

"It was deeper, toward the centre of the mine." The tunnels stretched and twisted for hundreds of miles, following long-forgotten veins of silver ore.

"Kira knew the Virus was alive," Fazura said. "Why didn't she tell us?"

"Maybe she was afraid. Her powers have given her nightmares for months, and they've been getting worse."

My unspoken accusation hung between us. *Which you would have known, if you weren't always away. . . .*

Growing up "different" had been hard for me, but it was a breeze compared to raising a metahuman child. Kira's powers manifested early, and it had been enough to drive a father insane. How did you punish a child who always knew exactly how far she could push without crossing the line, one who could foresee the best way to play Mommy and Daddy against one another to keep herself out of trouble? The day before her fourth birthday, before I had even finished wrapping her gifts, she started to cry, shouting, "I don't want a dumb purple Zap Girl. I wanted a Red Phoenix doll!"

The nightmares were a more recent development. Night after night, she jerked awake, screaming about unstoppable armies sweeping across the country. Other girls her age worried about boys and makeup. Kira spent her nights worrying about the deaths of heroes and an evil strategist who repulsed every attack, wiping out soldiers and superheroes alike. When I asked her who was leading the army, she only cried harder and said she couldn't see. Her enemy was protected even against Kira's premonitions.

The last time I fought the Virus, he had designed a nanovirus that synthesized controlled doses of narcotics from the victim's own blood chemistry. Instant supersoldiers, but far from foolproof. The Virus also had a nasty habit of experimenting on his own people. Several of his soldiers had fled rather than risk his lab. They had nearly died of withdrawal, but in the end, they were the ones who led me to him.

Iman hadn't acted like the soldiers I fought before. He had the same strength and speed, but there had been a dullness to his voice when he warned me away from the mine. Had the Virus engineered a better disease, one that would create true slaves?

If so, what would happen if he captured Kira? I prayed she had come because she'd seen a way to beat the Virus, but what if she hadn't? What if she had come because she *didn't* know how to fight him? If her nightmares had driven her to despair, and she had surrendered to the future she saw as inevitable? Imagining an army of slaves who obeyed the Virus's will, I could understand Kira's desperation.

The tunnel forked in three directions. The leftmost way sloped downward, while the other two continued flat. I checked the ground for footprints, but there was less dust here and I couldn't tell which way Kira had gone.

Fazura strode ahead, taking the left tunnel. "You said his lab was deep underground, yes?"

"That's right."

"Stay behind me," she said.

I know that she was only trying to protect me, but it burned just the same. "I can take care of myself."

"The Virus is not like the street thugs you arrest."

"I know that. I'm the one who beat him."

"*Stormcloud* beat him."

That was when the Virus's defences whirred to life. Black tubes popped out between the slats near the ceiling, and bullets tore through the air. They targeted my wife first, sending hundreds of rounds through her body. I covered my ears and leapt back.

Fazura coolly turned from one gun to the other as the bullets passed through her. Wood splintered as she marched onward. Directly between the guns, she leapt straight up. She disappeared into the ceiling, and the guns eradicated each other in a burst of sparks.

She emerged about ten feet up the tunnel, diving headfirst out of the ceiling and somersaulting to her feet. Then she was running back to me, fully solid as she held me down and examined me. "Are you hurt? Russ, answer me."

"I'm okay." My ears were ringing so badly I could barely hear.

Her hand tightened around mine, and she pulled me to my feet. She kissed me on the lips, then murmured, "You should wait here. It's not safe."

"Kira's my daughter, too. I'm going."

"It's too dangerous. I can't protect you. If you were Stormcloud . . ."

If I were Stormcloud, I would be encased in heavy armour, with enhanced strength and built-in weaponry and equipment, all powered by my body's bioelectric field. Stormcloud was a glowing figure of gold who could have torn those guns from their mountings with his hands, and the bullets wouldn't have scratched his armour.

But if I were Stormcloud, I couldn't have spent the past thirteen years raising my baby girl, trying to give her a normal childhood.

I walked to the shredded wall and climbed up to the ruined gun. The metal still smoked. I avoided the gun itself, reaching instead toward the twisted power cable behind it.

"You need me," I said as I pinched the wire between my fingers.

An illuminated web appeared in my mind. As the electricity flowed over my skin, my senses expanded through the Virus's power grid. The main generator pulsed like a white sun, deep underground.

I hopped down and brushed myself off. "There are more guns ahead, about a hundred meters. And I know which tunnels to take now."

Fazura's slender, gloved fingers clenched into fists. "It's not safe."

"You take care of those guns." I pulled out my semi-automatic and flipped the safety. "I can still take care of myself."

I set off without waiting for a response.

I sensed the current in the speakers an instant before a tin voice crackled to life. "Greetings, old friend. Nice of you to bring the family."

"Who are you?" Fazura asked.

"I am the Virus, my dark beauty. This is my home. I'd ask you to leave, but we know that's not going to happen. Stormcloud here just has no respect for the sanctity of a man's home. Oh, yes, that's right. Kira told me who you are . . . who you used to be. You have no idea how much I'd hoped to meet you again."

Until I heard his voice, I hadn't completely believed. Now I did. The Virus was alive, and he had our daughter. "I'll kill him," I whispered.

"Our place is not to punish," Fazura said sharply.

"She's quite the prize, your daughter. She told me when you would arrive and which way you'd go. She even described what you would do to poor Iman back at the entrance."

"I don't believe you," Fazura said firmly. "Kira would never help you."

"Not right away, naturally. Like Iman, she needed a bit of persuasion. But I've developed a number of new potions, and she responded beautifully to one of them. I guess it would be fair to say she's *my* daughter now. . . ."

Sparks of rage danced between my fingers. I had to holster my gun out of fear that I would accidentally ignite the bullets. "If you hurt her —"

"You sure have gotten grumpy with age, haven't you?"

"Let her go," Fazura said, "and we will leave you in peace."

I spun. "We can't. If the Virus gets loose, he'll —"

"He has Kira!"

Suddenly I understood the conflict Fazura must have felt as Phantom. Night after night, she left her family behind because the safety of all was too important. Now I was in her shoes. I knew what the Virus could do. Last time, he had killed thousands and threatened millions more. I had seen his victims, the ones we were too late to save. I couldn't let it happen again.

I gripped her shoulder, feeling the hard muscle beneath the slick black material of her costume. The anguish in her dark eyes matched mine.

The Virus chuckled. "I'm not about to give up my favourite new toy. But if you like, you can come visit. In fact, I insist."

I heard the metal *clunk* of a door swinging open, deep within the tunnel. Moments later, a group of dark figures came into view.

"He wants to use Kira's powers," I whispered. I had fought this man. I knew him. "He won't hurt her. He's too smart to give up a potential weapon."

She nodded. My hand tingled and slipped through her arm as she dematerialised. She drew her sticks and stepped into a fighting stance.

I put my gun away and grabbed my nightstick. No doubt these were innocent victims of the Virus's serum, like Iman up above.

"Kira told me you'd choose the hard way," the Virus said as his slaves advanced.

Fazura struck first. Immaterial, she dove through the attackers and rolled to her feet behind them. Before they could react, she lashed out, solidifying only long enough for her sticks to strike. The Virus's men tried to fight, but their blows passed through her. They ended up pummelling one another more often than not.

The Virus had selected his soldiers for size and strength. A huge man with a wrestler's physique lunged at me. I slapped him on the wrist with my nightstick, then dropped him with a jab to the solar plexus. Another man dove for my legs.

I fell, and thick fingers wrapped around my wrist. I sent an electric jolt through his arms, then kicked him against the wall.

I grabbed a canister of mace from my belt and took out a third man before he got within five feet of me.

My wife was a black streak as she dispatched the rest. She vanished into the floor, then dove from the wall, sending two men to the ground before rebounding like a ball from the far wall. Even I couldn't follow the movement of her sticks. It looked like she flung the last attacker onto his back with a simple wave of her arms.

We glanced at each other, communicating without words. She gave me a quick nod, letting me know she was okay. I did the same. Together, we ran down the tunnel toward the Virus. Toward Kira.

It came to me as we ran that *this* was what Kira had feared. She had seen an army led by an unstoppable villain, one who seemed to know every counterstrike before it happened. Someone Kira herself couldn't see in her visions. She had seen herself, a slave to the Virus's will.

I knew Kira could change her own future. No, not change. She could *choose* her future. No doubt that was how she had made it into the Virus's lair, by avoiding those paths that would lead to her death.

But why had she chosen a future that turned her into the Virus's servant?

A darker thought plagued me. For every Sentinel, there was a Kreuzritter, one who chose to put himself, his glory, his security, over everyone else's. But I couldn't imagine Kira ever making such a choice. Unless . . . unless she had *no* choice. Unless all paths led to the same point.

I ran faster.

"The generator is up ahead," I said. I slowed to a walk and pointed. "More guns."

Fazura never slowed. She leapt into one wall, then to the other, destroying the trap without breaking stride.

"There are more," I said as we rounded a corner. Up ahead, a steel door guarded the entrance to the Virus's lab. Two armoured guards stood with automatic rifles. Several more of those ceiling-mounted guns tracked us as we came into view.

I leapt back behind the corner as the guns fired. They went silent an instant later. Had Fazura taken them out so quickly?

"Here's an idea, old friend," said the Virus. "Nice as it is to see you in action again, why don't you and Phantom come quietly? You're right — I wouldn't kill my newest pet. On the other hand, I've any number of nasties that will leave her powers intact, but her body . . . damaged. You wouldn't want your little girl to end up looking like me, would you?"

Fazura stepped out of the wall beside me. Her face was pale. "He has Kira. He's holding some kind of compression injector to her neck."

I knew what it had to be. As a child, the Virus had been exposed to a mutated flesh-eating virus that had nearly killed him. It had left him scarred and crippled, in constant pain even after he repaired his broken body with prosthetics. It would give him a twisted sense of pleasure to inflict the same fate on my daughter.

The Virus sighed. "I give you to the count of ten. One . . . two . . ."

Another voice interrupted his. Weak and flat, Kira's voice still called to me as she said, "It's okay. They're about to surrender."

Even as the Virus's guards trotted over to seize my arms, I knew I had failed. If Stormcloud hadn't retired, would the Virus have been able to remain hidden all these years? How many innocent people would suffer because of my mistakes?

My wife's fingers brushed mine for an instant. Then we were led through the steel doors and into the Virus's laboratory.

I hadn't seen him since our last fight, but he looked unchanged. His face was wrinkled leather. White tufts of hair sprouted above overlarge ears. Most of his skin was pink scar tissue. The infection had taken his left arm and both legs when he was a child. The power sources inside the plastic prosthetics were heavily insulated, protected by multiple circuit breakers. In our first battle, I had managed to disable those prosthetics, leaving him paralysed. No doubt he had improved his protection over the years. Even at my best, I doubted I would be able to stop him that way again.

Beside him sat Kira. Her wrists were strapped to the armrests of a plush recliner. No doubt she was quite comfortable, as long as she didn't try to escape. The Virus held a small, streamlined pistol to her neck.

"Your guns, Officer."

I unbuckled my holster and gave the semi-automatic to my captor, then bent to retrieve the revolver strapped to my ankle. Another man took Fazura's sticks.

"Does he have any more?" the Virus asked.

Kira shook her head.

"Kira, it's us," yelled Fazura. "Be strong. Fight him!"

Our daughter blinked, but said nothing. She was still wearing the clothes she had worn to school, a tight green sweater and black hip-hugger jeans. My eyes teared. I had sent her back to her room to change into something more appropriate. She must have waited until I left for work to change back. It was the kind of thing she would do.

"Did he hurt you?" I asked.

Kira's eyes remained fixed. The Virus laughed. "Answer them," he said. Only then did she shake her head no.

"Why would I hurt her?" asked the Virus. "I can use her. I can use all of you, come to think of it. That's the trouble with research, you know. Never enough lab rats."

He chuckled and summoned another guard, this one an older woman so dishevelled she looked half-dead. He pressed the gun into her hand, steadied it against Kira's neck, and said, "If they disobey, pull the trigger."

He waited until she nodded, then walked away. His lab was a huge, roughly circular room with a shallow dome of a ceiling. Granite countertops lined the walls. Pipes and plastic conduits covered the ceiling like a web. I could feel the electricity pulsing through the wires. Galvanized vents drummed softly as they circulated clean air through the room. The disinfectant smell made me think of a hospital.

The Virus walked to a huge steel refrigerator, one of four built into the walls. I had to turn to follow him. He opened the door, and I saw racks upon racks of slender glass tubes, each one full of a white liquid. He took another step, disappearing from my view. When he emerged, he had another gun in his hand and he was loading it with a blue capsule.

He held the gun for me to see. "This is another project I've been working on. A combination retrovirus and nanojuice designed to break down metahuman DNA. You and your wife could create far too much trouble if you weren't tamed. Your daughter assures me the serum will function perfectly." He grinned at me. "You wanted to give up the superhero business, eh? Well, in about forty-eight hours, you'll be as mortal as the rest of us."

"What of your other toxin?" Fazura demanded. "The one you used to enslave these people? Does that work as perfectly?"

"Of course," he said. Movement caught my eye. I craned my neck to see Kira shaking her head no.

"You lie." I barely recognized the words as my own. "What will it do to our daughter?"

The Virus tilted his head and smiled. "All tools wear out in time." Then he pointed the gun at me and pulled the trigger.

Kira's birth only heightened the conflict that had tormented me since the day I married. Russ Fiedler had decided that he wanted a normal life with a family. Stormcloud wanted to protect the innocent. Working as a police officer had allowed me to toe the line, to serve justice without sacrificing my family. Every time my wife went out as Phantom, a part of me saw it as a betrayal of Kira and myself. Yet, deep down, a part of me burned with envy each time she went.

Now, for the first time in my life, Stormcloud and Russ Fiedler were truly one. As the Virus fired, a jagged arc blazed from my hand, incinerating the dart in midair. The Virus screamed and fired again, but I ducked aside. My captors staggered, stunned by the secondary shock from my bolt.

I had already launched a second strike. The gun at my daughter's neck spun away, as did the woman who had threatened her.

My clothes smouldered as I advanced on the Virus. Another of his guards tried to stop me. Jagged light leapt from my back, knocking him to the ground.

I heard Fazura moving as well. Even without her weapons, my wife was an unstoppable fighter, and I trusted her to watch my back. Soon those few guards who had stood between her and Kira lay unmoving on the floor.

The Virus backed away until he came to the steel door of the refrigerator. His gun clattered to the ground.

My voice was hard. "Can you cure Kira?"

He stepped to one side, and I sent a forked bolt of electricity into the wall beside him. He turned the other way, and I launched a second bolt. His eyes were wide. He looked around like a trapped animal. I didn't blame him. Even I had never known this much power.

I adjusted the flow, pouring electricity out one hand, sending it through the steel door, and pulling it back into my other hand to create a blazing cage that jumped and sparked.

"Is there a cure?"

The soles of my shoes began to melt, sticking to the floor as I walked. The blinding light danced closer to the Virus with each step.

The Virus knew me. He knew I had never killed an enemy. But he had never before seen Stormcloud unleash such raw power and fury.

He raised trembling hands in a sign of surrender. "Sure, there's a cure," he stammered. "Why don't I just get that for you?"

Before he could move, my wife grabbed my shoulder. "Russ . . ." She pointed to Kira.

The Virus's second dart, the one that had missed me, protruded from my daughter's stomach.

★   ★   ★

We turned the Virus over to the Guard in Empire City. As they took him to be locked him up at the Carousel, we drove Kira to Doctor M's apartment and waited as he examined her.

After an hour, he stepped back into his living room. Our clasped hands tightened. Kira followed a few seconds later.

"She will survive," he announced.

"I told you so," said Kira. "I'm fine." Her pale face gave lie to the spunk in her words.

Fazura and I reached her at the same time. We hugged her so tightly a part of me was afraid we would hurt her. But her thin arms squeezed us just as hard.

"The Virus's serum was effective," Doctor M said in that same toneless voice. "Even now, her power fades."

Fazura was crying. "I'm sorry we weren't fast enough. We tried —"

I touched her arm and studied our daughter. "You knew." My stomach was stone. "You knew what he would do to you. That's why you went."

"I'm sorry, Dad." She pulled away and wrapped her arms around her body.

"We could have found another way to stop him," Fazura said.

"It wasn't just the Virus."

"What do you mean?" I asked.

"The Virus wasn't the only one in my visions. There were so many people trying to control me. I wasn't strong enough to fight them all."

"Why didn't you ask us for help?" I squeezed her shoulder, but she still wouldn't look at me. "Kira —"

Doctor M cleared his throat. "Tell them the rest, child."

"The rest of what?" I asked.

Kira raised her head. "The Virus was only the first. The others . . . Janus threatened to kill you and Mom if I didn't obey him. I — I didn't, and —" She jerked her head away and wiped her face. "Jade Naga was even worse, and there were more. This was the only way to save you." Her voice dropped to a whisper. "I knew you'd save me."

Doctor M left the room and shut the door, leaving us alone. The apartment felt oddly silent. At least, it did until Doctor M cranked up *London Calling* in the other room.

"I saw something else in my visions," Kira said. "You and Mom . . . you need each other's help. You need to help each other the way you did in the Virus's lab. Otherwise —" She took a deep breath. "Otherwise you'll both be dead by the time I graduate from high school."

I stiffened.

"I'm *thirteen*. I can watch out for myself. Even without powers."

"But the Virus knows who we are," Fazura said.

Kira grinned, the first genuine grin I had seen from her since we left Nevada. "That's right. And do you really think the Guard are going to let him tell anyone?"

Fazura and I looked at each other. "It's not that easy," I said. "I haven't been Stormcloud for so long."

Kira shrugged and hopped to her feet. "It doesn't matter. You're going to go back. I already saw it, before the Virus captured me."

Fazura frowned as only a mother can. "This is not the kind of decision your father can make all at once."

"Sure," Kira said cheerfully.

"Kira, I don't know —"

"I dug your old costume out of storage before I left," she added. "It's in my room."

"Your mother and I need time to talk about it," I protested weakly.

"Yeah, I know." Kira's grin grew, and the fear and weariness almost disappeared from her eyes. "I saw it last week. You'll wait until I'm asleep, talk for ten minutes, and end up making out." She made a face at that. "I'm almost glad to lose my powers. I didn't want to see *that*."

Before I could figure out what to say, she added, "The only reason you're even going to talk about it is because you're both too stubborn for your own good."

I held up my hands in surrender, knowing in my heart that she was right on all counts. I saw the same recognition in Fazura's eyes.

"So let's get back to the hotel and let you get some sleep," I said, grinning. My fingertips sparked as I blew my wife a kiss. "The sooner you're asleep, the sooner your mother and I can head back to our room to 'talk.'"

Sometimes even a superhero has to bow to the inevitable.

THE
WHISPERING
WARS

BY LUCIEN SOULBAN

The three smugglers attacked in clumsy unison, their footing slick on the tug's deck, their vision framed by the black ski masks pulled over their faces. Corbae slipped past their intended blows, always keeping one smuggler between him and the other two. His movements seemed choreographed, his footing sure despite the choppy waters smacking the tug into the docks with jarring thuds.

To the smugglers, Corbae was a winged devil, a figure half-cloaked in night's array of purple and black. What blows he didn't avoid, his body armour softened. Pipes and tire irons, clenched in the assailants' white-knuckled grips, could mete out little punishment. Corbae, in turn, struck with polyceramic hard points along his elbows, forearms, knuckles, and shins, knocking each attacker for a dizzying loop.

Inside Corbae's helmet, the battle was a different beast entirely. Advanced biometric programs analysed each attacker in turn and streamed data into Corbae's HUD. The information translated shifts in weight as a spectrum of blues and reds overlaying the smugglers' bodies. Advanced wire-frame vectors predicted the path of incoming swings according to an attacker's stance and position.

Fighting was simply a matter of not being there when the blow arrived.

Corbae redirected a tire-iron swing, sending the lead attacker's thrust into a compatriot's face. He then launched a vicious sidekick into the third assailant, who dropped to the deck with broken ribs.

The lead attacker swung again. Corbae ducked beneath the blow and spun, sweeping the smuggler off his feet with an outstretched black wing. The metal deck smacked the sense from the attacker. He was out cold.

From the first swing to the last man down: *8.7 seconds* — or, at least, that's what the suit's chronometer indicated. Immediately, a string of data ran past the HUD's synthetic diamond veneer goggles, displaying PSIs per blow, Corbae's maximum heart rate, adrenal output, and overall efficiency of his performance.

62% of maximum potential, the display announced.

Corbae would have to do better next time. He mouthed *Standby*. Microphones in the armour's mandible guard registered the command, and the HUD's displays obediently clicked off. Corbae drew his wings in close to his body, forming a cloak, and walked to the smuggler who gripped his side in pain.

"*Snimeite vashu masku!*" Corbae said in Russian.

The smuggler obeyed quickly. He removed his ski mask, revealing the ugly sculpture of a man with a cratered, bulbous nose and a single stretch of brow. Corbae's sensor net snapped into action, scanning the smuggler's face, creating an image; the computer opened a wireless Internet connection. It rifled through criminal files in Interpol's database. Within seconds, the smuggler's face appeared, along with his personal data.

"*Vui daleko iz Samara.*"

The smuggler nodded, stunned by Corbae's knowledge: He *was* a long way from Samara, Russia.

Off in the distance, DC police sirens wailed.

"You'll cooperate," Corbae told him in Russian. "You'll cooperate or I'll come back." With that, he pushed himself skyward, wings exploding out in a rushing gust. By the time the smuggler stood on uncertain legs, police cars had blockaded the pier. . . .

Corbae set his head against the wind and swept low across the dark Potomac River, toward Washington. In his ear, he could hear a flurry of police banter concerning the smugglers and their cache of street-ready AK-47s.

A prompt-icon appeared on Corbae's HUD goggles, then:

Greetings. . . .

"What the hell?" Corbae said, and pulled up from his flight to hover over the black waters.

Forgive the intrusion, the message read.

"Who the hell are you?" Corbae demanded, watching his words appear across his HUD in concise little rows.

I would ask the same. I think Interpol would be interested to know how you're breaching their secured site.

"Are they asking?" Corbae said. "Who are you?"

An admirer, actually.

"I doubt that."

Truly. I appreciate your struggles. Especially against the Vorovskoi Mir . . . the Russian mafiya.

"I know the *Vorovskoi Mir*. Get to the point."

A digitised photo appeared in Corbae's HUD. It was a middle-aged gentleman in a business suit, sporting a moustache to shame Einstein. Corbae immediately noticed a small, handwritten note stencilled at the bottom of the picture: *Intertourist Hotel, Moscow. 1990.* He would put that into context later. At the moment, he was more concerned that someone was sending him messages over what was supposedly a secret and secure tap.

Recognize him?

"Say I don't." Corbae glided toward Lady Bird Johnson Park, just in case his mysterious visitor foisted another surprise on him, like downloading a virus into his armour or triangulating his position.

Dmitri Gordievsky . . . a former minister of finance.

"Let me guess. With the Communists' fall, he used his connections to buy state property and sold it to himself at reduced rates. Now he is *mafiya*."

A familiar plot, true, but no. Gordievsky vanished with the mafiya's *killers after him.*

"What is it to me?"

Much, I would think. He's being chased by a torpedo named Akula. You know him?

Corbae held his tongue and landed between a cluster of trees. He knew Akula; the thug worked for the Arkhangelsk gang lead by Yaponchik. He was among the few metahuman *mafiya* assassins — or "torpedoes" — around. Corbae knew these criminals well. Yaponchik was the reason he wore this suit. He was the reason his sister would never speak again and why his parents lay rotting in a Moscow cemetery. Corbae made a special effort of targeting Arkhangelsk members.

From your silence, I am thinking yes.

"This still doesn't concern me."

Possibly not, but I leave it to your sense of fair play. Gordievsky stole over three billion rubles using forged bank notes. I have it on good authority that he's attending a private auction at the Istanbul Arms Show in three days.

"Auction?"

Three billion rubles buys many things, I would think. If Gordievsky and his cronies are to survive war with the Arkhangelsk gang, they need weapons. My network says Gordievsky will meet with the Aaro brothers — they're Albanians who have a booth at the show.

Corbae thought about it quickly, then activated the suit's core purge, wiping out its AI and operating systems, eliminating any Trojan Horse viruses or tracking programs. The suit powered down, severing the Internet connection and bringing the internal displays to low ebb before they finally blinked out. Corbae pulled a black cell phone from a hidden thigh compartment, and dialled.

"I need a pick up."

"It's a trap."

"Maybe," Rustam said, stripping the chestplate from his suit in the back of the van.

"Well, shouldn't you be calling in heroes like Sentinel or Red Phoenix? Maybe they can contend —"

"Bad earthquake down in Columbia two days ago. Remember?"

"Oh, right — relief efforts."

Mattie McKinley continued driving for a quiet moment, pausing long enough to scratch the soul patch on his chin. Tattoos up to his neck, piercings from eyebrow to nose to ear and back, and short, spiky black hair were all enough to frame Mattie as a street primitive. Rustam would have never given him a second glance had Mattie not been a keyboard maestro, mastering programming code with Beethoven's finesse on the keys. Mattie and Rustam spoke the same language.

Rustam, his armour shucked, slipped into the van's front seat. He watched the streetlights stream by, stretched and pulled against the glass. He ran his hands through his sweat-slick black hair and sighed.

"So what's the plan?" Mattie asked.

"I'll go to Istanbul by car, by way of Sofia."

"Greece?"

"Bulgaria. It doesn't take a genius to check the passenger rosters for flights between Washington and Istanbul over the next three days. Once they do that, they have a better chance of gauging my identity."

"Maaan, are all you superheroes so paranoid?"

"I'm not a superhero," Rustam said, objecting.

"Don't start up with the 'it is job' crap," Mattie said, doing his best movie-Russian accent.

"It is."

"No, man. Your software company . . . that's a job. *That* pays the bills."

"Can we get back to the topic, please?" Rustam pleaded.

"Fine," Mattie said, though his tone made it clear he considered himself the victor of this verbal skirmish. "So? What do I do while you're vacationing?"

"First, this isn't a vacation. But, we need to download new programs into the suit. I purged the old ones as part of the safety protocols. Second, I need a new firewall to keep unwanted visitors from piggybacking on the suit's connections. Third . . ." Rustam said, pausing while several thoughts shot past his black eyes. "I need everything you can find on this Dmitri Gordievsky."

The Atatürk Convention Complex was a shimmering oasis of glass and blue steel framed against the city's normal backdrop of chalk-white minarets and Ottoman grandeur. It was also a huge gamble for the Turkish government, a multibillion-dollar enterprise built to host various international conventions and summits. Specifically, its chief purpose was to house Turkey's international arms and air show, in direct competition with Russia's Nizhny Tagil and Britain's Farnborough expos. With Istanbul straddling the Middle East and both eastern and western Europe, it proved a capable host for Oriental and Occidental . . . familiar and relatively inoffensive to both.

Inside the main pavilion, the air conditioning stifled the humidity carried by the Bosporus and Sea of Marmora, but few complained of this decidedly Western luxury. Turkey prided itself on being a forward-thinking Muslim nation with dreams of entering the European fraternity.

The blue-jacketed convention staff greeted visitors with professional, civil smiles, which was somewhat atypical when compared with the natives' normally jubilant and honest grins. After momentarily savouring the cool air, Rustam studied the pavilion's carapacelike, high-ceilinged lobby and the khaki-clad *emniyet* security forces carrying M16A1 assault rifles. Istanbul wasn't taking any chances, if the vehicles on display in the lobby were any indication of the hardware in show. A spit-polished T90 Russian battle-tank and a French Super Puma assault helicopter drew many appreciative stares from the rivers of brightly clad humanity streaming by, but Rustam knew the really high-end models waited inside.

The arms show was a legitimate convention, drawing dealers and military contractors from across the world. Arabs, Americans, Asians, Europeans . . . all gathered by the mutual siren song of destruction. It seemed more tragic than ironic that even these moments of coexistence still entailed someone's misery. Rustam felt like shaking his head; he remembered the arms business. Everybody dealt in death but few truly appreciated its impact on the individual. A weapon's potential to inflict casualties had somehow become part of the hardware's vital specs, mentioned in the same breath with make and model.

Rustam circumnavigated the bustling main pavilion and made his way to one of the many annexes linking the seven adjoining halls. The crowd thinned, the general public only able to purchase tickets for the air show and hangar tours, not the weapons exposition itself. Rustam flashed his laminated badge — one purchased against a future favour for an old friend — to the *emniyet* officer, and entered the four-story-high hall with its seashell domed ceiling. Immediately, his eyes scanned the sprawl of exhibition booths and displays, the multihued banners and camouflage-drab equipment highlighted against the hall's white and blue plaster walls. Rustam took in the spectrum of attending companies. The eastern Europeans were in rare form today, with impressive booths displaying the corpse of Russia's military for sale. Ukraine's Bronetekhnika and Russia's Central Scientific and Research Institute for the Precision Machine Building Industry both flaunted the latest light-frame exo-armours. Sweden's Oerlikon Contraves displayed their newest fire-control system, while Pratt & Whitney showed computer simulations for a scramjet engine that could fly at excesses of five thousand miles per hour thanks to thrusters that remained lit at supersonic speeds. And the list of notables continued, from powerhouses like General Dynamics and Raytheon, to smaller business enterprises selling this technological trinket or that firearm.

Despite himself, Rustam's gaze skittered over the many booths and television screens hawking technology's latest, lethal enterprises. He pocketed a few pamphlets for future reference, and mentally gauged the feasibility of adding some of the present technology into his own suit. At the very least, he ascertained the threat of tomorrow's arsenal, an arsenal he'd face in one form or another quite soon.

Eventually, Rustam manoeuvred himself near the Aaro booth. The Aaro brothers were Albanian "businessmen" whose meagre wall-booth drew its share of the curious. On display were dismantled Russian weapons — AK-74s, 9 mm PM automatic pistols, and 7.62 RPK machine guns — stripped down to their nuts and bolts behind bullet-proof glass display cases. These were paltry samples of the small arms that the Aaro brothers were ready to sell, weapons probably looted from the Albanian military when rioters broke into twelve hundred army depots in 1997 and stole over seven hundred and fifty thousand weapons. The brothers, Rustam learned, had been attending the expo ever since, selling small arms from what seemed like a bottomless supply pit. Word among arms dealers was that the brothers ran the syndicate responsible for looting fourteen of the army depots. Rustam, however, was more interested in their private auction, the one where Third World countries bid on "special items" stolen during the riots, including some particle-beam weapons and liquid-propellant guns. Unfortunately, he couldn't afford to wait around until the auction. His target remained Dmitri Gordievsky.

Bending down to tie his shoelace, Rustam palmed an opaque, tiny microphone bug stashed in his shoe's tongue. He then casually walked over to the Albanian booth and smiled at Yorgi Aaro, older of the two brothers — a cherry-faced, heavyset man with a twitchy white moustache. Yorgi returned to his conversation, speaking in broken Farsi with an Iranian gentleman. Rustam squatted down to study the AK-74 display more closely, and brushed his hand under the trim of the table's white skirt. He affixed the microphone to the cloth, then stood again. The hidden receiver in his ear immediately crackled to life, allowing Rustam to eavesdrop on the conversations near the table. He was about to leave, when . . .

"Rustam? Rustam Konanykhine?" a voice called out.

Startled to hear his name, Rustam turned. A man strode forward, a twinkle in his old green eyes and a wide smile stretching his bushy moustache to the breaking. "Rustam, can it be?" he cried. Then he latched on to Rustam's hand, pulling him into his soft frame.

"Marcus Yegorov," Rustam said, kissing Yegorov on the cheeks. "How are you?"

"Fantastic." Yegorov was a bundle of energy, almost nervous in his movements and gestures. "What brings you here? I haven't seen you in ages."

Rustam shrugged with casual aplomb. "I couldn't stay away."

Yegorov clapped Rustam on the shoulder hard and led him down the aisles. "Yes, yes. Last I heard," he said, "you were developing a tactical combat suit for the military. The *Pika*, was it? What came of that?"

Rustam smiled sadly. "The same thing that comes of all Russian enterprises these days, my friend."

Yegorov stopped and nodded appreciatively. "Yes, yes . . . the bloody *shpana* ruin everything. These thugs caused me problems, too, you know."

"Really?"

"Yes. I ran a computer company in Moscow, but I couldn't compete against the KGB. They were bringing in computers by the shipload. Anyone who got in their way paid the price."

"Then it's a good thing you left."

"No," Yegorov said. "I was forced to leave. They almost ruined me. Imprisoned me for two years," he added, emphasizing his incarceration with two pudgy digits.

"I'm so sorry. . . ."

"Fah." Yegorov dismissed Rustam's concern with a paternal grin that creased his chubby cheeks. "Prison in Moscow was better than being sent to the Gulag."

"True, but still —" Rustam said, before realizing Yegorov still stung from the sordid adventure. He quickly changed the topic. "So, what are you doing now?"

"Still in Moscow," Yegorov said with his chin two notches high. "Selling computer security programs to banks and the government."

"Really?"

"Yes, yes. Today's crooks aren't so smart . . . not when it comes to computers. I merely moved into a field with fewer real competitors."

"And nobody's tried forcing you to work for them?"

"Of course they try. But I have friends now. Important friends."

Rustam understood the comment's gist easily enough.

"And you?" Yegorov asked. "What are you doing these days?"

"I'm troubleshooting for computer companies," Rustam said in a blatant, but sincere sounding lie. "I go where there's work — London, Prague."

"Ah. Well, I would offer you work," Yegorov said, "but I don't think you'd like my partners."

"It doesn't sound like you like them much either."

Yegorov's smile was a sad, pained labour at best. "There are no more ideals left for men like myself, Rustam. All around me are sharks, so I must be one, too."

"Then leave."

"I . . . cannot. I am too good at what I do. So good, in fact, that I can do nothing else."

Rustam nodded and the pair bid their farewells with a hug. Rustam watched Yegorov walk away, back the way they had come.

I don't get it. Mattie's message materialised into small letters on Corbae's HUD.

Rustam attached his gauntlets and checked the chair jammed under the door handle. It wouldn't stop most serious intruders, but the laser-emitters hidden around the hotel room would register any trespassers who broke their beams, alerting Rustam immediately.

"If Yegorov is a simple programmer now," Rustam said, "then why is he here?"

Maybe he misses the biz?

"Doubtful. Anyone in that pavilion has the right connections to get in . . . political or military connections. And he was trying very hard to lead me away from the Aaro booth."

You think he knows who you are?

"No, unless he's a better liar than I remember. He's protecting someone. At

139

the same time Yegorov led me away from the booth, someone approached it and spoke to Yorgi Aaro in Russian. The voice was familiar, but I couldn't place it. I'll bet Yegorov went back to pick him up."

What did they say?

"It was about an auction."

Okay, Aaro is having an auction. We knew that.

"No. Someone was *inviting* Yorgi to an auction later tonight. I overheard the location."

Cool. Listen, I dug up some stuff on Dmitri Gordievsky from the economic crimes division of Moscow's Ministry of Internal Affairs. I'm downloading the file now.

A flurry of information streamed past the HUD, including photographs and a personal history. Gordievsky was part of the late Communist party and had been well situated among their upper strata, the so-called "*nomenklatura.*" Nobody advanced into the ranks of Russia's social elite without a nod from them, even after the party's fall. They ran everything and were the best positioned to shift from communist to capitalist when the Soviet Supreme disintegrated. It was an "old boy's network" spanning the breadth of an entire empire, and Gordievsky had been part of it . . . until he stole billions in rubles.

"Interesting," Rustam said, paying note to one picture in particular.

What?

"Gordievsky. They caught him, though they never recovered the money. Looks like they didn't even bother trying. His prison sentence was for show only. He served three years in Matrosskaya Tishina, long enough to fade from the public spotlight, before his rich friends arranged his release."

What's Matrosskaya?

"Matrosskaya Tishina. It's a white-collar prison for economic criminals, and it's in Moscow," Rustam said. "Yegorov also said he went to prison in Moscow."

Big coincidence, huh?

"I'm an atheist when it comes to coincidences. I don't believe in convenient happenstance."

The Sea of Marmora pushed away the diesel-reeking smog of Istanbul, while aluminium scavengers took to the night streets on rickety bikes, carrying jangling bags of cans to be recycled. High above them, brushing Heaven's belly and staring straight down at the rooftops, Corbae soared and glided on warm Turkish gusts. His HUD lay dormant, this unspoiled moment his alone. But it was only a moment. Corbae sighed and studied the convention complex far below; the auction would begin soon. His HUD flared to life, encasing the urbanscape in digital wire-frame. The AI highlighted one building, and Corbae's wings pushed him toward that structure.

The Sultan Mahmut II Building was a glass braggart in stature; the second-story windows alone rose three floors high and overlooked the blue Marmora on two sides. Inside, conference rooms and ballrooms hosted dinners, functions, and lectures for the arms show after the main floors closed. This is where delegates sealed weapons deals for their country and spoke business openly, now that the crowds had gone home.

Corbae homed in on the wedge-shaped Anzac Salon that dominated one corner and played host to the private auction. The Anzac Salon was large enough to seat two hundred people comfortably, but when Corbae passed the windows he saw a mere two dozen participants milling about the room. Corbae swept upward, toward a sufficiently wide ledge on the floor above the Anzac's glass wall. He pulled in his wings, allowing momentum to carry him up.

Corbae flipped at the last second and planted his feet on the ledge's bottom. Spring-mounted pitons on the soles of his feet bit into the stone with a snap. . . . The pitons held. He crouched, upside down, looking directly into the Anzac Salon from the back of the room. Not even the auctioneers, who were facing his position, could see him. The interior was well lit, and the glass reflected the room back at the people inside.

With a smile, Corbae activated the microphones that he'd hidden throughout the salon. Knowing where the auction was being held had allowed him to bug the room at various points, earlier; keeping the bugs inert until he signalled them rendered them invisible to any sweeps. The sound filter program also came on-line, suppressing background noise while he listened to one conversation or another.

Inside the salon, people gathered in several small groups, mostly at or near the wet bar or the buffet table bedecked with a Christmas pageant of cold meats, cheeses, vegetables, caviars, and breads. Yegorov and Gordievsky discussed bidding strategies between mouthfuls of food. They dressed very conservatively, in black and grey suits, their expressions particularly grave. Standing next to them was a familiar figure with a squat frame, square shoulders, and a pompous swell to his large chest. A heavy beard, auburn and dusted with age, crowned his jaw.

"Mattie?" Corbae said quietly, after listening for a few minutes.

Here, Mattie responded.

"Prepare to receive multiple facial composites. I already see Gordievsky and Yegorov. I'm using you as a secondary firewall, for the satellite uplink, in case someone's waiting for me to tap the system."

Got it. Should I run through the standard channels?

"No. Try the Russian agencies first — in particular, the MVD and Moscow police."

Will do.

For the next fifteen minutes, Corbae flit between conversations, listening to different people and gauging the nature of the auction. Several attendees, including the Aaro brothers, drifted in and out of Yegorov's group; half the room seemed too well acquainted. Yegorov looked sullen, unhappy to be there. He walked away from everyone several times, ordering vodka from the bar and drinking alone. Gordievsky and the squat man exchanged glances, and spoke in quick whispers. Yegorov was losing his composure, they said. They'd have to deal with him after they'd returned to Moscow.

Finally, a thin Turkish man with dagger proportions to the sharp cut of his face and lean frame entered the salon carrying a briefcase. Accompanying him were two armed members of the *emniyet*, with their M16A1s, and a female assistant of svelte proportions who carried a high-end laptop, judging by the titanium housing. Corbae was intrigued, if not mystified; what auction required an *emniyet* presence when the auctioneer wasn't carrying any visible samples? The secretary casually brushed away long locks of her black silken hair and plugged her laptop into a wall terminal, then booted up the machine. After a moment of typing, she nodded to the auctioneer, who launched into the meat of his business. They were professional, Corbae had to admit.

Yo, Mattie interrupted.

"What do you have?"

Half the people in there seem legit. No records so far.

"And the other half."

Several were part of this nomenklatura *thing you keep mentioning. All part of the old Russian regime . . . all new money now.*

"And how many were in Matrosskaya Tishina."

Including your buddies Yegorov and Gordievsky? Four.

"Who are the other two?"

Andrei Koltsov, former administrator of something called the Liquidation Commission.

"They were responsible for disposing old Soviet property when Russia became democratic."

That makes sense. Says he was indicted for undervaluing state property, then selling it high and pocketing the difference. He was unit chums with Yegorov and Gordievsky.

"And the fourth?"

A former general. Pavel Burbulis.

"Damn it," Corbae said, re-examining the squat man. The beard and the bulk had thrown off Corbae, but it was him, down to the peacock thrust of his chest. "I should have realized he'd be here. . . ."

What? Who is this guy?

"I worked under him briefly during the *Pika*'s development. That's who Yegorov was trying to get me away from — protecting me from. He knew Burbulis would recognize me. The guy wanted my head after I vanished with the suit's schematics. Last I heard, he'd been implicated in the Paldisky Submarine Base scandal."

Yeah, it's right here. Officers deliberately sank two torpedo boats so divers could strip them of the titanium, copper, and aluminium. Burbulis was caught trying to buy the recovered torpedoes.

"But he had enough connections with the *nomenklatura* to mitigate his sentence from military prison to Tishina, of course. From what I heard, though, the scandal destroyed his reputation with the *nomenklatura*. They refused to touch him afterward."

Better make sure he doesn't spot the suit.

"The *Pika* design was completely different from the Corbae armour. It didn't even have flight or a polyceramic shell."

What next?

"Keep looking. I'll bet if you search deep enough, you'll find connections between Gordievsky, Yegorov, and several others in the room. They seem too well acquainted. Expand your search to our business databases."

Business?

"I'll explain later."

Corbae continued watching while the auctioneer deftly conducted matters. It wasn't the typical American affair, where the bids flew by at breakneck speeds, but the auctioneer was certainly nimble-tongued. In turn, the bidders raised numbered paddles for their lots, with some bids climbing into the millions of American dollars. Corbae didn't need the microphones to follow the action in which he was most interested. He merely watched Yegorov, Gordievsky, and Burbulis coordinate with their associates; they used a slight nod or nose tap to bring the bidding to a halt or to combine their assets for specific lots. They were cornering the bidding in their favour and blocking the others from landing deals. Some of the items were too expensive for them alone, but together, Gordievsky and company were securing all the choice picks.

Corbae, I turned up more on the business databases. At least three guys there are Russian or Russian satellite. They all ran into financial troubles and were ousted by larger competitors.

"Competitors in Russia usually means other members of the *nomenklatura* or . . ."

The mafiya.

"Right."

So what are we up against here — a mutual grudge society against the Russian Scarfaces?

"No," Corbae said. "I think it may be a power struggle. The *nomenklatura* on one side, the *mafiya* on the other. . . ."

And these guys in the middle — what are they doing?

"They're bidding on lines of credit. It's a currency auction."

A what?

"They're bidding on blocks of American dollars. The Central Bank of Turkey is offering them as lines of credit."

They're bidding on money? *That doesn't make sense.*

"Sure it does," Corbae said. "Listen, it's a beautiful idea. The Turkish Stock Exchange nearly crashed in 2001 following a political dispute, and the Turkish lira plummeted as a result. The International Money Fund is currently helping Turkey recover. Meanwhile, the state banks offer these auctions to encourage businessmen to invest in their institutions. The same thing's happening in Russia. Burbulis, Yegorov, and Gordievsky use their ill-gotten wealth to purchase lines of credit with the bank, thus laundering their stolen rubles. I'll bet you they then loan the money to businessmen in Moscow at higher interest rates, for profitable gains. This way they secure a foothold with legitimate Russian enterprises, thereby giving them a powerbase from which to operate. And they have the capital to fight the *mafiya* for the same territory, but by drawing on outside resources."

So this is all on the up-and-up?

Corbae studied the auction-goers, watching them quietly bid on lots. "Only if you ignore the fact that their initial investment came from stripping Russia's carcass."

Wait . . . what about the Aaro brothers? Are they bidding, too?

"No, they haven't," Corbae said. Neither the corpulent Yorgi nor the younger, black-haired Igor was even holding an auction paddle. "I'll bet they're being offered one of the credit lines as payment for weapons. In fact —"

Corbae didn't finish the sentence.

The microphones sizzled and popped in Corbae's ears; the lid of the cabinet-podium where the auctioneer stood exploded upward, throwing the man back. A soda can-shaped object sprung out from the podium.

It was a remote-activated Bouncing Betty, a nasty anti-personnel mine.

Almost in slow motion, the bomb exploded, sending out a shower of pellets. The buckshot peppered the room, gutting chairs of their stuffing and knocking them over, puncturing walls and blowing out windows. Its effect upon the auction-goers was no less destructive.

Corbae retracted his anchoring pitons, immediately dropping from the ledge. One push of his wings thrust him through the shower of plummeting guillotine glass. He pulled up from the dive into a barrel roll, toward the shattered window. At the same time, the salon's double doors exploded inward on the heel of someone's silver-green metal boot.

Akula stepped in, his black-mesh costume hugging the contours of his well-defined frame. Silver-green metal guards covered the *mafiya* torpedo's shoulders, elbows, knees, and groin. Forearm-length gauntlets likewise encased his arms, with triple shark-toothed blades lining the underside of both forearms. A motorcycle-style racing helmet covered his head, though the visor was a solid plate with a single, high-impact sensor lens planted dead centre.

Behind Akula came four men in Western street clothes — jeans, leather jackets, and sneakers. They all held Uzis. Corbae swept past the intruders, his forearm guard popping up to reveal a miniature Gatling needle gun beneath the housing. He peppered the area with a stream of flechettes. Akula, however, vanished in a blurred surge of hyperkinetic speed. He moved like a shark . . . fast, but only in bursts. His men were not so fortunate; all four fell to the attack, and now lay moaning and clutching at the metal shards protruding from their flesh. Akula grabbed his compatriots, two at a time, and tossed them out the room, saving them from further punishment.

The gesture surprised Corbae. He banked sharply and hovered a moment, studying the carnage. Akula rushed into the room's centre, a blur until he was at Gordievsky's throat, one arm cocked to deliver a slash to the neck. Corbae was about to fire his grapple, but it was Burbulis who came to the rescue, grabbing Akula's forearm with his gloved hand.

A metallic snap echoed through the salon as one of Akula's arm blades broke under Burbulis's grip.

"So, *suki*," Burbulis said, his voice a triumphant roar. "Surprised this fish has teeth, too?" A series of small magnetic plates exploded out from a nearly hidden ring around Burbulis's neck. They shot up to cover Burbulis's head. His face and neck were now fully protected.

Akula swung at his adversary's chest, shredding his jacket and shirt. Instead of blood, however, Akula drew a spray of sparks. Burbulis laughed and threw the torpedo to a wall, but he flipped and hit the wall feet first. He landed on the ground.

Damn, Corbae thought, *Burbulis is wearing an exo-frame.*

Then he recognized the skeletal-carapace housing of the *Pika* beneath the tattered clothing.

Burbulis lifted the stunned Yegorov to his feet. "Here," he said to Akula before he pushed Yegorov at the assassin. "Here's something to bite into."

Akula, however, was uninterested in Burbulis's offering and batted the stumbling Yegorov away. Burbulis, Corbae realized, was going to use the fight to dispose of his ally.

Corbae headed straight out one of the shattered windows and banked around quickly, re-entering through another window, accelerating with each wing beat. In the salon, the survivors of the Bouncing Betty scrambled or crawled to safety. Akula and Burbulis danced around one another, dodging or blocking each other's blows. Both men were experienced in hand-to-hand combat, and while Akula proved the better, more nimble fighter, he could barely dent the *Pika*. Burbulis, in turn, despite his strength, could not land a telling blow on Akula. It was a stalemate of sorts, one that would cost many civilian lives, including that of the stunned Yegorov, who was in danger of being trampled under foot.

Corbae hesitated for a moment, sorting out which was the greater good as he hurtled toward the combatants. By saving Burbulis and Gordievsky, he allowed for a power struggle in Moscow, one that might claim innocents when the war spilled into the streets. Letting Akula kill his targets was not an option either. A life was a life. . . .

Corbae fired his talon grapple; the braided wire-cord wrapped around both Akula and Burbulis, pulling the two men in, chest-to-chest, when Corbae flew toward the window. Corbae brought his wings and arms to his sides. He shot out the window like a bullet, yanking the two men behind him.

The manoeuvre wrenched Corbae's left shoulder, even through his armour, but he managed to pull up and disengaged the grapple from the forearm housing. Akula and Burbulis tumbled to the beach below. Corbae returned to the salon's broken windows and hovered momentarily, catching the eye of an *emniyet* guard currently tending to the injured auctioneer and his assistant.

"I'll handle the villains," Corbae said, "but detain everyone here. Especially those men," he added, pointing to the unconscious Yegorov and the stunned Gordievsky. "They're Russian criminals."

With that, Corbae dove for the beach, loading a spare talon grapple as he flew. Akula was already free of the wire, thanks to his forearm blades, but his escape had also liberated Burbulis. Akula was relentless in his assault, using hyper-bursts to pummel Burbulis at every opportunity. Corbae watched the two men fight for a quick moment, then silently dove with a hawk's grace, dive-bombing the two combatants. He fired a rapid stream of needles at both men, scoring hits on Akula. Burbulis's armour withstood the spray, but Corbae had anticipated that. At the last moment, he pulled up from his dive, washing the two men in biting sand kicked up by his jets.

Corbae understood all the *Pika*'s weaknesses, including the suit's vulnerability to adverse environmental conditions — like sand. The Corbae flight suit was ceramic and plastic polymers, providing it with integrated and overlapping joint seals. The *Pika* used metallic alloy plating over an insulated body suit, but its vulnerabilities lurked in the spaces between the armour and its insulation, where the micro-servos were housed.

Akula spun and raced directly under Corbae, who was still pulling out from his dive and relatively close to the ground. The assassin leapt the three-meter gap easily, grabbing Corbae's legs and smashing both boots into Corbae's face.

Corbae wheeled out of control. He felt Akula drop away, but the pain drove white hot spikes through his skull, blinding him. A moment later, he hit the ground, shoulder first, in a jolt that robbed him of his breath. Thankfully, between the soft sand and the armour's padding, nothing broke.

In between the heartbeat flashes of blinding pain, Corbae saw Akula crouching in the sand. He was assessing the situation: Which target was the greater danger? Corbae didn't wait for him to decide. He raised his needle-gun arm, feigning to fire. Akula moved suddenly, leaving a dust cloud in his blurred wake, racing for Burbulis, who was trying to escape. Burbulis was slowing, each heavy step a laboured process, as the *Pika*'s micro-servos groaned and grated from the invasive particulates.

Corbae had one hope left. He fired the last grapple line at Burbulis. The cord wrapped around Burbulis's legs, bringing him crashing down, face first. Corbae pulled hard, dragging the former general through the sand like a worm on a hook.

Akula took the bait. The assassin grabbed Burbulis by the *Pika*'s collar ring, intending to deliver the killing blow through the gaps in the plates. Corbae, however, activated the grapple's miniature batteries, sending two consecutive jolts of electricity through the cord. The *Pika* conducted both charges beautifully; Burbulis and Akula went rigid from the shock before both fell unconscious.

Corbae stood, his HUD displaying a stream of diagnostic information.

31% of maximum potential, the display announced.

Corbae snarled at the HUD, shutting down the diagnostics. He limped to the two villains. His face still throbbed with each heartbeat, but he had bested them. In the background, sirens wailed their familiar melody.

The doorknob rattled briefly before Nicolai Arbatov opened the office door, a Styrofoam cup of coffee in his mouth, his teeth digging deep into the cup's soft lip. Quickly pocketing the dangling set of keys, he pulled the cup from his mouth, dropped a sheaf of worn papers on the small desk, and manoeuvred his linebacker frame around the cramped office to reach his chair. The Moscow sun was bright today, offering a rare punch of morning light through the office's cell-like window. Arbatov felt its warmth against his balding pate as he sat down with a huff. He flicked on his computer and waited for the soft purr of the boot-up sequence to finish. The computer's speed and software capabilities were incredible, thanks to Arbatov's tech wizard of a son. Arbatov activated the voice-encrypted software and logged on to the Internet for Interpol's daily reports. He rarely touched the keyboard these days.

A message prompt flashed on his screen. Someone was trying to contact him. Arbatov opened the dialogue box.

Hello, Arbatov. Remember me?

"Who is this?" Arbatov asked, his words appearing on the screen.

Dmitri Gordievsky is in custody, as are Akula, Marcus Yegorov, Pavel Burbulis, and Andrei Koltsov. Recovered from their PDAs and personal computers were dozens of bank accounts with billions of rubles in each. Turkey is contacting Interpol to handle the return of these funds to Russia. Marcus Yegorov, however, might be willing to help you in exchange for his safety. Otherwise Gordievsky and Burbulis will see to his execution.

Arbatov sat back and sighed. A weight he had never realized existed lifted from his shoulders suddenly. Arbatov allowed himself a smile before studying the message again. He finally said: "Thank you for telling me about Yegorov. Now, how did you find me?"

It's what I do. That's why you used me to get to Gordievsky, isn't it?

Arbatov waited, trying to think of a response.

From your silence, I am thinking yes.

"Yes," Arbatov replied. "You have me. But I'm curious — how?"

It was easy. At first I thought it was a trap, but why lure me all the way to Istanbul just to attack me? You knew where I operated and that I targeted the mafiya. *It would have been simpler to come here without alerting me.*

"I never intended to harm you. I was honest when I said I was an admirer."

Still, that you were an enemy was a possibility I had to consider, albeit an unlikely one. Once I discovered Dmitri had served in Matrosskaya Tishina, along with several others present at the expo, it was easy to find the connection between their arrests and the man who had access to Interpol's files. Besides, the picture you showed me of Dmitri Gordievsky was the same one in the arrest report you made . . . complete with your handwritten notations.

"So, you know I arrested Dmitri and some of his compatriots."

And that you paid for it. I know you headed the Economic Crimes Division before your rivals arranged for your political exile for being too efficient. You've been relegated to working for the Moscow Drug Squad with barely a staff and virtually no power to enforce the laws.

Arbatov shook his head bitterly, his voice unleashing sentiments he never thought he'd share with anyone. "Russia is ruled by the *nomenklatura* . . . the same bastards who were in power during the Communist regime. They sold all the state property at a pittance back to themselves when *perestroika* came. They never lost power. They simply changed suits and used their connections to rob Russia of her wealth. They're auctioning off our oil to Europe for profit when we barely have enough to heat our stoves. They allow Moscow's buildings to fall into disrepair so that the value drops and they can earn a windfall selling them to desperate companies. Anyone who disagrees with them falls victim to their whispering wars. The right word in the wrong ear, and suddenly you're a pariah or, worse, dead. I didn't know what to do anymore. Nobody would *help* me. Nobody *could* help me."

So, I became your proxy for justice.

"Because I have no one else. Muzhik protects the nation, but not the individual. Snowgirl and Saturn fight the *mafiya*, but not the bureaucracy, and others like Akanidi escape to America rather than face the realities here. Everyone else is too afraid to fight corruption at its root. Instead, they fight the symptoms, believing they're making a difference. Some even switch sides. . . ."

You knew I would move against them because I do not fear them.

"I knew you would be my hero . . . and I am sorry."

I'm no hero, Arbatov. This is about justice.

"If I can't call you a hero, who then?"

Yourself, perhaps? Without powers, you fight a system you know is dangerous, one that may eventually kill you in retaliation.

"No," Arbatov said, shaking his head. "I'm not a hero. I'm only doing my job."

There was a momentary pause on the line before Corbae finally responded.

Then these are sad times, if doing what is right is considered heroic . . . beyond the bounds of the common people.

Arbatov smiled. "Not so sad," Arbatov replied, "when you realize you're no longer alone."

HARDBALL

BY JOHN OSTRANDER

It was the bottom of the ninth and Iowa was down a billion. The actual score was 6 - 0 in favour of Tucson but it might as well have been a billion; the game was as good as over and everybody knew it except the man stepping up to the plate.

Robertson, the Tucson pitcher, glared at the batter and swore to himself. Why did the last out have to be Terry Mitchell? Not an easy out. The guy always kept coming at you. It's not like Mitchell's career was going anywhere; he'd been bouncing around the minors for almost a decade on drive and hustle, which only took you so far. Robertson was meant for the Bigs, but he needed this shut-out, this complete game, to help convince the Suits.

The southpaw wiped the sweat from his eyes, his arm tired and aching. Mitchell crouched in the batter's box, crowding the plate, making the strike zone as small as possible. His eyes locked with Robertson's, challenging him.

Robertson swore softly; the guy just didn't know when to quit. Well, he was going to teach him. . . .

The pitcher shook off every call the catcher signalled but the pitch he wanted — fastball, high, inside. Brush that blond head back a bit.

The pitch was wrong. Robertson knew it the moment it left his fingertips. He tried to reach for it, to call it back, but it sped at over ninety miles an hour right for the batter's head. The crack of ball hitting helmet smacked around the ballpark. Terry Mitchell dropped like a stone. The dugouts emptied.

It took ten minutes to restore order on the field. Robertson was replaced, a runner took Terry's place on first, and the next batter popped up for an easy out. Tucson went to the bus the winner. Terry Mitchell went to the hospital.

★ ★ ★

Terry was in Wrigley Field, just as he was always meant to be. The sun was golden and warm on his skin and the grass was sweet beneath his feet. It was a day game, played as God intended baseball to be played, in the bright sunlight. The stands were full and everyone was chanting his name. The feel of wood was a caress in his hands as he faced the pitcher in a classic one-on-one duel. The ball came in slow motion, looping high and then coming down, to cross chest high in front of him.

In a languorous move, Terry pulled the bat across his body and felt that wonderful shudder as it caught the ball right at the sweet spot, launching it, slowly, inevitably, up and outward, reaching for the sun, arcing out over the outfield, out over the stands, out of the park onto Waveland Avenue. Terry watched it go through the golden light as he began his sprint around the bases. This was what perfect joy felt like.

When he woke up, he was in a hospital bed. It was night and his coach, Shep Fletcher, sat there. Fletcher had a dumpling shape; there were those who, when they saw him in uniform, described him as a sack of flour wearing a cap.

"Hey, skip," Terry croaked, his mouth dry and unfamiliar, like he hadn't spoken in a while.

Fletcher nodded. His eyes, big behind the bifocals he wore, seemed more guarded than usual. "Terry. Docs said you were starting to come 'round. Wanted to check on you before we went out on the road."

Terry nodded slowly, thoughtfully. "Well, soon as the docs cut me loose, I'll catch you up —"

"No, Terry, you won't." What Fletcher had to say pained him, so the coach did what he always did in these cases and said it direct. "You're not coming back to the team. Skull's cracked. Docs fear another shot in the head like that might kill you. Club's not going to take that chance. They'll cover you while you're laid up here, but that's the end of it. They're cutting you loose. . . ."

Terry looked at the ceiling, his jaw tightening, fighting it. "I can catch on somewhere else. Maybe some AA team or . . ."

Fletcher's voice was soft and sad but final. "Son, they'll all want to see your medical history. It's not going to happen."

Terry swallowed hard and was silent for a moment. "I can play this game, skip," he whispered.

Fletcher put a hand on Terry's shoulder. "Sure you can, kid. I never seen anyone with more heart than you. Never saw anyone play so hard. You never quit on me, son, and you never backed down, and I admire that. I do. But it's not enough. You're just never going to make it to the Bigs, is all."

This was always the worst part of Fletcher's job, to have to tell someone who was giving their best that their best wasn't good enough. Terry stood it, the collapse of his world, and lay quiet.

"You going to be all right?" Fletcher asked him softly. "You got some place to go?"

Terry nodded. "I'll go home."

"Where's that?"

Terry looked at the older man with surprise, as if home could be any other city in the world.

"Chicago," he said. "I'll go home to Chicago."

"Baseball?"

The eight-year-old fixed Terry with that look children reserved for truly demented adults. "You're saying you want me to play *baseball?*"

Terry nodded. "National pastime, Jorgé. Greatest game in the world."

Jorgé rolled his eyes. "What world you *talking* about, Terry? Only thing lamer than baseball is hockey!" Terry just smiled. The kid sighed and shook his head again, but he threw Terry a wave as he left for home; Terry caught it and returned it. Still friends.

"Looks like you struck out, son," the Reverend Aloysius Gray said as he stepped out of the doorway. Gray ran a small, non-affiliated church and the youth centre attached to it. Like Terry, he had found a world in the neighbourhood surrounding the place.

The lanky blond turned to his friend, and his smile reached from ear to ear and into his eyes. "Jorgé'll come around. He's a good kid. Besides, he knows I won't quit bugging him until he does."

Gray chuckled. "You really don't know when to quit, do you?"

"Winners never quit; quitters never win, padre." Terry's eyes narrowed and his voice took on a flat hardness Gray rarely heard in him. "My dad quit on my mom and me when I was Jorgé's age. Up and left. Walked away. It killed her, but it took six years to do it." Then Terry took a deep breath, coming back to himself. He glanced at Gray with a touch of defiance as he continued his argument. "Heroes don't quit. Look at Sentinel. He's been at it since World War II! And Lady Starbright — she never quit at Mount St. Helens, even though it cost her life."

Gray sighed. "Ever hear of the Raven? Chicago's Defender? He quit. No one's seen him since the late sixties."

Terry shook his head stubbornly, as reasonable as a bull. "I don't buy it, padre. Maybe he changed his name and costume; some of those folks do. Wherever he is, if he's alive, I'll bet the Raven is still fighting the good fight."

"Maybe," Gray cautiously agreed.

The older man looked around him, past the asphalt play-yard attached to the crumbling church, out into the broken streets and battered buildings that made up the Jungle. The city had long since given up on this neighbourhood; cops showed up rarely and never stayed long. Here the local gang, the Crypts, held sway — a mongrel mob of thugs led by a sociopath calling himself Killa Klown D.O.A. Gray operated his mission and youth centre as an alternative to the Crypts, although lately it seemed he held it more in defiance of them.

"We could use someone like the Raven right about now," he said thoughtfully.

Terry flashed him another grin, a burst of sunlight in a grey day. "I'm telling you, padre, the answer is baseball! Front office down at Wrigley promised me some used equipment. I'm going to pick it up and bring it home after the game tonight. I'll drop it off on my way home. You going to be here?"

Gray nodded. He had some paperwork to do — grant applications to fill out. Most likely they'd be ignored, but he had to make the effort.

Terry gave him a wave and headed for Wrigley Field. Gray watched him go and thought, *You're a little crazy, Terry Mitchell, but I'm glad of that. You have to be a little crazy to have any hope around here. . . .*

Reverend Gray borrowed some of that hope and went back inside to tackle the paperwork.

Terry sat in the front seat of the first car of the elevated train as he went down to Wrigley. He caught snatches of peoples' lives in their apartment windows as the train rattled by, and followed the pattern of the tracks, crisscrossing one another. Watching the tracks was like watching people's lives, too, Terry thought; they met, joined, separated, moved on, headed toward — what? Where was his life headed? So long as he'd had baseball, he'd always had a direction. Even after the cancer took his mom, baseball had given him a goal.

Not now. He wasn't a part of the game anymore, except as a groundskeeper. It was a part of him, but he wasn't really part of it. So what was he?

He'd moved back to the old neighbourhood, looking to pick up some threads, but it wasn't his neighbourhood anymore. It had become a desolate, abandoned, hopeless place — an alien landscape. Terry never knew many people there when Mom was alive, and those few had long since moved out. The people there now were trapped, unable to escape because of their own poverty.

The Reverend Gray was different. He chose to be where he was. Terry didn't have much use for God. After his mom's death, somebody said it was God's will, and Terry decided then and there that God was a jerk and, personally, he wanted nothing to do with Him. The Reverend Gray was something different; his God believed in social justice and hope, and that's what the old man tried to put into practice. Like much of the neighbourhood, Terry had been drawn to the black preacher and his message. He needed the hope.

As the train lurched to a stop at Addison and Terry scrambled out, the young man realised he needed that sense of direction for himself. He needed to figure out what he was doing, where he was going, what he wanted to do with his life. What he was doing now was just marking time. That was all right for a little while. In the long run, it wasn't enough.

The game that night went into extra innings, but eventually the Cubs eked out a win. It made the groundskeepers a little late leaving the park. Still, the front office had come through on their promises and Terry left with two equipment bags filled with bats, balls, some gloves, even a catcher's mask, shin guards, and a chest protector. The latter might be a little big for the kids, but Terry thought he could use it to catch for them. He'd done a little of that in the minor leagues. He'd done a little of everything in the minors.

In the youth centre's meagre basement locker room, Terry inventoried the equipment before locking it away in the cage. Curious, he tried on the chest protector to see if would fit him, then found himself putting on the shin guards and the catcher's mask, as well. Looking in the mirror, Terry saw a ghost of what he had once been and abruptly turned away. He was about to remove the equipment when he heard coarse laughter upstairs. Something was wrong. Instinctively, the former player grabbed a bat and chased the sounds.

Five Crypts had broken into the mission and were busy applying a lesson to Reverend Gray. Two of them held the minister's arms while two others watched the thug calling himself Puff Dawg Z jam his fist again and again into the older man's stomach. They laughed as blood spurted out of Gray's mouth. The laughter pleased Dawg and pumped him up.

"You been talkin' trash 'bout the Crypts, old man," Dawg growled in Gray's face. "Tryin' to get the sheep riled up against us? D.O.A., he don' like that. He wants a lesson applied and — guess what? I'm your teacher!"

The others all found that hysterical, and Dawg grinned; he was notorious for his contempt of school. But under the laughter he heard the whisper of feet running toward him. He saw movement, too, out of the corner of his eye. As Dawg started to turn, a strange figure in baseball gear smashed a bat across the shoulder of one of the Crypt bystanders, breaking his collarbone. The figure then swept the bat into a second thug's stomach like he was hammering out a line drive. Without breaking step, the man in the catcher's mask pulled the bat to his shoulder, catching Puff Dawg Z with the backswing. The blow landed on the tip of his chin and flipped him onto his back.

Dawg gasped, trying to keep focus. Who was this guy? Didn't he understand? They were Crypts! Didn't he know who he was messing with?

If the guy knew, he didn't care. Dawg stared dumbly, still trying to gather his scattered wits, as the two punks holding the preacher released him to lunge at the intruder. The first threw a punch at the guy's face but jammed it against the catcher's mask and yelped in pain. The pain got worse as the bat-wielder put a knee to his groin and threw him into the path of his brother Crypt. The two went down together. The masked man then grabbed the second thug by the scruff of his neck, picked him up bodily, and slammed him against a wall. That took both the breath and the fight out of him.

It took the fight out of all of them. They stumbled for the door, scrambling over each other, all except Puff Dawg Z. He was still trying to get to his feet when rough hands grabbed him and shook him. A face behind wide wire mesh met him almost nose to nose. Two blazing blue eyes scorched him like an August sun.

"The man you hit is a man of God," the masked man snarled at Dawg. "You touch him again, and I'll send you to hell! Do you understand me?"

Dawg mumbled that he got it, he really did. Then he felt those hands picking him up and propelling him out the door. He tumbled to the ground at the feet of the other Crypts.

Dawg looked up into four pairs of eyes as filled with fear as his own, and mumbled, "Let's get outta here."

The battered gang members lurched off into the safety and reassurance of the dark.

Terry ripped off the catcher's mask and went to Reverend Gray, who still knelt at the centre of the floor. The minister managed a weak smile through bloodstained lips and said, "Pretty impressive, son."

Terry's mouth was a grim line as he examined the minister. "C'mon, padre. We're getting you to the hospital."

Gray just shook it off. "Had worse than this. Just . . . the wind knocked out of me. Get that stuff off and put away, and help me tape up my ribs. We need to talk."

Down in the equipment room, under Gray's instruction, Terry taped the minister's ribs. For a man in his sixties, Gray was still slim and his body taut, but his torso showed the scars of other battles, all quite old. Terry looked at them thoughtfully. "I guess you *have* had worse. Vietnam?"

The reverend pulled his black shirt back on and nodded. "Other battles, too. Before 'Nam." The shirt, still unbuttoned, hung draped on Gray as he sighed and looked up at Terry. "You remember the Raven? Well . . . that was me."

Terry stood there, dumfounded. The Raven was a figure of legend. Dressed in black from head to toe, with a wing-shaped cape and beaked cowl, he'd been the Chicago Defender. Immune to bullets, or so some said — though to look at Gray's scars now, that seemed not to be entirely true. What was true, what no one could question, was the way the Raven had fought crooks, crooked cops, and the political machine throughout the sixties, until he'd become a symbol of the city, almost as famous as the Water Tower.

Until, one day in 1969, the Raven had just disappeared.

And now he sat on a small cot, in a threadbare room, in a rundown church, in a dying neighbourhood? The Reverend Al Gray dropped his eyes and allowed himself a soft chuckle. "Hard to believe, isn't it?"

Words were never Terry's strong suit and they tumbled over themselves now. "No — I mean, yes. I believe you, of course — I do. But how — why —?"

"How did I become the Raven, or why did I stop?"

"How. Then why."

Gray sighed. "It's in the blood, I suppose. My grandfather was Red Summer, back just after World War I. Fought the Klan and race riots here in Chicago. Always kept his identity completely concealed. No one knew he was black, although some later suspected. My father was a fighter pilot in World War II. One of the Tuskegee Airmen. Flew bomber escort until he got shot down over Germany. I was only four, maybe five. My grandfather took care of me after that. He made sure I had a good education. I knew about him being Red Summer and all, but he wanted better for me."

Gray paused and shook his head. "Of course, 'better' was hard to come by. I was supposed to be a scientist, but this was back in the early sixties and black folk didn't have many options that way.

"And then Lady Starbright came on the scene. You weren't alive back when she first showed up, but she just made everything seem . . . possible. Hopeful. And she was black. I can't begin to explain what it meant to me at the time — to be a young black man, and there she was — beautiful, strong, brave. Shining. Black.

"There'd been heroes before her, of course, like my grandfather. But after World War II a lot of them retired, or went into hiding when McCarthy went after 'em. By the early sixties, it was time for heroes again. And I decided I wanted to be one of them — make a difference. I became the Raven. My grandfather had taught me to be judged by my deeds, not the colour of my skin, so I made sure no one knew that the Raven was black. Seems foolish now. At the time, it seemed important."

The two men were quiet for a while, until finally Terry asked, "What happened? Why did you stop being the Raven?"

Gray shuddered, almost as if he had been startled out of his memories — or disturbed by them. "JFK happened," he said softly. "Martin, Malcolm, and Bobby happened. It seemed the country was killing its best. The riots happened. I tried to calm things, and it got me shot at by the police and set on fire by my own people. It didn't seem like I was doing any good. . . ."

"Then I got drafted. My choices then were to go to Canada, go to jail, or go become a soldier. I laid aside one uniform and took on another. By the time I got back, Lady Starbright was dead and my heart just wasn't in it anymore. So I went and got myself ordained and took up God's work in the neighbourhoods, doing my best where the need seemed greatest."

He gave Terry a tired smile. "So you see, son, you were wrong — sometimes heroes *do* quit."

Terry shook his head slowly side to side. "No, I was right." He grinned. "You changed your name and your costume, but you're still fighting the good fight, padre."

"Maybe." Gray fixed a look burning with conviction on Terry as he added strongly, "But maybe it's time for the Raven to rise again."

"I dunno, padre. I mean, you're in good shape but —"

"Not me, Terry — you. I know what I saw, son. You're a natural. You stepped up without a thought and took on five punks — five — then laid them flat before they knew what was what! You didn't even think about it, did you? You just did it. I've seen more than a few masks, worked with some of the best, and I'm telling you that I've seen few with your God-given talent."

Gray touched the younger man's shoulder. "I'm not going to kid you. It isn't easy, what I'm suggesting. Taking up a mask is hard and you pay a price for doing it. But I swear to you that I'll be there with you. I'll help guide you and train you, and maybe together we can make a difference. What do you say?"

It was insane and Terry knew it. Not the part about being a hero. This was, after all, a world of heroes. No, Terry remembered what the docs had told him about his injury. It was the reason no other team would hire him; nobody would take that sort of risk. Certainly Gray would not have suggested this, had he known, but Terry had never gotten around to telling him about it. That made the decision, and the responsibility, his alone.

And Terry Mitchell had never wanted anything so much in his life.

During the fight with the Crypts, everything seemed to slow down and he saw — he felt — everything with a crystal clarity. Terry knew every move they would make, every response he would need, before it all started. It was part of a big picture, and doing it gave him a purpose.

Terry remembered what Shep Fletcher once said to him: "Nobody gets out of this alive, kid. Nobody. Live long, live short, it comes down to the same thing. We die. So you'd best live while you're alive and make it mean something."

Right now, Terry figured, his life didn't mean much. So why not take up Gray's offer? Part of him, however, still balked. He told himself it was nuts. It was suicide. It was just plain stupid. But, then, he'd done stupid things before. . . .

"I can't be the Raven," he finally told the minister. "That was you."

"Fine," Gray replied. "Be somebody else. Be you. But be someone! This neighbourhood needs a hero to inspire them, to bring them together. That's the real power of Sentinel, Lady Starbright, the Guard, and all the rest — they inspire others and make the impossible seem possible. You should do this, Terry, unless there's some specific reason you can't. I mean, you never said why you quit baseball. Was it an injury —?"

"No," Terry interrupted.

He wasn't a good liar. Fletcher used to kid him that he didn't talk enough to know how to lie. More than anything else in his life, however — even more than baseball — Terry wanted what Gray was offering. If he was willing to die to do it, he was willing to lie, as well.

"I wasn't good enough. That's all," Terry said, then hurriedly added, "Okay, you're on. Who shall I be?"

Gray walked over to the bat Terry had carried to the room, picked up the wood and examined it. Then he grinned and showed it to Terry. "I think this has your name all over it: the Louisville Slugger."

Terry grimaced. "This isn't Louisville. Besides, I think that name's trademarked. How about just Slugger?"

Gray made a face. "No sense of style at all. All right, all right — you're Slugger."

"I got name. Now what?"

"Now we get you ready for battle."

First up, Gray wanted to create a "look" for the Slugger. Since Terry had already introduced himself to the Crypts with a baseball bat, the minister decided that they should build on that. The baseball equipment also allowed some protection. The cap would cover the colour of Terry's hair and the catcher's mask made it hard to make out the details of his face. It also allowed more visibility than many masks. Gray used the blacking ballplayers wore under their eyes against sun glare to fashion a "war mask" for Terry, just in case the catcher's mask came off in a fight.

The chest protector would offer padding for the torso. Underneath it, Terry would wear a long-sleeved turtleneck warm up shirt, and, over it, a blue satin warm-up jacket. Gray would stitch the name *Slugger* on its back, where the team name would have gone. Batting gloves would help protect Terry's hands.

The real dispute came over the bottom half of the ensemble.

"No tights," Terry said adamantly.

Reverend Gray looked nettled. 'What's wrong with tights? I wore tights. Lots of masks wear tights! You need to be able to *move*, boy!"

Terry was unmoved and unmoveable. "I'm not wearing tights. I'm no dancer."

They argued this for the better part of an hour, until Gray finally gave up. They settled on camouflage pants and combat boots. "They'll hear cleats a mile away," Gray insisted and Terry conceded.

The minister also tried to make a case for using an aluminium bat, something the former ballplayer just wouldn't consider. "Purist!" muttered Reverend Gray, but Terry was unmoved. Tradition was important in baseball, and, so far as he was concerned, that meant a bat made of wood.

Gray had one last item for Terry — something left over from his days as the Raven. It was an odd-looking tangle of wires and three-inch-diameter black metal plates. "This was my own invention," the minister said softly, running his fingers over the device. "I kept it secret. Called it a pulse field. It generates a small anti-magnetic force field for a few seconds, one strong enough to deflect high-velocity projectiles — like bullets. Buys you only two or three seconds, and does squat against a fist or a knife, but this little beauty can save your life. It certainly kept *me* alive more than once."

The Cubs were going on a road trip. Terry had little work to do at the ballpark for the next few weeks, so he and Gray spent time in the gym next to the church — as many as twelve hours a day — honing Terry's fighting ability. In addition, they mapped out a strategy and marked off a turf, six city blocks by six city blocks, that the Slugger would claim as his own. Finally, they decided it was time for the new hero to make his presence felt.

"I've taught you as best I can, Terry. Tonight's the night you make it your own. *Vaya con Dios*, Slugger."

Terry grinned from behind the mask. "Batter up," he said softly.

For the next three weeks the Slugger tore up the Jungle. Reverend Gray devised the strategy and called the plays, and Terry executed. The street-level dope dealers were first up, and the pimps were second. A bat upside the head and a flurry of blows elsewhere all underscored a fundamental message: *Take your business elsewhere. These are not your streets.*

Next the Slugger uncovered a group of thugs extorting from the few local businesses in exchange for "protection." The thugs wound up needing protection themselves. By the end of the week, the Crypts were starting to look over their shoulders and the locals were certain to grin when they heard the cry, "Batter up!"

"Now we start hurting the Crypts directly," Gray told Terry as a new week began. "We know where their chop shops and crack houses are. That's where we strike first."

"And to do this I just go up and knock on their door — their re-enforced, heavily guarded, barricaded door?"

Gray grinned. "In a manner of speaking. First, we get you some bigger balls."

Gray had spent the previous week devising trick baseballs. Some spewed smoke. Some were explosive, set on a three second delay. "Or you can make them explode on second impact. Hit one with the bat and it's primed. Second impact will make it blow."

Terry grinned wolfishly. "I *like* it!"

First to go was the local crack house. A smoke baseball to the front door obscured the guards' vision while Terry stood out in the middle of the street and popped up some of the explosive balls on to the roof, then hit screaming line drives with them through the windows. The explosions spewed debris on the empty lots surrounding the crack house and sent the Crypts inside running out into the street, coughing and yelling. Terry had on a gas mask instead of the catcher's mask that night. He waded through the smoke, laying the Crypts low left and right with swings of the bat. The building burned as the Slugger cornered the last gangster standing and told him simply: "We play by my rules now. And I say the neighbourhood doesn't want you here any more."

A crystal meth lab followed, as did the local chop shop. The Slugger got the Crypts' attention and they set a trap for him — a phony victim and three gunmen. Fortunately, the Raven's pulse field worked just like he said it would. The Slugger charged the assassins, and they went down with cracked heads and ribs, broken knee caps and arms and collarbones. After that, word spread that the Slugger was bullet proof. Others claimed that he swatted the slugs away with his bat. Either way, the Crypts stopped treating Terry as a joke.

As the third week of their private war began, Gray warned Terry that it was going to get a lot more serious. "They'll be hunting you this week," he warned. "The trap was just the beginning. They see you as a specific threat and they're going to respond that way. You've got to be ready. . . ."

The Crypts' response was a fighter who called himself Running Dragon, who fancied himself a martial artist. Nunchakas faced the Slugger's bat, and if Running Dragon's skills had matched his mouth, the outcome might have been different. Through the alleys, up onto the elevated train tracks, across the roofs of the buildings, the battle played itself out. In the end, it was Running Dragon who went down, his leg broken. But Terry had taken some punishment, as well, including some blows to the head. He barely stumbled back to the youth centre before collapsing.

Gray stripped him of the costume and got him to the hospital ER, explaining that Terry was the victim of a mugging. The minister had known of this possibility, but still felt tremendous guilt at having gotten the younger man involved. The whole thing was his idea, after all — at least in his own mind. So the minister stayed with his friend as all the tests came back and revealed the full extent of his injuries, past and present.

When Terry woke up, he found Gray staring at him angrily. For the moment, the two men were alone in the ward room.

"Why didn't you tell me?" the minister whispered angrily.

Terry found it hard to focus, hard to mouth his reply. "Tell you . . .what?"

"They did some X-rays of that thick head of yours and found an earlier fracture. A bad one, right by the temple. Damn it, Terry, you lied to me! You could wind up paralysed or brain damaged or just plain dead. If I'd known, I'd never have you let you start this. Well, it's over now. . . ."

Terry's lips, swollen as they were, pulled into a thin tight line. "Not your choice. My choice. I don't back down, padre. I don't quit."

It took everything Gray had to keep from shouting. As it was, his voice got cold and hard. "Fine. But you're not going to kill yourself with my help. You play this game again, you play it alone. You hear? This partnership is over."

With that, Gray walked out. Terry closed his eyes and let his wits scatter until finally sleep came.

The Reverend Gray wasn't the only one angry with Terry. The leader of the crypts, Killa Klown D.O.A., had also had enough. When he got word that Running Dragon had been beaten, D.O.A. trashed the Crypts' headquarters. He howled, making his painted face look even more distorted. It was a clown's face, but the mask, instead of being chalk white, was blood red. The exaggerated smile, the painted eyes, were all done in black. The scars crisscrossing his face, however, were the thug's own creation. His skull was shaved and white against the paint, his eyes mould green against bloodshot whites.

D.O.A. stood six-four and tipped the scales at two hundred and forty — all of it muscle. He'd risen to the leadership of the Crypts through violence and maintained his position through more violence.

When he was done destroying the room, D.O.A. beat the messenger who had brought him the news of Dragon's defeat.

"I want this Slugger freak dead!" D.O.A. screamed. "I want every one of you out on the streets hunting this creep. When you find him, shoot him! Shoot him and whoever is standing near him! I don't care if it's your mother — you shoot them all down! Dead! I want him dead!"

"You don't want to do that."

Deadface's voice was quiet, but he was always heard. No emotions ever showed on the man's bronze face. It was only in his eyes that you saw something, a dark and reptilian intelligence that paused and considered before Deadface spoke. Smaller than D.O.A., slighter, he was the Crypts' brain, second in authority only to Killa Klown. So long as D.O.A. was in charge, that's all Deadface would ever be — number two. He knew it and D.O.A. knew it. It made for a wary alliance.

D.O.A., still fuming, turned toward his lieutenant. "Why don't I want them to kill this guy?"

The lieutenant shrugged. "Kill him like that, you make him a martyr. The sheep maybe stop being sheep. You, personally, have to do him, *jefé*. Then everyone knows again that your word is the law here."

D.O.A. smiled and all his teeth, filed into points, gave him a shark's mouth. "You're the smart one, bro. How we do this?"

"Meet him one on one. You have a bat, too, but we make sure yours has an iron bar down the middle of it. Meet him and beat him so the entire Jungle knows about it."

"And we get him to come — how?"

The only change of expression on Deadface's features was in the glittering of his eyes. "The first person he helped was that minister. We put a snatch on him, then put out the word for Slugger to meet us at a time and place we choose. Let him know — just one on one. You and him. Tell the sheep to come watch. Let it be known that if their guy wins, he not only gets the padre back but the Crypts vacate the Jungle. He refuses and the man of God goes to God."

"And when he loses?"

"Do we really need to say, *jefé*?"

D.O.A. stood there looking at his lieutenant — his rival — for a time, looking hard. Then a nasty grin spread over his face, made more broad and hideous by the make-up and his shark's teeth, until he threw back his head and roared with laughter. "I love it!" he shouted.

Deadface's eyes narrowed and grew hard. "I thought you would," he whispered.

The cops came and went at the hospital. Terry claimed he never saw who mugged him. The two patrolmen just went through the motions. Life in the Jungle, after all.

The hospital turned the bruised victim loose in the morning. Terry didn't have insurance and didn't seem to qualify for aid, so they decided he was well enough to send home. Head aching, he tried stopping at the youth centre on the way back to his place, but his key no longer worked. He thought at first that maybe he couldn't work the key, but when Reverend Gray didn't respond to his knocking, Terry gave up and stumbled home to his one-room basement apartment.

Once in bed it took the battered hero two days to get out again. The only message on his answering machine was from his boss at the ballpark: "Your minister called, Mitchell, and said you wouldn't be in on account of you got mugged. But management's noticed that you been 'mugged' a lot lately. You used to be reliable, but not any more. . . . I got no choice, Mitchell. I'm letting you go. We'll mail you your last check."

Terry sat on the edge of his bed, trying to remember when things had ever been this bleak. He hadn't felt this bad since his mom died, and maybe not then. Up until now, Terry had always believed that he could make something happen. Now? Maybe he had to face it. His best wasn't good enough for baseball; maybe it wasn't good enough for this, either.

The front door buzzed. Hope spasmed in Terry and he thought, maybe it was Reverend Gray. Maybe he wasn't so mad any more. Maybe he was coming to say it was okay. . . .

It wasn't the padre at the door; it was Jorgé. The kid was scared, and seeing Terry so beaten up scared him more.

"Aw, jeez, man!"

Terry forced a small smile. "Looks worse than it is, kid. Whassup?"

"The Crypts took Reverend Gray! His office is all trashed and everything! Word on the street is that they want the Slugger to meet them tonight, midnight, at the main baseball diamond at Sheridan Park! If the cops show, or if the Slugger don't, they'll kill the padre!"

The blood pounded in Terry's temples and fear grabbed his guts. "Okay. I'll help get the word out, Jorgé. The Slugger will hear. I'm sure he'll do what he —"

"C'mon! Who you kiddin'?" Jorgé, eyes big with fear and hopelessness, grabbed Terry's arm. "You're the Slugger!"

Terry took a second to let that sink in. "How did you — does anybody — who else. . . ?"

Jorgé shook his head impatiently. "Naw, naw, man. I mean, me — sure. It wasn't hard for *me* to figure out, 'cause I know you and your thing about baseball. Rest of the neighbourhood don't have it doped. But how you gonna help Reverend Gray? You can't hardly stand up straight!"

Terry leaned heavily against the wall. For a second, Jorgé thought the man was going to keel over. But Terry stayed like that, eyes closed, until he finally took a long slow breath, forced himself upright, and looked at the boy.

"Get the word out. Tell 'em the Slugger'll be there. Nobody else shows. No other hostages. No audience. That's what the Klown wants, an audience."

Jorgé eyed Terry anxiously. "You sure you can do this?"

Terry fixed the boy with a long stare. "What have I always told you, Jorgé? Before you can win, you've got to show up. . . ."

The baseball field had been abandoned by the park district like the rest of the Jungle had been abandoned by the city. Terry had done his best to rescue it, keeping it clear of debris, planting new grass, but it was mostly baked and dusty earth, cracked and dead.

D.O.A. looked at his lieutenant and snarled, "Where're the sheep? The idea was I smush this creep in front of the neighbourhood. . . ."

Deadface lit a cigarette. The flare from his cupped match cast stark shadows on his expressionless face. "Don't matter, *jefé*. We leave the body where they have to see it, like at the church, and they'll get the message just the same."

"And if the asshole don't show?"

"Leave the priest's body. Works all the same. You win, no matter what goes down."

D.O.A. grunted and went back to his waiting.

Over in front of the pitcher's mound, Gray lay on his side, his hands tied behind his back and attached to his ankles. He had not gone quietly and his captors had enjoyed making the minister pay for his resistance. All around Gray was dark; the gang had shot out most the lights illuminating the park. As much as he wanted to live, the minister prayed that Terry would stay away.

Reverend Gray knew a moment later that his prayers had been in vain.

Slugger came in street-side, carrying his bat over his shoulder, striding through the detritus of urban decay. The Crypts had their wheels just off the infield, clustered around second base, facing inward, and they hit their brights as Terry walked around the backstop. The lights stabbed at him, and their brightness was like needles in his eyes; he flinched for a moment. They could've shot him dead then and there, but Terry counted on there being other plans. He raised his hand to shield his eyes a bit, and searched the infield until he saw where his friend lay in front of the pitcher's mound.

Behind Gray, on the pitcher's mound itself, stood Killa Klown D.O.A., stripped to the waist, backlit, monstrous. His own bat rested on *his* shoulder. "So, you heard the word?" he bellowed. "Good. Gonna teach your punk ass who is the king of *this* jungle, and I'm gonna do it playin' *your* game!"

Slugger gestured with his bat toward the figure huddled on the ground. "Not until I check on the minister, Klown. Then you get your ups."

D.O.A. smiled a big, toothy, shark's grin. "Be my guest," he sneered and backed up toward second base.

Without hurrying, the Slugger walked out to his friend and knelt beside him.

"You shouldn't have come," Gray whispered urgently. "D.O.A. means to kill you and, one way or another, I'm dead, too. No way they'll ever let me walk away from this."

Terry worked the knots binding Gray's hands to his ankles. "Told you before, padre. I don't quit. I don't walk away." The knots came loose. "Can you stand?"

Gray nodded. Slugger had his hand under one arm, helping his friend get up, when D.O.A. decided he had waited long enough. With a bellow, he charged, his bat raised high. Slugger barely had time to push Gray to one side before D.O.A.'s bat came thundering down. The gang leader riposted with the handle to Terry's temple. The blow was like an explosion in the hero's head. Only by instinct and reflex was Slugger able to roll with it and scramble back to his feet.

D.O.A. was on top of him again. Slugger brought up his own bat to parry, and the two bats met in a sharp *krak*! A flurry of blows followed; the two men were like gladiators in an arena, swinging broadswords. There were fists, there were elbows, kicks, and headbutts. D.O.A.'s bat not only had an iron rebar down its core, it was studded with hooks and razors that cut and grabbed at Terry's clothes and flesh wherever it made contact.

D.O.A. himself was nothing like the Slugger had ever faced before. He wasn't a more skilled fighter than the street scum or Running Dragon; he was a savage, a berserker — psychotic and heedless of pain and always on the attack. Terry heard ribs crack as he connected with the Klown's midsection and side; D.O.A. let out a grunt, took in a breath, and charged again.

One swipe tore the catcher's mask off Terry's face. Repeated blows had already ripped open his chest protector and shredded his jersey and the skin beneath it. Now blood trickled down over the blacking on the Slugger's face, into his puffy eyes, threatening to blind him. Killa Klown D.O.A. smiled. He was arrogant, certain of himself, and that meant this victory needed to be drawn out so he could savour it.

A kick to the Slugger's midsection drove him down to one knee. D.O.A.

raised his bat with both hands over his head and, with a roar, brought it down. Slugger roused himself and raised his own bat, left hand on the handle and right hand on the sweet spot, to block the attack.

The two bats met near Terry's left hand. D.O.A.'s blow splintered and broke Terry's bat and the stroke continued down. Terry heard a dull crack, then felt searing pain as his left collarbone split. The Crypt leader put a boot to Terry's face, and the Slugger sprawled to the infield dirt, unable to defend himself.

Gray, surrounded by Deadface and the rest of the Crypts, watched helplessly as D.O.A. kicked the prone figure again and again, until the Slugger stopped moving. D.O.A. laughed, throwing his head back, bellowing like a beast. Gray's tears ran down his cheeks and into the thirsty dirt. "No," he whispered, certain that his friend was dead.

"Batter up!"

The words caught D.O.A. by surprise, caught them all by surprise. The Crypts' leader wheeled to look in the direction from which they'd come, out past the wire backstop, flanking home base.

The neighbourhood returned his angry stare. Under the cover of darkness, with all eyes focused on the battle, no one had seen how, one by one, the people of the Jungle had come. Men and women, young and old, every colour and nationality, they had come. They were already fifty strong, with more arriving every moment. Some wore jerseys. Some had catcher's masks. They all carried bats, and now they used them to pound the earth, the backstop, the benches. "Batter up!" they called, the cry rippling up and down, repeated with the drumming of the bats until it became one unified roar, over and over again. "Batter up! Batter up! Batter up!"

D.O.A. gawked at them for a moment, dumfounded, before he howled his defiance, like the animal he most certainly was.

Deep within the crimson haze where he drifted, where all was pain, Terry Mitchell heard the neighbourhood's cry, too. The sound reminded him of something: It was like the rumble you heard from the stands when it was the last of the ninth, two outs, game tied, and the crowd was chanting, calling to him, calling him back. Last bats. Batter up.

Terry's hand closed on the broken handle of his bat, the end of which was now a sharp wooden point. In front of him, his back to Slugger, D.O.A. continued to bellow in defiance of the crowd. Gripping the shaft of wood, Terry forced himself up to his knees, then plunged the wooden dagger deep into D.O.A.'s right thigh.

The Crypts' leader shrieked with pain and surprise, and dropped his bat. Terry lurched to his feet and delivered a haymaker to the brute's jaw, staggering him. Then he picked up D.O.A.'s fallen bat, felt the iron in it, and applied it to the Klown — arms, back, ribs, knee, shoulder. The blows came fast and furious until it was D.O.A. who lay sprawled in the dirt, moaning.

For a moment, all was silent, then Terry turned to the Crypts and growled, "Get out of our neighbourhood. This is over."

"No!"

D.O.A.'s bellow startled everyone as he lurched to his feet and staggered toward his men. "Kill them!" he screamed.

Deadface caught the Crypts' leader, steadied him, and looked him in the eye. "Too many witnesses, man. Too many victims. He's got them united. Let it go. There are other neighbourhoods."

D.O.A. stared at Deadface for a moment, mouth agape. He pushed away again, roaring at the Crypts, "This is my turf! I'm the boss here, and I'm telling you to take out your guns and shoot them! Kill 'em all!"

D.O.A. knew then how much he had lost when the Crypts hesitated, then glanced at Deadface for permission. They were his gang no longer. With a maddened snarl, D.O.A. lunged forward, seized a gun from a former minion, and swung back to point the piece at the Slugger.

Terry had never had the chance to get the pulse field generator back from Reverend Gray. All he had to shield him from the bullet was the defiance in his eyes. But he did not waver. Never quit, never back down, never give an inch. Live or die — it's all he knew. His eyes locked with D.O.A.'s, like they had locked with Robertson's, that punk pitcher from Tucson. *Bring it on. . . .*

There was a single shot. The back of D.O.A.'s head exploded, and he fell forward. Deadface held the gun at full arm's extension a moment longer, then let it drop to his side.

"Grab up the body," he told the Crypts, and three of them leapt to do it. "Doc Cimitière may have a use for it down in New Orleans. As for you, Slugger . . ." He stared at Terry. "These are your streets now. Hold them if you can."

He waved his hand. The Crypts ran to their rides and took off, gunning their engines, tearing up the packed earth of the infield. Terry waited until they were gone before letting the darkness swallow him up. He fell like a stone and was caught by his friends.

Word got out to the media that something had happened in the Jungle: A mysterious figure called the Slugger had driven out the local street gang. When the cameras came searching for footage of the Crypts, they found the people of the neighbourhood, armed with baseball bats, patrolling the streets, watching out for their homes and for each other. They all said that they were "the Home Team" and that they were "pinch hitting" for the Slugger.

The media exposure put pressure on the city. Police patrols increased. Crime plummeted. The neighbourhood came back to life.

Gradually, so did Terry.

Favours were called in; donations were raised. No questions were asked. Slugger belonged to the neighbourhood, and the neighbourhood protected him now. Six weeks in a hospital gave way to a rehab house not far from what used to be the Jungle.

Reverend Gray found Terry in the rehab home's glass-walled day room, soaking up the waning October sun. "Good news, Terry," Gray told his friend. "The physical therapists figure you're good enough to go home in a few days."

Terry nodded, a slow smile spreading across his battered face. "Yeah, they told me. It *is* good news." To Gray's eyes, though, Terry seemed thoughtful and a little too pensive.

The minister moved in closer, laying a hand protectively on his arm. "Son, have you considered what you want to do after you go back? I want you to think real hard about this. I know you don't quit, but even the great players retire when their bodies tell them they've had enough. . . ."

"The Crypts went somewhere, padre. Some other neighbourhood. They're doing the same stuff they did to us, just to people we don't know. It's not right."

"Then maybe somebody else will rise up and kick them out. But it doesn't have to be you who does it, Terry. You hear?"

"I hear, padre. I hear."

But do you agree? wondered Reverend Gray.

In the end, though, even the minister had to admit that it didn't matter. Whatever the answer, whatever Terry's decision, Gray would be there for him. They were partners. They were friends.

For now, the two men talked about other things, in particular the sort of miracle it would take to get the Cubs into the World Series, and how to convince God to let it happen. After a while, with the Reverend Al Gray watching over him, Terry Mitchell fell asleep in his chair and dreamed of Wrigley Field and baseball played under a warm summer sun.

Evening With the Minotaur

by Jon Hansen

The server at the Forbidden City had just refilled Jayne's water glass when her blind date walked in, guided by the hostess. She'd never seen him before but recognised him at once. Her cousin, who'd set them up, described him thus: "Big guy, nice dresser, has the head of a bull — y'know, with horns?"

From *Explaining Asterion's Condition to Children* (Gov't Pub NIH 05-789-a):

We know something is wrong because of the way you've been feeling. Your head hurts a lot of the time and seems a lot heavier. Your face is growing hair where it hadn't before. You don't feel like doing the things you used to do and you seem to get mad all the time for no reason.

Because of this we want to try to help you. So that's why you have come to the hospital for a check-up.

The bull-headed man stooped as he passed under the gold-filigreed ornamentation of the arch, his horns almost but not quite catching on the red tassels hanging from it. He looked around before spotting Jayne; she was the only woman alone, the other tables empty or occupied by staring couples. Them, he paid no mind.

The server paled as he walked up, but recovered enough to dash away. The bull-headed man looked down at Jayne. "I beg your pardon, but are you Jayne Halbert?" he said. His voice rumbled like a idling truck.

"Yes. Are you Robert?" She stood quickly to stick out her hand. He took it, his giant hand almost swallowing hers, but his touch gentle.

Robert said a quick "thank you" to the hostess, who nodded once before disappearing back to the front. Then he pulled off his tan raincoat and draped it over an empty chair. Another waiter appeared long enough to drop off a second menu and a glass of water before vanishing like the first.

"You look great," said Robert. He pointed at her dress, a simple cut in burgundy. "I like that colour."

"Thank you." Jayne pulled a hand through her hair. Dark curls fell forward. "I was beginning to worry."

"I'm sorry," said Robert as he picked up the menu. "I had a little trouble catching a cab in the rain. I'm not usually late for things. In fact —" he laughed, a sort of snort that ruffled the menu "— I usually find it useful to arrive early when meeting someone for the first time. Gives them a chance to get away clean, if they suddenly change their mind."

"Oh, no," she said, laughing a little herself. "Don't worry. My cousin said you and I would be a good match."

You will meet a lot of different people at the hospital: doctors, nurses, psychologists, and social workers. They will ask you a lot of questions. It's important for you to answer them as best you can so they can help you.

The hospital is a big place. It is easy to get lost, so don't go anywhere alone. There is plenty for you to do. We have toys and games for you, a TV you can watch, and a computer you can use.

While you are at the hospital, you will be given a lot of tests. Your mom and dad can be with you during most of these tests, but someone from the hospital will always be with you.

"So, have you lived in Empire City long?" asked Robert. He picked up the soy sauce dispenser, grasping it delicately in his long fingers as he poured a quick dollop into his bowl of egg drop soup.

"I actually grew up here. Well, Brooklyn. Not in this restaurant." She picked up a fried wonton wrapper and popped it into her mouth. "I know, I know, Empire City is the sort of place most people move to, but there are plenty of natives."

"I can see that," said Robert. "But not me. I'm from Kansas City." He lifted the spoon, lips pursing just long enough to quietly sip the soup. Jayne paused to watch him. For a second, the inside of his mouth was visible. He had no upper front teeth, only something resembling a ridge.

Robert stopped. "Everything all right?"

Jayne blushed, warmth rushing over her face. "I'm sorry. I was staring. That's so rude."

"It's all right. I'm used to it."

"I know, but —" Jayne stopped and took a deep breath. "I'm sorry. Let's start again. Sharon said you work in IT?"

He nodded. "Yeah. Been doing that for a few years now. Mostly back-end development work. Growing up, I always thought computers would be a good field to get into. Good pay. Don't have to interact with a lot of people. Besides, my *condition* —" he emphasised the word "— pretty much ruled out any chance I had of going into the family business."

She paused, spoon halfway to her lips. "Really? What do your parents do?"

"They run a china shop."

The purpose of these tests is to see if you have Asterion's Condition.

Children with Asterion's Condition can go to school. They can play and eat with other children. You can't give the condition to your friends by sharing things like toys or clothes. You can't give it to your relatives by hugs or kisses.

Then how did you get Asterion's Condition? Asterion's Condition is caused by a problem in your DNA.

"I like this place," said Robert, looking around. The décor was traditional Chinese restaurant: lots of red and gold, a large mural covering one wall, and the tabletop covered in glass. A bamboo shoot plant sat beside the soy sauce.

Jayne smiled. "Me, too. It's not as fancy as Peking Duck, but it's not as crowded either. Besides, I love their sweet and sour prawns. And afterward, we can walk a couple blocks down to the Chinatown Ice Cream Factory."

"I like the sound of that."

The waiter reappeared, whisking away the empty bowls. Robert watched him go. He raised a finger to point toward a scowling grey-haired man beside the kitchen door. "I see the manager hasn't moved. He's watching us like you were his only daughter."

"Maybe they don't get a lot of metahumans in here."

"I think he thinks I'm going to eat the bamboo if he doesn't keep an eye on me." His eyes sparkled.

Jayne smiled. "You're a lot funnier than I expected."

"With a face like mine, a sense of humour helps."

They both fell silent a moment, the only sound Chinese orchestral music piped through the restaurant. Then Robert leaned forward.

"I know you're curious, so I'll just tell you, get it out in the open. This —" he gestured at his face "— happened when I was twelve. Up until then, I looked completely normal."

Jayne hesitated before asking the question. "What caused it?" Her voice was quiet, as if ashamed at her curiosity.

Robert sighed. "Turned out our family doctor had got some of his vaccine stock from a distributor who'd bought it from the great kingdom of Thule. Turned out it did more than immunise us against rubella. It also rewrote our DNA." He held up a hand. "It didn't affect everyone who got the shot. My younger brother, for instance. He's just fine. Married with two kids and living in Springfield. But there were quite a few of us by the end. A lot of people think that Thule was field-testing some sort of experimental warrior serum, but there's not a lot of proof. Thule claimed they had nothing to do with it, that the vaccine became contaminated after it shipped. The distributor disappeared along with the paper trail. There's a big class action lawsuit still tied up in court."

Jayne crossed her arms and shivered. "That's terrible, losing your face like that. I can't imagine . . ."

Robert shrugged. "Could've been worse. There were some variations in the, ah, breeds we resembled. I've met a few guys who ended up looking like Texas Longhorns. Poor bastards had to have their horns taken off so they could hold their heads up, let alone walk into a room. If you're curious, I resemble a Toro, the Spanish fighting bull." He clapped his hands together and struck a pose from an old Bugs Bunny cartoon, eliciting a snort from Jayne. "So, no vacations in Pamplona for me."

"How did your parents take all this?"

"Pretty hard, actually. Mom blamed herself and Dad had trouble looking at me. He used to raise beef cattle before. Then he couldn't do it anymore. Sold everything. Said he couldn't bear to slaughter something that looked like his son."

Jayne gave a little smile. "Is that when they bought the china shop?"

Robert grinned. "Oh, good. I was afraid I was bringing you down. I must admit, I don't eat a lot of meat myself. Too hard with this mouth. Haven't got the front teeth for it." He took another sip of water. "Which is a shame, because I loved my mother's meatloaf.

"Still," he said, sounding a little more cheerful, "it wasn't all bad. Got to go to college for free because of this. Lot of schools offered to pick up the tab for anyone affected, just 'cause we bore a strong, ah, resemblance to their mascots: Texas, Marshall University, South Florida, Buffalo, among others. I ended up at Nebraska."

Jayne frowned. "Didn't that make you feel — well, exploited?"

Robert said nothing, then finally shrugged. "It was my only chance to go. My grades were good, but we didn't have the money. So I made the most of it, got the degree, and got out. I'm satisfied."

At that moment another waiter appeared, tray loaded down. The air suddenly smelled of hot food, spicy and intoxicating. Robert rubbed his hands together. "At last. I'm starving." As the waiter distributed dishes, Robert looked at her. "Is there anything else you'd like to know?"

Jayne cocked her head. "Where do you buy your shirts?"

DNA is a word that describes all the little things that make up you. For example, whether you have black hair or blond hair, or whether you have blue eyes or brown eyes. Your DNA controls those details. Your DNA will also tell us if you have Asterion's Condition.

Asterion's Condition is passed on through your chromosomes. Your chromosomes are made up of DNA you got from your mother and your father. Asterion's Condition only appears along the Y chromosome. This means only boys can have it, not girls.

If you would like to talk to a boy with Asterion's Condition, just ask someone at the hospital.

★　　★　　★

"So, have you seen many masks?" Robert was ploughing through his eggplant with Peking sauce and extra steamed rice, Jayne only nibbling on her sweet and sour prawns.

"Oh, all the time," said Jayne. She stabbed another prawn with her fork. "Superhero spotting is an Empire City tradition. Seems like a few of them call Empire University home base."

"You've probably had a class with one or two."

Jayne shook her head. "I'm in plasma physics. It's a small department, and we're all practically in each other's laps. It'd get around. I haven't had a really big class where I didn't know everyone since I was an undergrad, and that was at Brooklyn College." She leaned a little closer. "I still can't believe you've never seen any of them."

He shook his head, the waggling of his horns forcing a retreat by the server refilling water glasses. "The closest I've come was watching that *Simpsons* episode last month, when Homer and Bart tried to join the Guard. I couldn't believe those were Sentinel's and Caliburn's real voices."

Jayne rolled her eyes, addressing the ceiling. "How is this possible? How long have you lived here — six months?"

"Hey, hardcore computer jockeying takes a lot of time." Robert shrugged. "And I spend all of my time at work."

"That's what Sharon said. She comes in, you're there, and when she leaves, you're still there. You work all the time."

Robert laughed, a giant laugh that echoed through the restaurant. Heads turned and faces appeared at the kitchen door for a minute before disappearing again. "She did, did she? What else did she say?"

"That you were a good guy. That you were smart, and funny, and nice. And that she had heard —" She broke off, blushing.

"It's not true," Robert said in solemn tones. "The only thing you can judge by the size of a man's horns is if he has to drive a convertible or not." He twirled his fork for a moment. "I met a lot of girls in college who thought that. Called themselves 'cowgirls.' They hung out in bars, hoping to meet guys like us, thinking we were, well, *different* elsewhere. Some guys encouraged it, but it's just a rumour. It's not true."

"Oh . . . really?" Jayne arched an eyebrow, a hint of smile tugging at one corner.

One hand came up in mock protest. "Hey, hey, now — don't get me wrong. I didn't say *that*." He laughed again, and this time she joined in. Finally he continued, sounding calmer: "I want you to know, I don't do that anymore. Not since college, and certainly not since I moved to the city."

"Good."

The word hung there for a minute.

Then Robert smiled.

The first test is a blood test. To test your blood, a nurse will have to take some of it with a needle. It may sting a little, but that won't last long. Afterward, you can pick the colour of Band-Aid you would like to wear.

You will also be given some other tests that will let us look inside your body. These tests are very important because they will tell us how your body is changing.

The first test is an X-ray. This will let us look inside you to see to see what is happening with your bones. The second test is called a CAT scan. This test takes pictures inside your head. The last test is called an MRI scan. This test takes special pictures of the inside of your body, like an X-ray.

These tests may be loud sometimes, but they won't hurt you and someone will be there with you the whole time. All you will need to do is stand very still.

The waiter set the check beside Robert. He didn't acknowledge it, just kept staring at Jayne. "Well, honestly, I don't think I'd make much of a superhero."

Jayne stared back. "Why not?"

Robert tucked his head down, suddenly uncomfortable. He hesitated for a moment before leaning forward, as if he were confessing. "I don't have any powers. Horns or no horns, having the head of a bull doesn't have much advantage. I can smell and hear pretty good, and my peripheral vision's better than most. So what? The Guard wouldn't be interested in me. Though Merrill Lynch might be. . . ."

Jayne looked at him, a slight frown on her face. Even sitting he loomed over her. "Well, you look strong. Are you?"

Robert shrugged. "I once dragged an illegally parked SUV out of a mall handicapped space so my mother could park there." Jayne whistled, clearly impressed. "She's got bad legs," he added. "But it's not like I could've bench-pressed the thing. Besides, I can't fly, and I've never heard of a superhero taking the subway. I'm certainly not bullet-proof like Sentinel."

"There are all kinds of heroes, Robert. Not all of them are bullet-proof, and not all of them belong to the Guard."

He wiped at his mouth with the napkin, then set it on the table. "Look, a lot of the guys, when they went into town, would get roaring drunk and start fights. People always got hurt by the end." He reached up a hand to the end of a horn. A thick rubber cap covered the tip, blunting it. "That's why I'm not much of a drinker. I don't like fighting much, and we *cowboys*," he said, "tend to start fights when we get drunk."

She reached out and put a hand on his. "You're not a cowboy. You're Robert. And you don't have to like to fight to be a hero."

Robert nodded, still quiet. Jayne pulled her hand back. Beside the check sat two fortune cookies. She claimed one and broke it open. "My fortune says, *Your happiness is intertwined with your outlook on life.* How nice. What's yours?"

Robert pulled out the strip of paper. "*Someone will invite you to a Karaoke party.*"

Later you will meet with a psychologist. The psychologist is a special kind of doctor. This kind of doctor will talk with you and ask you questions about how you feel. It's important to always tell the psychologist the truth. The psychologist will also talk with your parents. You will also take some tests, like the kind you have in school. You will come back and meet with the psychologist again in a few months.

You will also meet with a physical therapist. The physical therapist will be able to help you if you have trouble moving. You and the therapist will do all sorts of fun things together. You will play with toys, paint pictures, and even learn to cook just like your parents! The therapist may videotape you while you play, and may also talk with your parents.

★　　★　　★

Moving with a reluctance to bring things to an end, they headed to the register. The manager kept watching, a scowling statue, but the hostess smiled wide. "How was everything?" she asked in musical tones. The brass ID on her white shirt said *Michelle*.

"Everything was great," said Jayne as Robert passed over some bills.

"And not just the food," added Robert.

As Robert pulled on his coat, Michelle caught Jayne's eye. She looked pointedly back at Robert before winking one green eye at Jayne. Jayne blushed again, but said nothing as her date held the door for her, then followed her into the night. Outside, the rain had finally stopped, leaving the streets dark and wet. Neon gleamed in the puddles.

They walked down Mulberry, taking their time. Around them, the sidewalks were deserted, thanks to the rain and the lateness of the hour. They crossed Canal Street, where the normally bustling vendors had all packed up and left for the night. They hurried at the crosswalk to dodge a speeding cab, then continued on. Robert kept slowing to look in the shop windows.

"I can't get over how different things are in this part of town," he said. "It's like we're in Shanghai."

"Yeah, Chinatown's different. It's also pretty large. Stretches all the way past the Bowery." Jayne shivered. "I don't go over there much. That's supposed to be where Bloody Mary haunts."

"Bloody Mary?"

"She's like the boogeyman — takes bad kids and pulls them into Hell. Pretty scary, huh?"

From out of a nearby alley stepped six young men dressed in leather and wearing wraparound shades. They moved to flank Jayne and Robert, three in front and three behind. Metal gleamed in their hands. One of them, short with a small tattoo on his right cheek, stepped forward and pointed a heavy-looking pistol at Robert. "I think we're just as scary as any boogeyman," he said in a lightly accented voice.

Jayne and Robert raised their hands. "I don't suppose you guys are inviting us to a Karaoke party?" said Robert.

"'Fraid not." Shorty held out his other hand. "Now, gimme your wallet, cowboy, before I blow a big hole in that funny looking head of yours."

No one moved for a second, then it started.

Robert watched Jayne bring the palms of her hands together. There was a cracking sound and she disappeared. Shorty twitched, pointing the gun to where Jayne had been standing. As soon as the gun moved, Robert took his chance.

He lowered his head and charged, the movement shockingly fast considering his size. Shorty jerked the gun back and squeezed off a single shot. Robert felt the bullet graze his head. An instant later, he ploughed into the would-be robber, one blunted horn hitting him in the stomach.

Shorty gave a strangled moan as Robert straightened up and tossed him high into the air. Robert didn't stop to watch him land. Instead, he balled up a giant fist and punched another gang member, a gawking fellow with a shaved head, squarely in the chest. Shaved head went flying, arcing several yards away to crash into a nearby garbage can.

Robert turned to face the others. As he watched, two of the thugs suddenly stiffened, as though a gun had been shoved into their backs. Then they relaxed. Their weapons slipped from their hands as they collapsed onto the sidewalk, unconscious.

Robert raised up his head, flaring his nostrils wide. Then he bellowed, a deep, rumbling, rage-filled sound that shook the concrete. The two remaining muggers flinched.

Before they could move, the air around them filled with swirling colours that circled them like a swarm of bees. Robert looked around. Not far away stood a young Chinese woman in a green silk dress, her face hidden in shadow under a wide straw hat. In one hand she held a long pole, a lantern hanging from the end. It was from the lantern that the colours streaked, pouring out like a kaleidoscope gone berserk. Robert held up a hand to shield his eyes .

Then the colours stopped, as if a door had been shut. The last two gang members swayed back and forth, eyes glazed.

"Sleep," said the silk-clad woman.

The final two gang members collapsed onto the wet sidewalk. Robert looked at the young woman. Another sharp crack broke the night air, and Jayne reappeared beside him.

The Chinese woman inclined her head. "I thought you might need help, but I see that is not the case. Still, you must have better ways to spend an evening."

"Thanks," said Robert. "That was impressive."

"As were you both," the woman said. The silk of her dress whispered as she stepped forward to regard the unconscious gang. "Happily, the Fifth Precinct is only a few blocks away. I'll let them know."

"That's the Lady of the Lantern," whispered Jayne.

The Lady chuckled and turned back to them. "Yes, I am. But I don't believe that I've met you before."

"I'm Lethe," said Jayne. "And this is Robert. He's new in town." Robert turned to look at his date, one eyebrow raised.

"A pleasure," said the Lady. "Good evening to you both." With that, she disappeared back into the shadows, leaving the two of them alone with the unconscious muggers.

They picked their way through the bodies, continuing down Mulberry before turning on Bayard. As they walked, the familiar wail of sirens could be heard, headed toward where they had been. "Lethe?" said Robert finally.

"That's my superhero name," she replied. "It's the river of forgetfulness the dead have to cross in Greek myth. I can turn invisible and my touch can put people to sleep. When they wake up, they don't remember anything I don't want them to remember. . . ."

"You didn't tell me you were a hero."

"Well, I felt awkward. It's not something you bring up on a first date, usually. I'm sorry. I should have said something."

Robert looked away. "Does your cousin Sharon know? Is that what she meant by us having a lot in common?"

Jayne nodded. "Not just that, but, yeah, she knows. She even helped me come up with the name. She was a Classics major. But she didn't set us up because you look like the Minotaur." She put her hand on Robert's arm and pulled him to a halt. "She thinks you're nice and funny and that you'd treat me right — and that you'd understand."

For a long minute they stood there, quiet, until Robert finally sighed. He turned, shadows from the streetlight playing across his bull's head, as he looked at her. "You still want to get ice cream?"

"Yes."

"Good. Me, too."

They started walking again. Up ahead, a door opened, streaming light onto the street. Another couple appeared, each holding an ice cream cone and laughing as they headed down the sidewalk.

"So," said Robert in a lighter tone, "where did you get your powers? Do you have a great-aunt who's a Greek sorceress? Did you have an accident during an internship with GenTech?"

Jayne smiled. "I bought an amulet on eBay," she said, then burst into laughter. "Oh, it's a long story. Buy me a double scoop of adzuki bean and I'll tell it to you."

There isn't any medicine we can give you to change the things Asterion's Condition will do to your body. You should always remember, though, that what has happened is not your fault. And what happens to you as you get older is still up to you.

ARCANUM'S LAST CARD

BY BRADLEY J. KAYL

He felt a distant prick on his arm. As he woke to the dim light, a leaden heat burned in his veins, then a cool lightness filled his head. Doctor Fremin pulled the needle away and placed it on the night stand. The doctor stood tall over his bed, seeming to sway back and forth on his feet like he was rocking on his heels to a lazy Gillespie tune. The man pushed the blanket from his chest. After attempting to sit up in his bed, he sighed and let the soft pillow slowly have its way with his head.

What did that blasted doctor think he was doing now, just swaying there? If they would all just leave him alone, with their medicines and doctor talk. . . .

"Why is everything so damned quiet around here?" the man snapped with some effort, the words coming first to his throat and, finally, out past his thick tongue. "Put on some Parker or something. It's too quiet!"

"Good to see you too, Gabriel. You've been out for hours," Doctor Fremin said calmly, closing an old-fashioned black bag that he had sitting on the end of the bed. "You seemed to be in a bit of pain, so I gave you something to ease it. You should be feeling much better now." He straightened his glasses, thinking for a what seemed a very long time. "And no Parker for you — or Monk, or Mozart, or anything else you want to listen to, for that matter. You need your rest." The doctor's voice echoed as he spoke.

Rest! Why were doctors always prattling on about rest? There was no time for the stuff. He was out fighting villains that could throw a truck when the good doctor was still playing with toy ones. "Then go, and be done with it. Leave me alone!" he said defiantly. As if Doctor Fremin knew what was best for *him*. No Parker! "I fought the Iron Duke single-handed! I was there —!"

The doctor left the room without saying anything more, his black shoes oddly silent on the hard wood floor. Gabriel tried to turn over, but his arms were too heavy and he gave up the effort. The bed began to float as if it were on a calm ocean. His eyelids fell shut as it rocked back and forth on the silent waves; he fought the feeling for some time, but eventually let the darkness wash over his thin frame.

He lay on a hammock suspended between two brilliant palms. The dark water beneath him lapped at the bright trunks. There was no land as far as he could see — and he didn't care about that at all. He looked far out at the distant horizon, where the two blues met, and noticed a storm gathering there; small flashes like silvery moths played in the black clouds. He wondered how long he would take to reach them if he decided to swim the distance. He wondered if flying wasn't, perhaps, a better option.

He reached into his baggy pocket, searching for his flying Tarot, but he couldn't seem to locate it. Instead, a different card kept finding his fingers. Its pulse of energy was unfamiliar to him. He held the card up so that he could take a better look at it, but the moon was bright in his eyes and he couldn't quite make it out, no matter what angle he turned it. Which was it? If he could just make out a number, he would know. He became frustrated. Was it *la Force* — Strength? Or was it *l'Empereur* — the Emperor? Was that a tree there, or a shield? He couldn't be sure.

A cool breeze then sprang up and tugged the card from his hands. It spun end over end and landed in the water, floating face down. It was too far to reach down and fish out, so he abandoned it and shifted his attention to the wide fronds high above and listened to their papery rustlings. The sound became more and more strange, as if the trees were somehow calling him, calling his name. . . .

"Gabriel. Gabriel! It's time to get up," said the doctor standing over Gabriel's bed, gently pushing his shoulder. His coat was a different colour now. And so was his tie. He must have brought a change of clothes in his bag. He was such a clever doctor, always planning ahead.

"What is it? I was just resting my eyes for a moment. Can't a person do that sort of thing, or does your magic doctoring book forbid it?"

"It's time for your medicine," Doctor Fremin said. He placed a glass of water on the night stand and popped open a couple of brown bottles.

"You just gave me my medicine," he grumbled, trying to turn away under the covers.

"That was yesterday, Gabriel. You've slept the night through. It's midday now, the twenty-seventh." The doctor handed him his glass of water with some pills, which he took with a grimace on his face.

Gabriel frowned, trying to get a bearing on the time. "I know perfectly well what day it is," he lied. "What difference does it make? I'm an old man now — what use do I have for calendars?" His confusion embarrassed him in front of the doctor and he tried to change the subject. "Back in the day, though, I could dish it out. I'm sure you've heard of the Iron Duke? A terror, a real demon — well, I was there when it nearly defeated Sentinel. I was there. It is something I'll never forget for as long as I —"

A forceful knock at the front door interrupted Gabriel's train of thought. The doctor perked up and headed for the front room without acknowledging the story's beginning or its pause. Gabriel took another swallow of water, and a hot wave settled over his body. He felt warm and clammy. He wished someone would turn the heat down, or draw the shades. The shade always comforted him. . . .

"You have visitors," the doctor said dryly, stepping into the doorway.

A tall man walked in behind the doctor with an older woman holding onto his arm. He was a handsome man with broad shoulders and sharp blue eyes. A spattering of grey dusted his otherwise dark black hair, accenting his weathered, yet cheerful face.

"Who's that? Who is that over there?" Gabriel asked. "Is that . . . is that . . . it *is*. Maxwell. Max-well Li-ber-ty. It only took you, how long — twenty, thirty years to get here? So, you've come to see a sick old man."

Gabriel grinned mischievously at Max. That look of good humour betrayed Gabriel's chastisements as the friendly jabs they were. The two men hadn't spoken much since Gabriel quit the Guard, but not out of any animosity.

"It has been too long, Gabriel. I am sorry for not coming sooner — time goes so fast, as they say," Max noted. His voice was deep with concern.

Gabriel noticed that age had finally diminished his old friend's youthful appearance, but he still maintained the proud posture that would always mark him as Sentinel.

The woman at Max's side had also succumbed to age's march, even more heavily than Max had. Wide grey streaks lined her cascading black hair, and deep lines wove their way down her face. Her proud, brown eyes peered at Gabriel, directly, intently. The stare gave him a sense of warmth and kindness.

"And that could only be Katherine. How are you these days, Katherine?"

"The more important question is: How are you?" Katherine asked pointedly.

"Yes, how do you feel?" Maxwell walked over to Gabriel's bed side and looked down at him. His wide shoulders seemed to crowd the small room.

"We came right over when we heard . . ." Katherine's voice trailed off.

"Heard what? What did you hear, and from who? Nasty rumours flying around, is all." Suddenly a thought sprang up in Gabriel's mind. "It's that bird of yours, isn't it? Of course. What did he tell you? I'm perfectly fine — fit as can be."

"The Raven Spirit does not lie, Gabriel. He has seen your shadow roaming the plains of the ancestors." Katherine's tone was serious, and Gabriel felt it would be foolish to argue with her.

The doctor had been silent this whole time, which irritated Gabriel to no end.

"Well, Doc," he rumbled, "what are you doing standing around like that? Will you stop hovering and please inform them that there's nothing to bother about? It's not as if a little setback is the end of the world!"

The room grew hot again, and Gabriel felt his body become heavy against the bed. Dim lights massed on the edge of his vision and fluttered there like anxious moths. Then, more and more of the flickering flames gathered and fought for his attention, just beyond his direct view. He tried to shoo them away from his face, but quickly tired of the exertion — though he justified his inaction by telling himself that they weren't bothering him too much. Eventually, he even began to feel at peace with their strange movements, hypnotised by their wheeling and blinking.

The moths were certainly out in force tonight, flashing underneath the streetlights like tiny fireworks. He hated patrolling at this time of year — it was always so damned cold. There was no snow yet, but the air was frigid enough to freeze your breath solid and make you question why you were out on the street to begin with.

Gabriel pulled the collar of his trench coat tight about his face and stamped his legs to get some warmth in them. The moths collected and fluttered around the dim, yellow streetlight. It was strange, he realized, that the bugs should be out in the winter, especially in such numbers. He thought about reaching for one of them, but his mask began to irritate his face with its cold edges. He brought a gloved finger up under it to scratch and, in the same instant, felt another particularly sharp gust of wind behind him.

"Damn breeze," he muttered and hunched his shoulders against it.

"What was that?" came a deep voice from behind him.

Gabriel jumped and quickly wheeled, while drawing from his pocket one of his Tarot cards. He wasn't sure which one it was he drew, but he held the card aloft anyway, preparing to activate it. It began to glow with a warm golden light.

"There won't be any need for that," said the man. He held one hand before him in a supplicating gesture, but was obviously unafraid. "We're on the same side here. I apologise for startling you." His voice was smooth and sure.

Gabriel noticed the man's costume then: red, white, and blue, with a golden eagle iconically stretched across his chest. The surprise slowly wore off and his heart rate steadied in his chest. He had seen his visitor on the news countless times — delivering speeches before Congress, raising money for charities, fighting supervillains. He was Sentinel, superhero and self-proclaimed protector of the United States.

Gabriel had never been this close to a superhero in his life and the enormity of the moment weighed on him. He looked Sentinel over, trying to remember every detail. He was tall, but mostly he was just solid — solid like a brick wall or an eighteen-wheeled truck is solid. He stood on the sidewalk with his arms crossed, and Gabriel felt quite certain that if Sentinel didn't want to move, there wasn't a thing in the world that could move him.

"Sentinel," Gabriel stammered under his breath. He then said the first thing to come to his mind, and immediately felt stupid at his statement of the obvious. "Freezing night, isn't it?"

"Now that you mention it — yes, it is," Sentinel replied, smiling without showing his teeth.

"Well, what can I do for you? I mean, what brings you down here to my neck of the woods?" Gabriel asked. "I'm Arcanum, by the way."

"I already know who you are, Mister Major. It's a pleasure to meet you." He held out his hand.

Gabriel was only slightly surprised that Sentinel knew his real name — little slipped past the attention of the Guard. "It is quite a pleasure to meet you, too." Gabriel eagerly grabbed the man's hand and shook it. He could feel the immense strength behind the grip.

"I only want a couple minutes of your time. Then you can go back to your patrol."

"Of course. Take as much as you need."

"Good. Would you like a cup of coffee maybe? I know I'd like to get out of this chill. . . ."

Gabriel realised the man was just being polite — everyone knew that Sentinel was impervious to cold and just about everything else — but he was glad for the chance to get something warm into him anyway. "Sure, I know a place that isn't too far," he said.

The two men found their way to a spot named *Porter's* Gabriel frequented. It was a secluded, but warm coffee shop on the corner, and would afford the two men some privacy.

"Mister Major, let me get to the point —"

"Please, call me Gabriel."

"Gabriel, then. We've been watching you for some time," Sentinel began. "When I say 'we' I mean the Guard."

Gabriel looked up from his cup of coffee. He had followed the Guard as much as he followed Sentinel himself. He was fascinated with all the different members of the group: Mother Raven, Red Phoenix, Caliburn, Slipstream. In all honesty, it was the Guard that had gotten Gabriel to start patrolling his neighbourhood, using his powers with the Tarot to protect his family and a couple of square miles around his apartment complex.

"We are very impressed with your track record. For instance, we had been looking for the Hangman for quite some time in connection with the lynchings of thirteen transients." Sentinel took a sip of coffee. "You captured him not too far from this location, if I'm not mistaken. He's now safely in the Manhattan House of Detention, awaiting trial."

Gabriel tried to conceal his growing enthusiasm. He had a feeling he knew where this was going and he hoped his surprise didn't show too much.

"In fact, this feat alone would have been enough for us, but after your subsequent defeat of Red Minstrel, we were certain of your potential. I stand fully prepared, on behalf of the Guard, to offer you a position with us, Gabriel."

Sentinel crossed his hands on the table in front of his mug and waited.

Despite Gabriel's façade of cool, he was actually speechless. Finally he managed to get his mouth working again. "A position? What kind of position?"

"It would be only a junior placement to begin with. You'd be given specific patrols, asked to investigate misdemeanours and assist law enforcement — that sort of thing. If your performance continued to be so impressive — and it seems likely it would — you may be promoted to a more senior position, with time."

Gabriel was silent for a long moment before answering. He looked through the window of the diner as small snowflakes began to fall in front of the street lamps. "I . . ." he began. "I . . . don't know exactly what to say."

"No need to say anything at this time. We understand the gravity of what we're asking. Your whole life would have to change, if you accepted. Take a night to sleep on it. Then stop by the Olympian Tower tomorrow at ten o'clock and we will discuss any questions or concerns you might still have." Sentinel walked to the door of the coffee shop and turned: "Ten-sharp, Arcanum — don't forget." With this, he leapt into the sky and was instantly gone, leaving snowflakes swirling in his wake.

Gabriel pulled his coat tight and whistled to himself in amazement. Then he remembered that, in his initial surprise, he had actually drawn one of the Tarot on Sentinel. He reached into his pocket and fished it out. A painted jester wearing bright red, yellow, and blue stared at him sublimely: *le Mat* — the Fool. He laughed aloud when he thought of what might have happened if he had activated the thing. What was he going to do, juggle Sentinel to death? He laughed harder as he walked from the diner into the snowy night.

"The Fool. Anything but the Fool," he muttered.

"What was that, Gabriel?" Katherine asked. She leaned over the side of the bed and placed her hand on his arm. It was cold on his skin. "Did you want something?"

He felt thirsty, and his body was hotter than ever — it was as if he were resting in a bed of sticky, heated sand. He wanted to push it away from him, but the more he moved the more it seemed to cling to him, the deeper he seemed to sink in the roughness. He looked over at the woman who was speaking to him, feeling the pillow grate against his cheek as he turned his head. She was an old woman with deep wrinkles — fissures, almost — in her dark skin. Ripples of heated air seemed to pass before her face and obscure her from him. Then the waves briefly subsided and he could make out her kind expression.

"Mother Raven," he whispered. "It *is* you. Good to see you."

"And you, Gabriel. What is it I can get for you?"

"A glass of water or something. Someone must have turned the heat up in this house. That blasted doctor of mine I'd bet. Turn it down already, Fremin," he tried to call out.

She picked up a glass of water from the night stand and handed it to him. He took a few sips and handed it back. The water was like a thick, metallic syrup in his mouth; it did little to cool him.

He looked again at Mother Raven's face. Age had obscured her beauty, but could not touch her eyes. Those were as youthful, as beautiful, as ever, as if she kept a great and peaceful secret inside her, one that you could somehow glimpse through her eyes. Gabriel reflected that his own secrets were far from peaceful, that if he had somehow found peace in them, then they would have ceased being secrets; it was a destructive paradox. He kept only that which was violent and shameful close to his heart. Only those things did he keep as secrets. And those guilty things would be revealed if he died. The thought pained him; both the admission that he might be dying and that he might not have the time to tie up all of the loose ends of his life.

His mind hovered around that realization until a beautiful and bright light like a glowing butterfly drew his attention away. *What was it, exactly? Where was that radiance?* The defiant fact intruded briefly: *It must be Beth.* But before he would acknowledge the truth to himself, he yanked his mind back like a man pulling on the leash of an unruly dog, and turned his thoughts forcibly elsewhere.

"So many damned things have changed these past decades," Gabriel said, thinking mostly about himself.

"The world of man is always changing, Gabriel — a magnificent river amongst shifting stones. Sometimes murky, sometimes clear." Katherine was sure with her words, always sure.

Then his mind wandered again and alighted on the affiliation to which he had devoted so much of his life. It was strange to him to think of a devotion in the past tense. "How is the Guard these days?"

Katherine took a moment before answering. Her eyes seemed to soften as she spoke. "The Guard was disbanded years ago. The government decided it had little use for its heroes. Now they simply find young kids, those too ignorant or naive to question their orders. Expendable soldiers in replaceable military hardware seems to be the way of the future. With the right technology, anyone can function as a superhero. Once again, the river of man has become dark." Then something occurred to Katherine. "But, you already know this, Gabriel." She placed her hand gently on his shoulder and looked into his face. He looked back, and the embarrassment of his memory loss subsided before her cradling gaze.

"Yes, yes. Of course I —" he began to explain.

"So, how is he doing?" asked Max in a booming voice as he entered the bedroom. His shadow was large against the far wall. Gabriel turned his head against the rough pillow to get a better look at the man. He had changed into a black turtleneck sweater and brown slacks. Gabriel wondered how he could wear such a stifling shirt in all this heat.

"I am doing just fine, thank you," Gabriel tried to shout, but managed only a feeble whisper that seemed lost, even in the small room. "I'm just hot, is all," he finally admitted, sighing as he did.

Max pulled up a small stool and sat at the foot of the bed. From this perspective, Gabriel thought Max looked like an overgrown clown on what appeared for a moment to be a very small tricycle. He thought briefly of laughing, then decided he wasn't in the mood. Something else kept poking at his mind; the moth was back again, flitting around in his memories. He tried to run from it, even invited pain to sit in its stead, but the thought wouldn't leave him. Finally he vocalised what had been prodding him.

"Sentinel —"

"Please, Gabe, call me Max. Sentinel no longer exists. I'm just a fly-fisherman now, a retiree who lives happily in Montana." Max smiled at him with only a hint of sadness in his face.

"Max," Gabriel continued, lowering his voice, "have you heard from Beth?"

A sudden silence descended upon the room. At first, neither Katherine nor Max made a move against its force. Then, when the quiet had had its way with the both of them and they could bear it no longer, Max stood up and moved to the opposite side of the bed from Katherine. Slowly he crouched down; his height was such that he could still look Gabriel in the face.

"Gabe," Max said gently, "Beth is dead."

Gabriel closed his eyes tightly against the light in the room, which had suddenly become bright. The sweat on his forehead became gritty and unbearable. His mind scrambled for an anchoring memory, for reference, for anything.

"She died years ago." Max's words came in echoes that grew and subsided in volume as the truth pounded at some lost part of Gabriel's being. He felt as if his head were resting in a pool of sloshing water, a bottomless font of darkness.

"You were there when she died. . . ."

And then his head was plunged under.

It was raining hard and he was looking at himself in a deep puddle. A thick black mask and wide-brimmed hat covered his features. What was that dripping from underneath his mask? He reached up to his face and pulled back a bloody glove. His face was hot where he had been cut.

The blood dripped from his fingers and mixed with the water on the ground. He looked next to the puddle and saw a large piece of cement spattered with more blood — his, it seemed. He looked around, and his gaze was captured by the sight of a smoking car that was sticking out of a two-story window high above. Pieces of the building were still falling around him. Even as he gaped at the plummeting debris, he heard a woman's voice somewhere to his right. He couldn't quite make out what she was saying.

"Arrrrr . . . cccaaaa. . . !" screamed the voice.

Then the words were suddenly sharp in his ears: "Arcanum! Head's up!"

He looked for the speaker and found a slender woman dressed in a silver jumpsuit with a shimmering lace veil. She was gesturing at him frantically. His vision blurred for an instant, until he wiped the blood and rain from his eyes. Then he could see her clearly again.

Luna?

He could hear her, but it was as if she were calling him through a long, empty tunnel.

Beth?

"Dammit, Arcanum! Watch out!"

She gestured to a point some distance in front of him. Arcanum turned just in time to see the Iron Duke, a ten foot monolith of plated steel armour, pick up and hurl a VW bug his way. The blue beetle arced through the air, heading directly toward him. He tried to scramble left, but his boot slipped in the muddy street and his right knee came down heavily on the pavement. Pain flared under his kneecap as he tried to regain his footing. The bug was large in his vision now; he could clearly make out the *VW* on the hood as the metal flared in the glare from the streetlight. Then, above him, out of seemingly nowhere, a bright golden streak appeared and slammed into the vehicle. The car burst with a loud, metallic explosion and crashed into a nearby lamp post, where it landed with a tremendous boom. Sparks from torn power lines rained down on the car's hood and sizzled on the wet sidewalk.

"Get up!" Sentinel said, landing on the ground next to Arcanum. "I need you in this."

Arcanum pushed himself up as the Iron Duke picked up a Gremlin and flung it toward Luna. Sentinel took off in a golden blaze and redirected the car into a nearby park. It slammed through a fountain, then splashed down in a nearby duck pond, spraying water in a fan of white.

Luna fired two silvery rays of energy from her outstretched hands. The bolts shot past the Duke, missing his head by inches, and severed two more power lines. The black cables snaked to the ground in a shower of blue sparks, only to leap and dance like the lines torn from the light pole by the VW.

Arcanum reached into his pocket and felt the Tarot deck there. He ran his hand over the many edges, recognising each card by feel alone. Finally, he came to the one that he needed: *le Soleil* — the Sun. He drew the card and held it aloft. As he did, it exploded into a great fiery light. Stark shadows from the nearby cars and light posts leapt onto the building walls as blazing tendrils of orange and blue entwined Arcanum's body and transformed him into a locus of blinding radiance.

The Duke, a pick-up truck already high above his head, snapped his attention toward the bright light. His eyes flared a deep red, and he brought back one massive arm to throw the truck. Arcanum outstretched one hand and fired a searing blast at the truck's exposed underside. It exploded in a massive fireball, showering the street in burning chunks of metal and rubber. The concussion blew the frame of the car from the Duke's hands. His armoured body shrouded in flaming gasoline, he strode toward Arcanum.

Sentinel clenched both fists before him as he streaked toward the Iron Duke. He slammed into the iron monolith's midsection, sending both of them crashing through the glass doors of the First Interstate Building. A mass of people, who had mistakenly thought themselves safe inside, escaped into the rainy street, screaming and tripping over one another.

Luna rushed over to where Arcanum stood, and got as close as she dared to the figure, still burning like a miniature sun. Even though her face was covered by a shimmering veil, and flames leaped and danced around his eyes, Arcanum could still make out her beautiful features — her graceful jaw, her inviting lips, her bright azure eyes, which were now intent on the bank's entrance.

"Let's go," Luna said, starting toward the bank at a run. "'We've got to get in there."

Arcanum followed, his blazing form a contrast to her silvery light. As they approached the building, they could hear the battle raging inside.

They stepped over the broken glass and entered in time to see Sentinel slug the Duke with a massive right hook. The behemoth flew across the floor, crashed through the doubled bullet-proof glass above the teller's windows, and slammed into the bank vault door with a resounding *clang*. The reinforced door bent inward, and cracks spread along the plaster around the frame. The Iron

Duke stood up and ripped the massive steel door from its hinges. Luna fired two shining blasts of light from her hands, trying to knock it from his grasp, but the polished surface reflected the beams into the ceiling where they sliced open two neat holes.

The Duke hefted the hunk of metal and heaved it at Sentinel. Though he could have dodged the clumsy projectile with ease, Sentinel instead braced himself for the impact. Arcanum didn't wonder why — if the door got past Sentinel, it might harm someone in the crowd outside — but he flinched in sympathy as the missile caught Sentinel in the chest and drove him back through the far wall, into a large office.

Arcanum took the opportunity to level a flaming blast at the Duke. He put both hands together in front of him, palms outward, and summoned the energy forth. The blast hit the construct square in the abdomen, knocking him off his feet and driving him deep into the vault. Arcanum raised his voice in a shout of triumph, but even this small victory was not long lived. The Iron Duke lumbered into the vault's doorway, a bright mark glowing red where the blast had hit him. At the same time, Sentinel stalked from the office, brushing dust from his arms and chest. Faster than Arcanum thought possible for such a bulky thing, the Duke was on Sentinel. They both tumbled back into the office, smashing chunks of plaster from the already-gaping hole in the wall.

Gabriel signalled Luna to follow him to the breech. They both sprinted across the bank, but before they could get through the opening, the Duke appeared there, stopping both of them short. Beyond the hulking metal juggernaut, Arcanum could just make out a second large breach, in the exterior wall, but no sign of Sentinel. He must have been knocked out into the street.

Luna fired a silvery bolt, this time aiming for the Iron Duke's legs. The ray sliced through a cylindrical section of metal just behind the Duke's heel; it seemed to be some sort of piston assembly or hydraulic mechanism. There was a sharp hiss, and black liquid sprayed across the wall. The Iron Duke let loose a deep, hollow bellow — whether in frustration or in actual pain, Arcanum couldn't tell. Then the monstrous construct stepped forward in a large half-hop and, with a swing that scraped the ceiling, back-fisted Luna across the face.

Arcanum saw a spray of blood burst from Luna's mouth even as the Duke swung his other fist and connected with her jaw. The terrible sound of her neck snapping filled Gabriel's head, as if it were the only noise in an otherwise-silent world. Her body spun across the floor and careened into a desk, limp, her veil stained a deep red. Arcanum felt his heart tear in his chest at the horrible sight.

He looked from Luna to the monster before him with such fury that he thought the flames surrounding his body would consume him. The metallic beast simply glared down at him with its smouldering eyes. He knew he had a split second before the thing was upon him, too.

Stepping back, he fumbled in his pocket for another card. He thumbed their many edges, searching for the one that his heart now burned for. He felt for its tinge of rage, its particular moan of raw anger — and found it: *le Diable* — the Devil. Its power was unpredictable, destructive, and fearsome. He would only use this card at times when his heart was filled with uncontrollable fury, as it was now.

Arcanum drew the card. A terrible heat poured into him, filling him like he was a great, seething chalice. His eyes began to burn and tear, and his heart pounded stronger and stronger, driving his blood into a frenzy. He could feel the sweat begin to drip into his eyes, but he blinked it away, his gaze never wavering from his adversary. The monstrosity before him appeared different now — he could see its inner workings of steel gears and pipes. Valves opened and closed; pistons worked tirelessly in a strange kind of synchronization; fluids poured through tubes endlessly filling and releasing. Most importantly, he could see weaknesses where none had been apparent before; a tiny flaw — an internal leak — just below the Iron Duke's right shoulder. The monster must have suffered the injury in one of its collisions with Sentinel. It was no more than a tiny crack, but perhaps just enough.

Arcanum feigned fatigue and slumped, letting the thing approach him. Then, before the Duke could respond, he leapt forward and grabbed the beast by the right wrist. He placed his right foot against its waist for leverage and pulled with all the fury the card had granted him. Pain shot through the vibrating muscles in his back and shoulders, but Arcanum had resolved that either his enemy's arm or his own would tear free before he would ever let go.

From where his hands grasped the metal a bright reddish glow began to spread — the armour was heating up underneath his grip. Arcanum arched his back and locked his leg out; under the influence of the Devil card his muscles had grown and become dense; he felt that he could easily heft a truck and throw it a city block.

The Iron Duke, sensing the threat, grabbed his right shoulder with his opposite hand and tried to hold it in place. Arcanum looked through the thing's casing, saw that the smooth clickings and whirrings that had formerly controlled the movements of its right arm were no more. A visible cacophony of sliding machinery writhed beneath the Duke's metal exterior armour. Smoke rose from the joint and small squirts of fire leapt forth. The gap between the upper forearm and the shoulder widened.

The Duke shook his entire body, violently, from side to side. For all his efforts to dislodge his foe, he was unsuccessful; Gabriel had found a point of leverage and held on like a wild animal. If anything, the thrashing served to further tear the metal around the shoulder. Arcanum let out a grisly yell, a sound from hell itself, as the arm tore loose from its moorings. Sparks and blue flames spewed from the joint as the appendage and Arcanum fell to the floor in a great heap.

Once more the Duke threw his head back, and a grating, metallic cry echoed from a steel grill that served as his mouth. Flame and smoke continued to pour from the wires and tubes now protruding from his shoulder, but he focused his attention on the dazed hero sprawled before him heaving breath after laboured breath.

Arcanum did not even brace for a killing blow he dimly knew would fall upon him. But it never came. The Duke lifted his remaining arm above his head and flew up through the wrecked ceiling, his path marked by a trail of oil and smoke.

As the pain fog lifted from his mind, Arcanum heard the crashing of floor after floor recede as the Iron Duke fled up through the building's many levels. He barely flinched as the debris rained down around him. It felt as if his entire body were on fire. His eyes burned unbearably, and he knew that the fury flooding his heart gave him strength enough to rip down the building — and every other one that stood between him and the Duke. But if he waited any longer to deactivate the Tarot, he feared he might be lost forever in that ferocity.

With trembling hands he drew the card forth, then closed off its power to him. As the flow of energy left his body, he felt as if his skeleton were being pulled with it. He fell limp to the floor, entirely unable to move. He shivered uncontrollably. Then, after several long moments, his limbs responded to him one by one and he was able to slowly pull himself up.

He half-crawled to where Luna lay. Her body was twisted and bent against the broken desk. One arm was thrown up above her head, as if she were trying to defend herself even in death. Arcanum reached out a shaking hand and pushed her bloody veil from her face. All that greeted him was an expressionless stare.

He had expected there to be a certain beauty in death or, perhaps, for the last expression on her face to be one of defiance. But there was nothing.

He touched her cheek and tried to wipe away some of the blood, but his gloved hand only smeared the gore over her white face, transforming her blank visage into something sickening. Arcanum hung his head and wept.

"I loved you," Gabriel said.

"What did he say, Doctor?"

He could feel the room about him like a great black box. Faces blurred and faded before him.

"He's sweating terribly."

He could hear the voices come to him from far away.

"There's little I can do. . . ."

Someone had lit a candle near him. He gazed into its flame as it danced. There were only faces around him now — no bodies, nothing that could touch the ground. The fire grew before him; he could feel its warmth even through the heat of his skin.

"Could someone play some music?"

No one responded to him.

"We should have kept in touch."

As he continued to stare into the flame, it changed colour. First becoming golden, then subsiding into a cleaner, clearer silver.

"I'm here, Gabriel."

After some time, he resolved that it wasn't a candle at all, but the moon. Its rays touched him from far away and cooled his skin. He reached for the light and found that he could touch it; it felt cool and warm all at once, and his heart swelled with it. The light grew brighter before him, as if it were travelling to him, or he to it. His body was weightless, his senses focused on the radiance — save for a small part of him that felt a throbbing coming from his pocket.

He reached in and felt the familiar edges of his Tarot deck. Each card called to him with its particular song — there was galloping, and laughter, cold armour and crisp lightning, the points of a crown and a weighty sword; there was desire and the vastness of a night sky, an old man and deep despair. But he knew that these were all wrong for the task before him now.

He thumbed through and finally found the one — the one that was approaching now, the one that, this time, called to him. He was frightened to draw it. What would come of it? What would come of his life? But something prodded him onward.

He drew the card, and a blank silence greeted him.

The rectangle of heavy paper was utterly devoid of markings — an endless, featureless plain.

The light of the moon began to fade. Gabriel sighed; he'd half-expected to find Beth emerging from its brilliant silver. But there was nothing.

Finally the light diminished until it was a dim point, far in the distance. He felt a sharp disappointment, then watched as the Tarot card, too, faded before him and vanished altogether from his view.

MIRROR, RUST, AND DARK

BY ALEXANDER MARSH FREED

"I was doing okay," Ami said, smiling sheepishly as she twisted her fingers together. "I wasn't comfortable, but I was okay. I was having lunch, I was a little cold, and I was looking around. I heard someone laughing near the hot dog vendor, and I glanced over, and I saw this little kid who'd dropped his hot dog on the ground. Four years old, maybe. The kid was crying, and his brother — I guess it was his brother — was laughing. And everything about Dark came back to me, and I couldn't breathe."

Doctor Jacobs tucked a lock of brown hair behind her left ear — Ami wondered if she knew how often she did that — and cocked her head. "What happened then?"

Ami shrugged. "I froze. My chest hurt, I couldn't breathe. I just sat there, staring. Feeling panicky. I think I was shaking." She studied the creases of her knuckles. "Next thing I remember, someone was tapping my shoulder and asking me if I was okay. I ran off." *After hitting him, but not hard. . . .*

"What scared you so much?" Doctor Jacobs frowned, then amended, "That's not what I mean. What brought on that reaction from you? What triggered it?"

"It was the same thing," Ami said. "That was Dark. That was everything in Dark. Little . . . repulsive acts. Everywhere."

"And you thought you'd shifted universes again? That you were back there?"

Ami looked across the room, staring out the window at the grey clouds and jagged angles of the Washington skyline. "I knew where I was. I just thought there . . ." *There was no difference.* "I was afraid of seeing it here."

"That's understandable," Doctor Jacobs said. "So what can you do? You can't avoid people doing rotten things. So how do you remind yourself of the difference between their world and ours?"

"I don't," Ami said. "I teach myself to get used to it."

The session lasted another twenty minutes. When it ended, Ami headed through the white hospital corridors, glanced at the entrance to the residential wing, and walked by the front desk and out onto the street. It felt odd to leave Doctor Jacobs that way; after four months of walking directly to her old room, it was the second time in as many weeks that she'd left the hospital instead. It was hard to adjust to. Not the only thing.

She tugged at her jacket's zipper, mentally whispering to the metal to help it join its teeth as she moved down the sidewalk toward the metro. She did her best to ignore the silhouettes of people in her peripheral vision. If she kept her eyes low, she wouldn't see anyone, and if she didn't see anyone, she wouldn't be reminded of Dark. She wouldn't have nightmares, she wouldn't panic, and she'd make it to the next day.

It didn't work. Her eyes met those of a homeless man lying on a grate, and she half-tripped as she tried to keep from remembering how she knew him. Too late — in Dark, she'd seen a guy in a suit spend fifteen minutes genuinely trying to convince the man to find shelter. They'd been getting ready to go when a cyborg — the paper said it was a Kikai Ninja — came rampaging down the street. The guy in the suit won a half-second running start by pushing the homeless man into the cyborg's path. Flying Tiger had followed the cyborg and laughed, letting both men be cut apart before finishing the fight. Ami hadn't done much more to help the men herself.

She hurried down concrete steps, over black slate tiles, then to the lights bordering the subway track. When she boarded the train, she grabbed a pole, asked it to try to stay stable, and inhaled the odours of sweat, fast food, and newsprint. Tuning out the conversations around her, she went over her remaining chores for the day: buy food, figure out when she could afford to pay what bills, maybe start looking for a job.

When she reached her apartment, she tossed a slim handful of mail on the kitchen counter and hung her jacket on the door hook. As she poured a glass of water and tossed two white pills from an amber bottle down her throat, she listened to her voice mail play. One telemarketer, and one message from Mel, who wanted to know when Ami was coming to Empire City to visit. Ami made a mental note to call her back.

She looked more closely at her mail as she drank the water and rinsed her glass. Beneath the catalogues and other junk was a manila envelope with a Food and Drug Administration logo. She grabbed it and dropped into a chair as she tore it open.

Inside was a single sheet of paper. Ami skimmed the key phrases: *wish you well . . . overcome your recent health difficulties . . . return to your position as consumer safety officer, or help you find a different position in which you are more comfortable.*

She rolled the paper into a tube, and closed her eyes. The words weren't important, anyway. The intent was obvious.

The Ultra-Elites wanted her back.

As Ami sat in a steel chair in the dim lab, waiting for the drug to take effect, she wished there was something complicated about her mission for her to review. When she arrived in Dark, she would find the artefact, analyse it, and meet her contact at sunset. He would get her home. Simple. Mike and the other field agents would laugh if they knew she was terrified.

Ami rubbed at the sore spot on her arm, her fingers tingling and beginning to numb. Had the doctor said five minutes? She had a while to wait.

She'd made it abundantly clear to the director that she didn't want to go. She'd explained that she'd only slid to Dark a few times knowing it wasn't a nightmare. She'd asked why they couldn't find the artefact on this side — see if Egide or GenTech had salvaged it. If the artefact was big enough that it couldn't be moved from Dark, then it would be hard to conceal.

The director had listened patiently, and bowed his head. "We'll try what we can," he'd said, "but having you slide is our best bet. If you refuse to go, however, I won't force you."

So Ami had agreed, because somewhere in her heart she felt guilty for sitting at her desk while the field team risked their lives. And, though she'd never admit it, the thought of being able to help — to go out and do something good, even once — excited her. She wanted to do something good.

Her eyelids drifted shut. They felt sticky when she tried to open them again, and she realized something prickly was touching her face. The sounds of conversation in the hallway were louder, and — no, not just louder. The sounds were different.

She crawled onto her hands and knees, and stared at the grass below her. She felt a series of quick taps on her back, and thought it was rain until she looked up and saw three children on a park bench nearby, tossing small pellets of dirt.

She swore, brushing herself off as she stood. The children laughed and didn't stop their bombardment. *You made it*, Ami told herself. *Go. Find the artefact. Ignore the kids; it's not their fault they're Dark. . . .*

Ami bit her lip, pulled herself out of the park, out of her memories, and focused on her bedroom ceiling. *Right then*, she thought. Less than a minute in Dark, and it was enough for any secret excitement she'd harboured over helping to become self-loathing over her agreement to go. Not for getting in over her head, but for being careless and naive enough to think that going was a good idea. The first in a long string of good thoughts that had turned on her.

She flipped her pillow over, looking for a patch not damp from her breath, and rolled onto her side. She still had hours left until morning.

"They want you back?" Mel asked, scraping a French fry through the cheese at the bottom of a plastic basket. Her white dreadlocks looked orange under the neon window sign, and her sweatshirt's black sleeves dipped dangerously toward her plate.

"Apparently. I haven't talked to them yet." Ami smiled without feeling. She'd gone to an art museum in an effort to relax before coming to see Mel, and had gotten into a humiliating shouting match with a security guard when she'd tried to talk to a bronze bust. Touching it had been a stupid thing to do, rude and disrespectful. She'd never have done it a year ago. So she'd made an idiot out of herself, and now it was hard to get into a friendly mood.

"What are you planning to do?" Mel's tone was sceptical.

Ami bit into her hamburger, using the time spent chewing to consider her answer. "I don't know," she eventually said.

"You know they're using you. You were there, what — a month? — before they sent you to Dark Empire?"

"It was Dark Washington. Dark Empire is just where they tried to invade Empire City from. We call the whole place 'Dark.' It's shorter." Ami glanced around, in reflex. No one was listening, though. The restaurant was busy, and noisy, and no one there cared what anyone else was doing.

Mel leaned forward across the table. Ami resisted the urge to push her back. "Whatever," Mel said. "You join because they say they'll stop your slides, and then they *send* you there and don't retrieve you for months? That's the sort of thing mom told me about ELITE doing, and if anything, they're worse now."

"They didn't *intentionally* leave me behind. Mel, they're not bad people. We do important work. We —"

Mel was staring, her eyebrows raised. Ami put her hamburger down and sighed. "Okay," she said. "Let's not get into this. We've read the same articles. Your mother told you things, and I've been there. We disagree."

"Okay. I'm just being concerned."

"I know. Thanks."

"So how'd you get back?"

Ami bit her lip and whispered, "Let's not talk about it."

Neither woman spoke a while, until Ami forced herself to find a topic. "How's your career going? You keeping busy?"

Mel perked up, apparently forgetting her grievances. "Things are great. Got a job as a talent scout for a music company, and I have a flexible enough schedule that I can spend time as Silk. And *that's* going well, too. Even met the Lady of the Lantern the other week. She said she liked my costume."

Ami smirked and picked at the remnants of Mel's French fries. "Isn't she a criminal?"

Mel shrugged. "Wanted for questioning. You should come with me some night. Get an outfit, and I'll show you around. Did they give you a code name?"

Ami snorted. "I'd be a lot of use. I can ask muggers to get *really* close so I can tell their guns not to shoot me. And yeah, I'm Conductor. Like the guy who runs a train."

Mel didn't bother containing her laughter.

Ami's mood improved after lunch, as she wandered the city with Mel. She split her attention between her friend and the buildings, determined to ignore the cruelty and misery people around her were surely exhibiting. When sunset came, Mel invited Ami to stay the night, but Ami refused without considering it. The thought of sleeping in someone else's home, vulnerable . . . *no*.

They made it to the train station before Mel asked, smiling as her voice trembled, "Did you see me, when you were there?"

Ami slowly shook her head, and looked from the departures board to Mel. "No," she said. "I was in DC the whole time."

Mel hesitated, then went on, speaking fast. "I guess it doesn't matter. It wouldn't have really been me, anyway."

Ami knew that Mel was looking for reassurance, but she answered honestly anyway. "Yeah," she said, "it would have been you. You ever have a nightmare, where everything's gone wrong, and so you find yourself doing . . . things, since everything's wrong anyway and it just doesn't matter?"

"I'm sorry," Mel said.

"That's you," Ami said. "You're the same, but instead of being basically good, you do everything that's twisted and wrong and hurtful that comes to mind, and occasionally give in to an impulse to be nice. You regret *those* later, because they come back to haunt you."

"I shouldn't have brought it up."

"You're right. I'll talk to you later."

On the ride home, Ami sat with her knees against her chest, listening to the shriek of train tracks in her head to drown out her fantasies of mangling the loud passengers behind her.

During the week after her return to Washington, Ami spent hours every evening in front of her computer, bleary eyed and slow, reading about MK-ULTRA projects and ELITE Operations.

It wasn't that Mel had touched a nerve, Ami told herself. She just wanted to reacquaint herself with the Ultra-Elites' predecessors before committing herself again. MK-ULTRA had experimented on metahumans, brainwashed agents, and killed innocents before being revealed to the public and shut down. ELITE had committed assassinations, toppled governments, and attacked the Guard. Given all that, and her own recent ordeal, it seemed fair for Ami to have reservations.

But times had changed, and at least ELITE had been an attempt at doing real good in the world. Not only stopping villains, but making an impact. Ending problems before they grew large enough to hurt anyone.

As she stared blankly at declassified CIA documents, her offer of employment laying by her hand — was consumer safety officer even a real job? she wondered — Ami tried to remember when she'd realized with whom she was working. There'd been the free clinic, right after college and a year after the start of the nightmares, where all the doctors could do was shrug when they found her meta-active gene. Then the government testing centre, where they'd offered her money — *good* money — to study her, and make certain her powers were benign. She'd said no, maybe later — had she really been busy, or had she been suspicious even then? — and then she'd heard about her father. There'd been no one else to pay for the nursing home.

She missed her dad.

Not that far back, then. Maybe she'd been wary, but she couldn't have known.

It had taken the centre a week to warn her that the nightmares weren't nightmares. That she was sliding into Dark, and that the teleportation was a secondary power unrelated to her metal empathy. Three more months before they created the targeted inhibitor pills and the nightmares stopped. Somewhere in there, she'd realized who "they" were, and hadn't questioned it. By the time Mel had contacted her and tried to convince her to leave, by the time she'd started the months of training before being hired as an analyst, all she didn't know was the group's name.

She almost mentioned it to Doctor Jacobs during their next session — how she'd fallen into the Ultra-Elites without ever really considering it — but decided not to. Doctor Jacobs had a high enough security clearance that Ami could talk to her about the mission. But that also meant that what they discussed might make it back to Ami's employers.

Instead, Ami mentioned that she'd gotten the job offer, and that she wasn't sure what to do.

"Are you afraid they'll send you back to Dark?" Doctor Jacobs asked.

"Not really," Ami said. Which was true. "I think they'll keep pushing me to do more field and on-site work, but that's not something I need therapy for."

Doctor Jacobs smiled and tucked a lock of hair behind her right ear. "Then why are you reluctant to go back to them?"

"Because it would be a reminder," Ami said. "I think I need some distance. For a while." Also true, as far as it went.

"Well, there are plenty of other places where someone like you could get a job. The Ascension Institute. Aegis always needs volunteers. You could even transfer to the Order, if you want to stay in government work. . . ." Doctor Jacobs searched Ami's face.

Ami picked dirt from her fingernails while studying the window shade. "I was thinking something unrelated to my powers," she said. "Secretary, paralegal — something. Fast food."

"Would that be satisfying to you?"

"Probably not, but it'd give me time." Ami paused. "I just don't know if I'm right for that work anymore. Maybe I never was. I liked the *idea* of doing good, but . . . I never did much then, and I don't know if I still have it in me to try."

"From what you've said, they appreciated your work a lot."

"That's not the same thing." Ami frowned. "Haven't we had this conversation before?"

Doctor Jacobs shook her head. "Not that I remember."

After the session, Ami had to force herself not to walk to the train home. That morning, she'd noticed she was out of pills, and the empty amber bottle now lurked in her jacket pocket. It was the first time she'd needed a refill since moving out of the hospital, and she'd put off going to the testing centre as long as she could. She wondered why; she'd never run into anyone from the Ultra-Elites there, and she could be in and out in ten minutes. So why be more nervous about getting the refill than about having the nightmares come back?

Well, not come back, exactly — she had plenty of nightmares now. She just wasn't actually sliding.

She was distracted as she passed an apartment building's concrete stairway, where three teenagers were beating a boy half their size. She saw the boy's face hit an iron railing, his mouth jerking open and wrapping around a bar as blood dribbled from a cut in his forehead. *Well, that'll toughen him up*, she thought, and continued on her way. It was a block later, when she was beginning to piece together her reasoning again, that she realized what a sick thing that had been to think. Seconds after that, she realized that she could have tried to help, and wondered if she should go back.

Probably too late, and not her problem anyway, she decided. She returned to analysing her reluctance to get more pills, and bit her lip when it occurred to her why she didn't want to.

"Damn," she murmured. "I really don't believe they stop the dreams."

Before his pickup truck pulled up beside her during her walk to the bank, Ami had last seen Mike at the end of her time in Dark. She'd sought him at his home out of desperation, said things to him . . . asked his help because she couldn't stand the thought of being there any longer. She hadn't asked any more questions than necessary — she hadn't wanted to know what he was like, or what things *his* Ultra-Elites did, as much for what it would say about herself and her friends as it would say about Dark. She hadn't wanted to look into a mirror. She'd just wanted to go home.

Now she was being forced to look. Ami had felt uncomfortable refusing Mike's offer of a ride, and so she sat against the truck's grey vinyl seating, trying not to look nervous. The black fuzz of Mike's nearly shaved head looked like a shadow, and his brown jacket and jeans suggested he was leaving work.

"So, where're you heading?" Mike asked.

Ami flinched and tightened her grip on the window sill. No one had tinkered with the truck that it knew of, it told her, or installed monitoring equipment. *Good. Then he probably wasn't sent to spy on me. If he came looking for me, he was on his own. . . .*

She thanked the metal before withdrawing her hand, as Mike buzzed the window shut. "Just a few blocks down," she said. "Running some errands." A deep breath. "So. How've you been?"

"Work's been good. Got a few upgrades since you last saw me. How've you been?"

Always articulate, Ami thought, but she made herself smile. "I've been okay. Out and about again, at least."

"I heard you were sick . . ."

"Something like that." She studied his profile, and noticed the flush of his skin below his ear — and what looked like a surgical scar. He really had gotten upgrades.

194

"Sorry to hear it," Mike said, sounding like he meant it. "The team — the field team, I mean; no offence — we'd been making bets about when you were getting transferred to us. The director wanted to expedite it."

Ami's smile became a smirk, turning genuine. "I wouldn't have been any good, Mike. Trust me."

Mike shrugged noncommittally. "So, are you coming back?"

"I —" Ami hesitated. "Has anyone asked?"

"Not that I know of. I didn't realize you were on your feet again until today."

Ami opened her mouth, then waved a hand at the road and the convenience store they were about to pass. "Can you pull over here?" she asked, moments before her cell phone rang.

Mike slowed down, and Ami pulled out her phone, mouthing a *Sorry* to Mike before answering. "Hello?"

The voice at the other end was male, cheerful, and nasal. "Is this Ami Micheline?" He managed to pronounce both names wrong, souring Ami's mood further.

"Yes," she said shortly. "Who's this?"

"Dan Loubet. You dropped off a sample a few days back?"

"Oh!" *Oh. . . .* "Yes, that was me. Do you need something more?"

"No — I have your results, but I didn't know where to send them. All you left was your number."

Ami glanced at Mike, who'd pulled the truck over. He was staring out the windshield, oblivious or feigning disinterest. "Sorry about that," Ami said. "Can I pick them up?"

Dan's chipper voice continued. "Sure, but you don't have to. I can tell you exactly what the sample is."

"What is it?"

"Aspirin."

She had to get out of the truck soon, but she couldn't let Mike get suspicious. "Can you repeat that?" she asked, trying to force her heartbeat to slow.

"Aspirin. It's a placebo, I assume."

"You're sure?"

"No doubt."

Ami nodded tightly. "Well, thanks. That's a big help."

"Great. Drop by when you want a copy of the report."

"Okay. Thanks." She clicked off the phone, and looked at Mike. "Sorry. My dry cleaner messed up a dress."

Mike looked over at her so fast that Ami thought she heard his gears turn. "No problem. So . . . it's been good seeing you."

"You, too," Ami said. "Hey — do me a favour?"

"Sure thing."

Ami used the moment when she turned away to open the door to try to compose herself. "Tell the director that I'd like to talk to him about coming back."

Mike's expression didn't shift. "Okay."

"Thanks," Ami said and climbed out of the truck. "Take care," she added, slamming the door quickly enough to miss Mike's reply. He pulled away seconds later, and Ami repeated in her head everything that had just happened.

There was nothing that should have surprised her, she decided, digging her nails into her palms. Except that consumer safety officer really was a job.

Snow fell as Ami walked the short path to the squat, concrete building where she had once worked. The air was too warm for the flakes to collect, but they burned coolly where they touched Ami's nose and cheeks. She thought she felt traces of iron in the water.

She pulled her jacket tighter and hurried as much as her long skirt would allow her. Her memories of the last time she had walked the path — a different path? — intruded on her consciousness. She'd been blindfolded, with guns at her back and Mike — though again, a different Mike — nearby.

She'd been blasé about it. They'd gone inside, and she hadn't asked questions or complained when they sat her down, took her blood, and made her wait for hours. Then they'd brought her into the sublevels. . . .

This time she knew what she was looking for. She pushed back her memories and apprehension, pulled open the unmarked glass door, and stepped into the tiny foyer. The receptionist took her name and sent her on. Ami navigated the halls, descended a flight of stairs, and entered the control centre.

A half-dozen desks filled the concrete room, and two banks of monitors hung from the ceiling — one displaying news from around the world, the other showing feeds from cameras in the rest of the compound. Men and women — mostly men — sat and typed at their consoles, or crossed the room to speak with one another. A few waved at Ami as she walked in, but most didn't notice.

She stood where she was a few moments, and found her dread melting away. She liked being here. She liked these people. Most of them hadn't been tainted by her memories.

"Ami!" Karen ran toward her, her thick brass glasses bouncing on her nose. "Good to see you. The director's going to be a few minutes — we've got a bunch of crises going on right now, and he's briefing Langley and the team simultaneously."

"Anything major?" Ami asked, glancing toward the monitors.

"Mid-league," Karen said. "Owen the Binary Man is making a break from the Carousel, and we just learned about an arms shipment leaving Thule for somewhere in northern Africa. We can probably tip off the Untouchables about Owen without revealing ourselves, but Thule will have to be us or the Order."

"Should I come back another time?" Ami asked. "I'm sure I'm not even supposed to know that. . . ."

Karen laughed. "It's fine. Have a seat, some coffee, whatever. Just don't pay attention to anything you hear."

"Right," Ami said, much more sombrely than she'd expected. "I'll stay out of the way."

Karen watched her quizzically. Ami resisted the urge to snap at her. *She's not staring because she knows anything*, Ami told herself. *She's staring because you're being an ass.*

"I'll be at my desk if you need anything," Karen said. Ami nodded, then stalked to one of the black plastic chairs along the room's perimeter to seat herself. She shrugged off her jacket and smoothed her skirt over her legs, preparing to wait.

For a few minutes she watched everyone go about their work, and felt the back of her neck prickle as she did. *Maybe I don't want to be here*, she thought, as names of countries and supercriminals and terrorists were called out. The people here helped choose the fate of the world, and she'd seen what desires people hid. She'd seen what this place hid. And if — by some miracle — their intentions were pure, should *she* be here?

The sudden realization that she was going unobserved interrupted her speculation. She hoped she hadn't missed her chance, and walked to Karen's desk. "I'm going to use the rest room, if that's okay?" she asked.

Karen nodded, most of her attention on her earpiece. Ami walked swiftly out of the control centre, forced herself to slow, and pushed through the door into the women's rest room.

She listened for voices or movement, and heard only gurgling water. Grateful to be alone, she entered the far stall, slid shut the flimsy lock, and bent down on her knees. The stall was narrow, but she managed to edge between the wall and the toilet, and find the metal pipe leading into the floor. Biting her lower lip, she wrapped her hand around the metal.

The pipes branched and twisted through the building, passing near radiators and oil gauges and a thick steel door — *Don't go to that one, yet* — and listening to everything that happened. They complained about how the building had shaken when Byzantius had gone wild, and about the patch of rust near the septic tank.

"Shh," Ami whispered, stroking the metal with her fingertips. *Do you remember what I'm looking for?*

A water pipe connected her to a support girder through a magnetic field created by nearby wires. The girder, dull and powerful, reached into its molecules, searching for vibrations caused by words spoken in its presence years ago. "Transfer her at midnight," someone said. "Have her back by morning."

An emergency sprinkler, somewhere in the western wing of offices, had a more recent memory to add. ". . . feel bad for Ami, but if we could have retrieved her earlier, we would have." Another voice followed: "I just don't want to damage an asset . . ."

Ami swore to herself, then apologized to the pipes, coaxing them to keep going.

A gurney, crammed in a supply closet against a heating duct, remembered the sensation of Ami's skin on its back. It didn't understand time well, and the extent of its memory decay was hard to ascertain.

Reluctantly, Ami brought her attention through the sublevels to the steel door. She could feel what it had touched, feel layers of Dark peel off it and stick to her. But it was like reaching into a clogged gutter with a hand soaked in oil and mud. More filth was more filth, but she was already soiled.

When did you last open? What do you remember?

It responded to her memories first. It had opened, and she had stepped through to this side — a blindfold on, and her face — God, had she looked like that? The director had greeted her, but she hadn't believed she'd really returned. Once she'd been convinced, she'd screamed at anyone who would listen, asking why the portal was there, what it was for. Begging that they destroy it. . . .

Ami squeezed her eyes shut. *Was there anyone else? More recent?*

The door offered another image. From hours ago? No — days. There were guards and someone walking . . . in or out, it was hard to tell. A woman. Ami could see her face —

Ami abruptly withdrew and let go of the pipe. Her jaw was tight, and her ears were ringing. The truth was bad enough. That she hadn't noticed before now was infuriating.

She stood, ignoring her shaky legs and wiping her nose with her sleeve. She started to unlock the stall door, then flushed the toilet before continuing. On her way out, she still didn't notice anyone, and she hoped she hadn't been gone for more than a few minutes. She didn't think she had.

When she stepped into the control centre, the first thing she felt was an intense pressure on her neck, combined with a raking soreness in her throat. After that, she noticed that her feet weren't touching the floor. Then she saw that Mike was holding her in the air with his fingers wrapped under her chin.

"What were you doing?" he asked.

Ami tried to look behind Mike without turning her head. Most of the room was watching, but no one appeared ready to help. *Bastards, all of you.* She kicked at Mike's chest, more to gain leverage than out of any hope that he'd feel it, and slapped a palm against his temple. "Let me go," she wheezed, "or all those implants in your brain will get angry, dissolve, and give you *very* early Alzheimer's."

Mike's eyes narrowed, and Ami wondered if he believed her. She hoped so; she didn't *want* to go ahead with it.

"Let her go, Piston," a voice said. Mike paused, then dropped Ami. She fell on her hands and knees, catching her breath as she scrambled to stand.

Mike stepped aside, and a white-haired man in a pinstriped suit took his place in front of Ami. "Were you actually interested in meeting with me?" he asked. "Or did you just come to spy on us?"

"Director Hall," Ami said, and winced at the pain. The director stood with his body turned, orienting his missing ear toward her and forcing her to speak loudly if she hoped to be heard. Which meant everyone else was listening, too. "No, sir, not to spy. I came with the intention of meeting you."

"Then maybe you shouldn't be threatening to cripple your former co-workers."

"What?" Ami glowered at Mike. *He attacked me first!* — but she thought better of saying as much.

The director folded his hands together. "Do you still wish to discuss the possibility of your re-employment?"

Ami opened her mouth, standing agape as she tried to find her answer. How long had they been screwing with her now?

"Maybe," she said at last. "But not today."

It wasn't the answer she'd wanted to give, but she still had nowhere else to go.

Ami next met with Doctor Jacobs two days later. She'd gone over what she had learned in the Ultra-Elites compound again and again, and thought she was ready to confront the truth. She despised herself for having been stupid enough to seek it out.

"So," Ami said, after greeting Doctor Jacobs and dropping into a chair. "Which one are you?"

Doctor Jacobs hesitated, and Ami smiled inwardly as she noticed the woman reach for something in her pants pocket. Then she dropped her hand, and said, "Dark. When did you find out?"

"Recently," Ami said. "So, do you two switch off? Compare session notes?"

Doctor Jacobs shook her head. "We see each other's reports, but we've never met. We don't have the clearance to talk to unauthorized individuals, or to leave our assigned areas. Neither side wants the risk of pollution."

"At least you can share your toys. . . ."

Doctor Jacobs was silent a while. Then she tucked a lock of hair behind her left ear, and asked, "Is that how you see yourself being treated — like a toy?"

Ami scowled. "Did I *ever* have the power to slide, or was I just passed back and forth to see what would happen?"

"You were —" Doctor Jacobs glanced at the window. "Essentially, yes. Each side wanted to know what would happen to a subject exposed to the other world. You were picked — assuming I'm remembering your file correctly, and that your people told us the truth — because you lived alone, had few close friends, and were a low-level metahuman without ties to MK-ULTRA."

"What about when you hired me? What was the point of that?"

"Not us," Doctor Jacobs said. "That was entirely your side. My guess would be that they were trying to create a field agent who could return from missions on our side undamaged."

Ami cursed as she looked at the carpet. Why was it so hard to hear that? She knew what she was, and should have been glad for the honesty.

Her voice was hoarse when she murmured, "Guess it didn't work out."

"No," Doctor Jacobs agreed. "But if it's worth anything, they did try to retrieve you on time. We blocked it, along with other exchanges during that period. Political differences."

"What kind of differences?" Ami snapped, anger boiling up.

"It's complicated," Doctor Jacobs said. "Ami — we're not friends, your side and mine. We're not even allies. Ever since your people let us into Empire City to eliminate your Guard, and we invaded instead, we've had a sort of cold war going on. But we've been in touch, on and off, for over twenty years, and neither side can ignore what the other means."

"And what do we mean to each other? Tell me, Doctor. That's my problem, isn't it?"

"Promise me something first."

"What?" Even Ami wasn't sure if she was confused, or asking what to promise.

Doctor Jacobs reached into her pocket again, and withdrew a small black box. "This is a bug-killer and psi-deflector. I'm not authorized to have it, but no one can hear us. I need you to assure me that you won't tell anyone what we're discussing."

Ami bit her lip, then nodded. "Deal." Breaking promises was one of many things she'd learned how to do in Dark anyway.

Doctor Jacobs slipped the box back into her pocket. "You call us 'Dark Empire.' 'Dark Ultra-Elites.' 'Dark Jacobs.' Just 'Dark.' What do you think we call you?"

Ami shook her head.

"We don't," Doctor Jacobs said. "We don't talk about you in public, and, in private, we just say 'the other side,' or 'their.' 'Their Empire City.' 'Their Ultra-Elites.' We sent hundreds of people into your world, and you won't find any of their stories in newspapers or books. We burnt months' worth of propaganda pamphlets after the invasion failed, and most people were glad.

"Why do you think that *is*, Ami? You've seen our world. Can you imagine what it's like for one of us to see what you've done here, what your world is like, knowing what we have now?"

Doctor Jacobs was breathing quickly, and her hands were balled into fists. "You're tainted. You're dirty. You're damaged. Absolutely. But you could have it worse." She reached into her pocket again and added, "There are things you understand — things you can do — that no one else can."

"Maybe so," Ami said, her tone dull. Her body hurt, like she hadn't slept in days; she didn't have the energy to do anything more than shake.

Doctor Jacobs shifted a finger in her pocket. "Good," she said, her voice even again. "I think we're making real progress."

"Did you get it?" Ami asked, pulling herself up from the gravel-lined rooftop to look at Mel. Ami was surprised to see that Mel had come in costume; her black cowl and veil hid all of her face except for her eyes, and long ribbons of crimson fabric danced around her wrists.

"I told you I would. I owe some real favours for this; I hope you appreciate it. How do you plan to pay him, anyway?" A tendril of fabric drew forth a palm-sized sphere of silver from somewhere, its surface gleaming like a suspended raindrop.

Bitch, Ami thought. *I'm the one who needs it in the first place; don't complain about helping a friend.* She felt guilty for the notion almost immediately, but it also reassured her that she had made the best choice. She reached out and took the sphere, felt it sink into her hand.

"I looked over Artificer's files when I was with — when I was working. In the note I gave you, I promised him I'd impress my power on one of his recorders, if he lent me this." The sphere rolled up to her wrist, starting to wrap around her. *Not yet,* Ami told it.

"I hope you're doing the right thing," Mel — Silk — said.

Ami almost laughed. "Yeah," she said. "Me, too."

"What *are* you doing?"

"You don't want to know. Thank you for everything."

Silk glanced behind her, up at the buildings towering around them and stretching into the purple sky. Then she took a quick step forward and embraced Ami. Ami stifled an instinct to lash out before awkwardly returning the hug.

"Be careful, Conductor," Silk said and pulled away.

Ami smiled, pushed her domino mask farther up the bridge of her nose, and tugged at her zero-fibre sleeves. "I'm going by Rust now, I think. Take care, Silk."

Silk gave a small wave and lowered herself down the fire escape. Ami pressed herself flat to the gravel again, raised her binoculars, and resumed watching the Olympian Tower.

Sunset passed, and none of the Guard entered or departed their headquarters. Radio reports said Mother Raven, Red Phoenix, and Slipstream were off in space, which meant that they were presumably gone for a while. The others, though . . . it was all or nothing. If they were inside, Ami's chances were better in DC. And she'd already written that off; she wouldn't get through the Ultra-Elites compound unnoticed.

She waited another hour, her doubts eating at her resolve. *Was* she doing the right thing? Was she being manipulated? Was it a ploy on the part of the director? She could drop the plan right now, walk into the Tower, and tell the Guard everything she knew. The Ultra-Elites would be shut down within days.

She envisioned meeting Sentinel in person, and remembered the last time she had seen a close-up of him. The videos on the billboards playing over and over again, that face so bright while Janus twisted and screamed. . . .

She gagged at the image. Maybe it wasn't him, but it could have been. And even if she forgot that — learned to pretend that what she'd seen in Dark didn't matter to this world — she still had to live with herself.

So no playing whistleblower. No going back to her old life. Which left continuing as she was . . . or trying something new.

She wanted to try.

When she saw a red-and-white blur leave the top of the Tower, she shuddered, then stood. Caliburn might still be inside, but he was usually patrolling at this hour. It was time.

She sent gentle urges to the sphere, and it melted in her hand, spreading a web of silver coils over her body. She stepped to the edge of the rooftop and looked halfway up the Tower to the story she wanted. With a hard swallow, she leapt.

It was several seconds into the fall before she was certain the device was working. She plummeted upward, toward the Tower, cold air biting her skin and blood rushing to her head. She desperately tried to judge how far she'd fallen and when to decrease the gravity field around her. With the street below thinner than a pencil, she spoke to the coils again — and felt her back slam into the concrete of the Tower's upper floors. She moaned and raised her head, staring at the sky in front of her. She was alive. She had made it.

The end of a metal bolt was all she needed to gain directions to her goal. It led her to a window, whose lock opened with a few taps, and she hurried inside and through hallways as she adjusted the device to deflect sensors. A conversation with an elevator cable brought her to a grey door, twice-barred and lacking any obvious means of opening. It was two minutes before Ami coaxed it into tiring and swinging inward.

Past the first door was a short hallway, then another door, identical to the first. Just as easy to unlock, but Ami hesitated before opening it. It was the real one, it told her. Twenty years ago, it had brought an army of invaders to this world's Empire City.

She opened it anyway. Behind it was the same short passage in which she now stood. Standing in the passage was her.

Her mirror's costume was different, and her hair was a little shorter. Instead of silver webbing, her body was covered in a pale yellow aura spawned by a lantern-shaped pendant on a string necklace. But it was her.

"Hi," Ami said. She felt like she would choke on her heart.

The mirror glanced down, then stepped into the doorway in front of Ami and removed her necklace. "Here," she said. "Jade Hare will ask you for this. It'll disguise you until you get home."

Ami stepped forward as well, so that they squeezed together into the door frame. She urged her web to coalesce, and handed the sphere to the mirror before donning the necklace herself. "Thanks. You should trade a power record to Artificer for that."

They both stared for several moments. "I left some notes for you. In case you came," the mirror said. "The faucet on the sink will tell you. There's also a picture of a butterfly in your nightstand. Get it tattooed on your right calf as soon as possible."

"I will," Ami murmured. "I didn't leave anything for you. I'm sorry."

"It's okay," the mirror said. "Can you . . . tell me why?"

Ami laughed. "I'm not doing this for you. I mean, I thought about you, but I had no idea if you'd be here. I just — I wanted to do something decent. But I'm all empty, and I'm no good out there anymore. This is the only thing I can give."

"You're giving me everything."

"You deserve it," Ami said, and brushed a half-step past her mirror into the Dark hallway. Then she paused and squeezed her eyes shut. "Does that mean anything — that *you* deserve it?"

"Don't think about it," the mirror said, with her back to Ami. She briefly craned her neck around, and after a final, lingering gaze, she ran toward her freedom and her new life.

Ami did the same.

That night, in her apartment, as gunshots echoed outside and a couple screamed at each other in the room above her, Ami dreamed of something better. And for the first time in months, she looked back on something good she'd done, and didn't regret it at all.

One week later, with her hair freshly cut and a tattoo burning her calf, Ami rejoined the Ultra-Elites. There was no celebration, and a few scowls when she walked in, but the director seemed pleased to have her back. Ami felt confident that no one had any real agenda against her. She had her old desk back — they called it her old desk, anyway — within hours, and began analysing the wreckage of a spacecraft Iron Phoenix had destroyed near the asteroid belt. The work was straightforward, though no one would tell her how they planned to use her findings. That was okay. She had time to win their trust.

After lunch, Ami received an e-mail telling her to report to one of the labs to fill out a psych report. When she arrived, she wasn't surprised to find Doctor Jacobs there.

"Welcome back," Doctor Jacobs said. "Finally decided you were ready to return to work?"

"Something like that," Ami agreed. "I thought I could put my skills to better use here, after all."

"I'm glad to hear it. If you don't mind, I'd like to recommend you be promoted to the field team as soon as possible. I think you'd be a good influence on the others."

"That sounds fine," Ami said. "I think I'd like that."

Doctor Jacobs nodded and withdrew a pile of papers from a desk drawer. "I need you to fill these out," she said. "I know you've changed a lot lately, and I don't think the director — or anyone else — would be well-served by making requests of you based on out-of-date psychological and background information."

Ami took the papers, and glanced at the questions: *How do you feel about your powers? When did you learn about the Ultra-Elites? Explain your attitude toward the following organizations.* She'd figure out answers. Then she glanced up in surprise, as her thumb rubbed the bottom of the last page.

There, someone had written with a lead pencil before erasing it: *Do you want to change the world?*

"Yes," Ami said, and smiled faintly. "I think that's a good idea."

CONTRIBUTORS' NOTES

The power of words and images has always fascinated **BRETT BARKLEY**. As a youngster, he would write and draw his own comics, as well as penning, illustrating, and binding his own books. These "books" filled hundreds of pages and spanned the course of several years, incorporating friends and family alike in their labyrinthine plots. Two years ago, he left a "sensible" career in Corporate America to pursue his lifelong dream of drawing and writing. Recently he got his first job in the comics field. Other opportunities have since followed. His contribution to this anthology is his first professional prose fiction work.

ALEXANDER MARSH FREED has written and edited role-playing game sourcebooks, and his fiction has appeared in *The Book of More Flesh*. An avid reader of superhero comics for the past decade, he freely acknowledges the influence of such writers as Grant Morrison and Christopher J. Priest on his own work (including "Mirror, Rust, and Dark"). He currently lives near Philadelphia, where a dearth of costumed individuals ensures low mortality rates.

STEVEN GRANT started as a film and music critic in the Midwest, then jumped to New York City and fiction when he began writing for Marvel Comics in 1978. While over the past twenty years he has mostly worked in comics, for virtually all major comics publishers and on such major characters as the Punisher, Spider-Man, Batman, the Hulk, and Mickey Mouse, he has also written magazine articles, reviews, teen adventure novels, essays, short stories, and political commentary. He currently lives in Las Vegas and produces the weekly column Permanent Damage (www.comicbookresources.com/columns/?column=10).

Award-winning fantasy and SF writer, game designer, and columnist ED GREENWOOD has been called the "Canadian author of the great American novel" (J. Robert King), "an industry legend" (*Dragon*), and "one of the greats" (*Games*). Ed is the creator of the Forgotten Realms fantasy world, arguably the most detailed fantasy world-setting ever, and has published over twenty novels and more than one hundred game books, which have sold millions of copies worldwide in over a dozen languages. In real life, Ed is a large, jolly bearded guy who lives in the countryside of Ontario, Canada. He likes reading books, books, and more books, which more than fill his farmhouse.

JON HANSEN lives on the edge of Atlanta with his wife Lisa and four assorted cats. He's been writing and selling speculative fiction and poetry since 1996, and his work has appeared in a number of places, including *Strange Horizons*, *Black Gate*, and *Star*Line*. His chief superpower is the ability to match any T-shirt to a pair of blue jeans.

STEVEN HARPER lives in Ypsilanti, Michigan with his wife and son. When not at the keyboard, he sings, plays the piano and recorder, and collects folk music. In the past, he's held jobs as a reporter, theater producer, secretary, and substitute teacher. He maintains that the most interesting thing about him is that he writes books. He is the creator of The Silent Empire series for Roc Books, including *Dreamer* and *Nightmare*. Currently, he's working on *Trickster* and *Children*, the third and fourth volumes in the series. His web page can be found at www.sff.net/people/spiziks.

JIM C. HINES began his writing career with an award-winning story in *Writers of the Future XV*. He has since published a number of tales in *MZB's Fantasy Magazine*, *The Book of More Flesh*, and *Andromeda Spaceways*, among others. Last year he received an honourable mention in *The Year's Best Fantasy and Horror* for his story in *The Book of All Flesh*. He is also becoming a regular contributor to *Speculations* magazine. Jim maintains a web site at www.sff.net/people/jchines and welcomes e-mail at jchines@sff.net.

BRADLEY J. KAYL graduated from California State University at Northridge with a degree in Environmental Biology and as a lifetime member of the Golden Key National Honor Society. Incorporating his knowledge of the physical world with his interest in the abstract, he has achieved success as an internationally published author in fields ranging from graphic novels to short stories and poetry. He currently writes Archangel Studios' graphic novel series, *Assassin*, an incredibly filmic tale that is already creating greater industry buzz than his work on the critically acclaimed series, *The Red Star*.

DANIEL KSENYCH has written short fiction for a number of online and print magazines, including *PlanetMag*, *QuantumMuse*, *EOTU*, *The Online Reader*,

Opi8, *broken pencil*, and *On Spec*. He has also contributed to Atlas Games' Unknown Armies product line and to Eden Studios' *The Book of All Flesh* horror anthology, edited by James Lowder. Much of his current work has involved writing scripts for children's plays, produced locally through Putting It Together Productions, a company devoted to supporting community talent and arts education for young people.

ROBIN D. LAWS's most recent novel is *Honour of the Grave*; his previous titles are *The Rough and the Smooth* and *Pierced Heart*. Robin's most recent adventure is as a writer for Marvel Comics, with credits including the *Hulk: Nightmerica* limited series and a stint on *Iron Man*. He is also the designer of many acclaimed roleplaying products, including *Feng Shui*, *Heroquest*, and *The Dying Earth Roleplaying Game*. His potato salad is even better than your mother's.

JAMES LOWDER has worked extensively in fantasy and horror publishing, on both sides of the editorial blotter. He's authored several bestselling fantasy and dark fantasy novels, including *Prince of Lies* and *Knight of the Black Rose*; short fiction for such diverse anthologies as *Historical Hauntings*, *Truth Until Paradox*, and *Shadows Over Baker Street*; and a large number of film and book reviews, feature articles, and even the occasional comic book script. His credits as anthologist include *Realms of Valor*, *The Doom of Camelot*, and a trilogy of zombie anthologies for Eden Studios that includes the International Horror Guild Award finalist and Origins Award nominee, *The Book of More Flesh*.

A superhero and comics fan since he was old enough to run about with his arms outstretched, MATTHEW MCFARLAND has been writing horror for several years now, and the stain of that genre can be seen in "Ghosts of London." Matt develops the Dark Ages line of roleplaying games for White Wolf Game Studio, and has written books for several of their other game lines. His short story "Jilted" was included in the White Wolf anthology *Lucifer's Shadow*. He lives outside of Cleveland, Ohio with his wife, Heather, and his two shiftless, layabout cats.

For more than twenty years, Batman editor and writer DENNIS O'NEIL has put the "dark" in the Dark Knight and has been the guiding force behind the Batman mythos. A bestselling novelist and screenwriter, he has taught writing at the School of Visual Arts in New York City and lectured at numerous colleges.

JOHN OSTRANDER has been a professional writer for twenty years. Before that, he was an actor and playwright in Chicago, where he worked with such actors as Dennis Franz and William Petersen. His play, *Bloody Bess* (co-written with William J. Norris), toured Europe. In comics, he's most noted for *Grimjack*, *Suicide Squad*, *Legends*, *Firestorm*, *Wasteland* (with the late Del Close), *Gotham Nights*, *The Spectre*, *Apache Skies*, and *The Kents*. He currently works on Star Wars comics for Dark Horse.

ERICA COBB SCHIPPERS started writing stories almost as soon as she learned the alphabet. She owes her love of science fiction and fantasy to her father, who introduced her to genre classics. She owes her love of RPGs and comics to her husband, whose unflagging enthusiasm for both convinced her to get in on the fun. When not writing, she is enjoying the company and contributions of the other members of her writer's group, playing fiddle, or being sat on by cats. She also spends some hours every day making money as a ColdFusion programmer, which she finds surprisingly enjoyable.

JESSE SCOBLE has worked for Guardians of Order since 2000. His writing credits include the Origins Award-nominated Big Eyes, Small Mouth adventure *So We Have an . . . Obelisk?*, the El-Hazard roleplaying game, the world of Silver Age Sentinels, and an upcoming Orpheus supplement. He took over the position of SAS line developer after putting crushed glass in Lucien Soulban's coffee. Currently, he also manages the RPG lines tied to George R. R. Martin's *A Game of Thrones* and DC's *The Authority*. He doesn't believe in cats or children, except to feed them to his malamute.

LUCIEN SOULBAN supposedly lives in Montreal, a bachelor celebrating his everyday liberties. He's real for as long as God doesn't grow bored of him. Frankly, Lucien suspects he's already crossed that line between mortality and fertilizer, and doesn't like the way the worms are eyeing his carcass. So, he writes and hopes to amuse God for a few words more. There, he just survived writing his own bio . . . how depressing is that? He could have written about his work with White Wolf, AEG, *Inquest*, and Wizards of the Coast, as a writer and designer. But, no, he decided to share his death psy —

J. ALLEN THOMAS grew up in Dyer, Indiana and now resides in Greensboro, North Carolina. He graduated from Indiana University with a degree in Economics, then worked in the accounting department of a Chicago ad agency for too many years. He went on to become one of the founders of Crocodile Games, and co-creator of the miniature wargame, *War Gods of Ægyptus*. After leaving Crocodile Games, Allen joined Hero Games in May, 2003 as an assistant line developer.

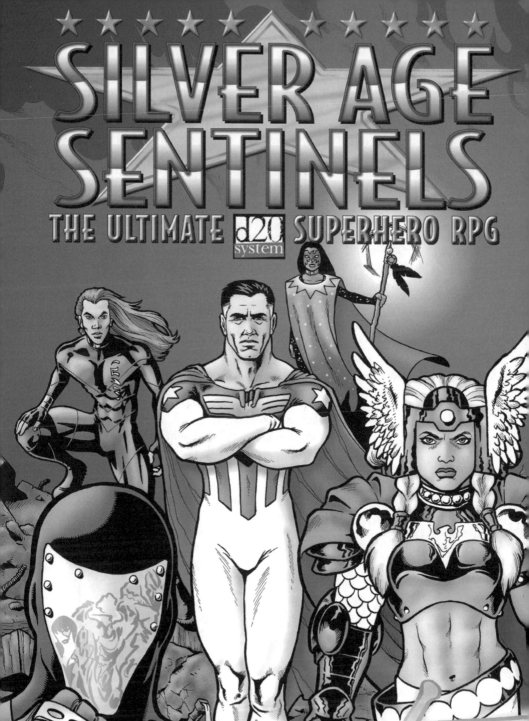